Robert William Fraser

Seaside Divinity

Robert William Fraser

Seaside Divinity

ISBN/EAN: 9783744716970

Printed in Europe, USA, Canada, Australia, Japan

Cover: Foto ©Andreas Hilbeck / pixelio.de

More available books at **www.hansebooks.com**

PILCHARD FISHING ON THE CORNISH COAST.

Frontispiece 1. (See page 353)

SEASIDE DIVINITY

SEA-WEEDS.
1. The Blood-coloured Delesseria.   2. The Spotted Nitophyllum.   3. The Scarlet Plocamium.
4. The Ruscus-leaved Delesseria.   5. Perforated Ulva of the North Pacific.

(See Chapters 7 and 8.)

MARITIME FLOWERS.
1. The Yellow Horned Poppy.   2. The Scarlet Horned Poppy.   3. The Sea-side Pea.   4. The Sea-side Convolvulus.
5. The Sea Lavender.   6. The Sea Buckthorn.   7. The Sea Rocket.   8. The Sea Chickweed.   9. The Sea Wrack-grass

See Chapters 9 and 10.)

Frontispiece 2.

SEASIDE DIVINITY

BY THE

REV. ROBERT W. FRASER, M.A.

AUTHOR OF
"SCIENTIFIC WANDERINGS;" "SACRED RITES OF ANCIENT ISRAEL;"
"DAY AND NIGHT;" "LEAVES OF THE TREE OF LIFE;"
"ELEMENTS OF PHYSICAL SCIENCE;"
"HEAD AND HAND;" ETC.

WITH ILLUSTRATIONS BY
HENRY NOEL HUMPHREYS, J. WOLF, G. H. ANDREWS, T. W. WOOD,
AND J. B. ZWECKER.

ENGRAVED BY DALZIEL BROTHERS

LONDON: JAMES HOGG AND SONS
MDCCCLXI

[*The Right of Translation is reserved*]

PREFACE.

SOME years ago the Author, at the desire of the editor of an eminent periodical, contributed a short series of papers on one of the branches of the Natural History of the Sea-shore. The extremely favourable reception which those contributions had the honour to meet with from persons qualified to appreciate them, has encouraged him to present the following work to the Public.

Its nature and object are perhaps sufficiently indicated by its title of "Seaside Divinity;" it may be added, however, that the work has not been written with the view of teaching geology, botany, or natural history, but of directing the reader's attention to the many very striking illustrations of great and impressive truths which those departments of science exhibit in the phenomena and productions of the sea-shore.

The studies to which the following chapters refer are calculated in no small degree to enhance the charms of a visit to the sea-shore, to yield recreation amidst graver toils, and to minister to intellectual and moral soundness, while the scenes in which they are pursued contribute to the increase of bodily health and vigour. It is the Author's earnest hope that the volume he now submits to the reader's perusal may conduce in some measure to such important results.

June, 1861.

CONTENTS.

CHAPTER I.

INTRODUCTION.

Charms of the Sea-shore. — Classic and Oriental Myths relating to the Sea. — Various Studies suited to the Seaside. — What is requisite for such Studies — an Illustration from Botany. — Advantages of such Pursuits . . . . . Page 3

CHAP. II.

MARITIME GEOLOGY.

Extent, Character, Variety of Aspect of our Sea-shores, and their Relation to Geological Structure. — General View of Geology. — Geological Tour from Cornwall and Devonshire along the Coasts of England and Scotland, exhibiting the General Features of our Sea-shores as regards their Structure 15

CHAP. III.

CHANGES IN OUR SEA-SHORE.

Mutations of the Earth's Surface indicated by Geology. — General View of their Causes. — Alterations which from Age to Age have occurred in various Parts of the British and Irish Coasts, and their Causes. — Analogous Changes in other Parts of the World 33

CHAP. IV.

FOSSILS OF THE SEA-SHORE.

General Views.—Fossils of the Palæozoic, the Secondary and the Tertiary Epochs, and various considerations regarding them . . . . Page 55

CHAP. V.

THE OCEAN.

Aspect of the Ocean.—Sunrise and Sunset.—Extent.—Relation to Rivers and Lakes.—Medium of Intercourse.—Depth.—Colour.—Saltness.—Circulation in the Ocean.—Coral Reefs, &c. 81

CHAP. VI.

WINDS AND TIDES.

Interest of the Subject.—Air and Water, Ocean and Atmosphere.—Theory of the Tides.—Tidal Phenomena.—Rise of Tide in various parts of the Coast.—The Bore.—Currents of the Sea.—The Winds 107

CHAP. VII.

MARINE VEGETATION.

Analogy between Marine and Terrestrial Vegetation.—Variety of the Algæ.—Marine Botany, its Classification.—Specimens of the three Subdivisions in which our Sea-weeds are comprehended 125

CHAP. VIII.

PHYSIOLOGY OF MARINE PLANTS.

Claims which they have on our Attention.—Fructification.—Peculiarity of their Structure.—Reproduction.—Their remarkable Structure as related to the Element they exist in.—Artificial Uses of Sea-weeds.—Their Relation to Marine Animals, &c. 137

CHAP. IX.

MARITIME PLANTS.

Seaside Flowers.—Interest attached to them.—Vegetation of Seaside less luxuriant than in Inland Places.—Seaside Grasses.—Seaside flowering Plants.—Examples of various Species . . . . Page 151

CHAP. X.

PHYSIOLOGY OF MARITIME PLANTS.

Adaptation of their Structure to their Places of Abode.—Special Instances of this Adaptation.—Analogy between Marine and Maritime Plants.—Functions of Roots.—Adaptation of Leaves to their Office, &c. 171

CHAP. XI.

CLASSIFICATION.

Number and Variety of Organic Forms.—Generalisation.—Classification of the Animal Kingdom 183

CHAP. XII.

RADIATA, OR RAYED ANIMALS — ZOOPHYTES.

Various Species of Zoophytes.—Tubularia.—Sertularia.—Sea-pen.—Sea-fan.—Actiniæ, "Sea Anemones," &c. . 191

CHAP. XIII.

RAYED ANIMALS — SEA-NETTLES.

Structure and Organisation.—Variety of Species.—Differences in Form, Colour, Modes of Locomotion.—Luminous Properties.—Reproduction, &c. 203

CHAP. XIV.

RAYED ANIMALS — STAR-FISHES.

Crinoideæ of Primæval Seas.—Different Families of the Starfishes—Their Structure, &c.—Ophiuridæ.—Feather-star.—Sun-star.—Brittle-star, &c. 219

CHAP. XV.

RAYED ANIMALS — SEA-URCHINS.

Antiquity of the Race. — Egg-urchin. — Complexity of Structure. — Method of Enlargement. — Mechanism of Spines, of Mouth, &c. . . . . Page 231

CHAP. XVI.

ARTICULATA, OR JOINTED ANIMALS — MARINE WORMS, ETC.

Their Structure. — Tubicolæ and Serpulæ, &c. — Nereis. — Sea-mouse 239

CHAP. XVII.

ARTICULATA, OR JOINTED ANIMALS — CIRRIPEDA.

"Curl-footed" Animals. — Balanus or Acorn-shell. — Barnacles. — Pentalismus anatifera. — Popular Error. — Young of the Barnacle Shell, &c. 249

CHAP. XVIII.

ARTICULATA — CRABS.

Structure. — Spider-Crab and various other Species. — Pagurus: Habits and Structure, &c. — Zoea 257

CHAP. XIX.

ARTICULATA — LOBSTERS, ETC.

The Shrimp. — The common Lobster. — Various Species. — Structure and Habits, &c. 273

CHAP. XX.

MOLLUSCA, OR SOFT-BODIED ANIMALS — BIVALVES.

Molluscs. — Bivalves. — Structure and Habits of various Species. — The common Cockle, &c. 283

CHAP. XXI.

MOLLUSCA — WHELKS.

The Whelk and its Varieties. — Structure and Instincts, &c. — The Limpet. — Structure, &c. 293

CHAP. XXII.

MOLLUSCA — CUTTLE-FISH.

Cuttle Fish: its Habits and Structure.—Varieties of Species.
Page 305

CHAP. XXIII.

VERTEBRATA — FISHES.

Form of Fishes: its Adaptation.—External Covering.—Colours.
—Locomotive Powers.— Respiration, &c. . . . 317

CHAP. XXIV.

VERTEBRATA — FISHES.

Fishes: Instances of remarkable Form, Structure, and Instincts. — The Lump-Sucker. — The Lamprey. — The Stickleback. — Pipe-Fishes. — The Fishing-Frog. — Shark. — Rays, &c. 329

CHAP. XXV.

VERTEBRATA — FISHES.

Edible Fishes: The Cod Family.—Flat Fish.—The Herring and Pilchard Family.—Pilchard Fishing 345

CHAP. XXVI.

VERTEBRATA — MARITIME BIRDS.

Swimming and Wading Birds.—The Curlew. — The Sandpiper. — Divers. — Grebes. — The Gannet: its remarkable Structure 359

CHAP. XXVII.

VERTEBRATA — SEASIDE MAMMALIA.

The Cetacea, or Whale Tribe. — The Dolphin.—The Sea Unicorn. — The common Whale: remarkable Adaptations of Structure, &c. — The Seal Family: Form and Habits.— Adaptations of Structure.—Conclusion . . . 369

LIST OF ILLUSTRATIONS.

PILCHARD FISHING ON THE CORNISH COAST . . *Frontispiece* 1
    From a Drawing by G. H. Andrews.

SEA-WEEDS:—1. The Blood-coloured Delesseria; 2. The Spotted Nitophyllum; 3. The Scarlet Plocamium; 4. The Ruscus-leaved Delesseria; 5. Perforated Ulva of the North Pacific.—MARITIME FLOWERS:—1. The Yellow Horned Poppy; 2. The Scarlet Horned Poppy; 3. The Seaside Pea; 4. The Seaside Convolvulus; 5. The Sea Lavender; 6. The Sea Buckthorn; 7. The Sea Rocket; 8. The Sea Chickweed; 9. The Sea Wrack-grass . . . *Frontispiece* 2
    From Drawings by Henry Noel Humphreys.

FOSSILS OF THE SEA-SHORE:—1, 2. Chain Coral; 3. Mushroom Coral; 4. The Fossil Flying-Fish; 5. A Fossil Fish of Permian Formation; 6. Fossil Fish of the Devonian Formation; 7. The Berry-bone Fossil Fish; 8. A Fossil Bat; 9. The Great-headed Fossil Lizard; 10. A Trilobite; 11. A Small Trilobite; 12. The Lily Encrinite Page 55
    From Drawings by Henry Noel Humphreys.

RAYED ANIMALS:—1. The Sand Star; 2. The Brittle Star; 3. Gemmed Sea-Anemone; 4. The Medusa Sea-Anemone; 5. A Jelly Fish; 6. The Sea Fan; 7. The Sea Pen; 8. The Sea Urchin . . . 191
    From Drawings by Henry Noel Humphreys.

JOINTED ANIMALS — SOFT-BODIED ANIMALS:—Lobster Fishing; Shrimping; Dredging for Oysters; The Hermit Crab; The Spider Crab; The Cockle; The Cuttle-Fish; Eggs of the Cuttle-Fish . 239
    From Drawings by G. H. Andrews and T. W. Wood.

FISHES:—Cod Fishing; Trawling for Flat Fish; Remarkable Fishes: 1. The Lamprey; 2. The Lump Fisher or Lump Sucker; 3. Fifteen-spined Stickleback; 4. Fishing Frog, or Frog Angler; 5. The Pipe Fish 317
    From Drawings by G. H. Andrews and T. W. Wood.

MARITIME BIRDS:—The Bass Rock; Terns, or Sea Swallows; Puffins; The Sheldrake; The Smew; The Gannet (adult and young); The Diver 359
    From a Drawing by J. Wolf.

SEASIDE MAMMALIA:—Seal Fishing in Greenland; The Seal Family: 1. The Common Seal; 2. The Grey Seal; 3. The Walrus; 4. The Harp Seal 369
    From a Drawing by J. B. Zwecker.

INTRODUCTION

SEASIDE DIVINITY.

CHAPTER I.

INTRODUCTION.

Charms of the Sea-shore. — Classic and Oriental Myths relating to the Sea. — Various Studies suited to the Seaside. — What is requisite for such Studies, — an Illustration from Botany. — Advantages of such Pursuits.

It is the month of June. The keen and withering blasts of Eurus, which blow with such direful pertinacity in April and May, are at last superseded by the soft west winds, fraught with health and oxygen from the luxuriant vegetation of the tropical lands where they have their birth. It must have been in this same month — the loveliest of the year — that "holy George Herbert" indited those lines so dear to quaint old Isaac Walton: —

> "Sweet day, so calm, so pure, so bright,
> The bridal of the earth and sky!"

In no other month does Nature exhibit so many and such varied evidences of that august bridal of which the poet so sweetly sings. Heaven, with its soft breezes and gentle showers and genial sunshine, is united with the smiling Earth;

and the happy bride has decked herself in her verdant garniture, and thousands of flowers rich in colour and perfume, and multitudes of living beings born of this union have sprung into joyous existence. Woods, meadows, rivers, hills, valleys, all vie with each other in presenting their various charms to the delighted wayfarer; but no scenes can advance stronger claims on his attention at this season than the sea-shore.

Let us wander along the beach. On one hand is the sea: its surface is rippled by the fresh breeze; the tide is gently encroaching on the sands; the wavelets falling in quick succession, utter their murmurs in a monotone not unmusical to a poet's ear. On the other hand, there are rocks whose bases have for thousands of years resisted the storms of winter, and whose summits are crowned with trees, and flowers, and waving ferns, and from a rift in which falls a clear sparkling runnel, that, after wandering through woods and fields, at length leaps over the rock and loses itself in the sea. Then, high overhead, the sky is of that same deep blue which we see reflected in the waters beneath; and here and there far aloft are clouds of that kind which meteorologists tell us never betoken rain, and which, as the rays of the sun light them up, seem lovely enough to realise the poet's dream, that

"Some angels in their upward flight
Had left their mantles floating in mid air;"

and the no less poetical fancy of the philosopher,

that such radiant forms might be the vehicles on which denizens of some of the planetary worlds might pass from place to place through the fields of ether. Then far at sea on the verge of the horizon there are a few ships, with only a speck of snowy canvas visible, for the convex waters interpose between their hulls and the spectator's eye; while only a few hundred yards off, a flock of gulls are floating on the waves, screaming to each other as if discussing the probabilities of a contemplated attack on the next shoal of small fry that make their appearance near the surface. None but very ordinary observers can resist the attractions which heaven, and earth, and sea thus unite in presenting to the visitor of the sea-shore; and so, without any disparagement to the special charms of purely rural scenes, we reiterate our conviction that in this lovely month of June no charms of natural scenery exceed those of our sea-shores.

Let us seat ourselves beneath the grateful shadow of this rock, and no longer resist the spirit of contemplation which whispers to us in these whispering waves.

What an inexhaustible fund of strange and marvellous knowledge does not that sea contain! What mysteries amid its depths! What wonders in the structure and habits of its denizens! In its tides and currents how much that is interesting and marvellous! In its storms and calms how much that is grand and sublime! In all that pertains to the great deep how striking and how solemn the lessons uttered as to Creative wisdom, and power, and foresight, bidding us

> " own
> The Hand Almighty who its channelled bed
> Immeasurable sunk, and poured abroad,
> Fenced with eternal mounds, the fluid sphere!"

Looking upon the sea on a day so lovely as this, one ceases to marvel at those wild and wayward fancies of Greek and Oriental mythology which loved to people the realms of ocean with nymphs and deities endowed with natures suited to the element in which they were presumed to exist. How favourable to the birth and development of such charming myths must have been the shores of Baiæ, or the isles that stud the blue Egean! With cloudless azure above, and serene waters below, and all nature breathing grace and beauty, how natural the idea that those bright waters were the abode of the Nereides, marine damsels, ever blooming in youth and loveliness, and who by the favoured few might sometimes be seen disporting on the backs of dolphins, or frequenting, on the sea-shore, caves and grottoes, adorned with flowers and sea-shells! How natural too, and how credible to a fervid imagination, the story of Ceyx and Halcyone, told in strains of such tender melancholy by Ovid, in which the faithful pair are reunited in the form of birds dear to the sea-nymphs, and which make their nests on the sea foam when winds and waters are at rest! The desire one feels to be able to take up one's abode beneath these mysterious waves would itself render perfectly credible in Classic times the history of the Bœotian fisherman who, perceiving that the fish he had caught on being thrown upon the grass were endowed with new life and enabled to regain their native element, imitated their example, and tasting the miraculous herbage, became forthwith a denizen of the deep.

How charming would it be if, as we are here seated contemplating those waves, we should suddenly find the Arabian myth of Abdallah of the Sea realised! How gladly should we accept a polite invitation to visit the caves of the ocean, protected by the enchanted unguent from all inconvenience which a descent beneath the waters would otherwise cause to our organs of respiration! How pleasant is this warm weather to visit in safety those crystal depths, where the finny tribes lead "their cold sweet silver life, wrapped in round waves!" Beneath the liquid crystal would await us scenes more wonderful than the fairy dreams of childhood.

It is hopeless, however, to await a visit from Abdallah; for that remarkable personage dwells, it is more than probable, only beneath those bright waves which bathe the shores of Yemen, and so cannot be expected to emerge from our hyperborean waters. We have nothing for it, therefore, but to content ourselves with what our sea-shores themselves present us.

Happily no preternatural aid or direction is required to enable us to perceive the objects with which the sea-shores furnish us. They are many and various. They all belong more or less to Natural History in its more comprehensive acceptation; and Natural History is itself a charming study.

Then we have to consider the aspect, the character, and the structure of our sea-shores; the ocean itself, with its special laws and history; marine vegetation and littoral plants ; and a great variety of living beings which either make their abode continually on our shores, or only visit them from time to time. Such objects, so many and so various, invest our sea-shores with the greatest novelty; for the most diligent and industrious observer cannot with all his labour exhaust the store even of the microscopic objects alone which the sea-beach affords. Be it observed, however, that to reap the full advantage which such studies are capable of conferring, some particular knowledge is requisite, as well as diligence and attention.

A very simple illustration will be sufficient to explain this. Let us suppose, for example, the case of a person entirely ignorant of the botany of field flowers. He never heard of the artificial system of Linnæus, or the natural system of Cuvier. He has no more acquaintance with one flower than another, as regards its structure, its functions, its habits, or its qualities. To such an individual a ramble through the fields or woods in spring presents little more than the fact, that the hedge-rows, the meadows, and the trees are again assuming their verdant garniture, and that, after the long sleep of winter, nature is once more exhibiting a cheerful aspect. The want of special and particular acquaintance with the science of botany deprives him of numberless pleasing impressions, which would otherwise be made upon his mind by the reappearance of those objects in the vegetable kingdom to which he had given attention in some preceding season.

> " A primrose by the river's brim
> A yellow primrose is to him,
> And it is nothing more."

The Book of Nature has opened its pages before his eyes; those pages are distinctly printed and gloriously illustrated; but to him they are in a great measure written in an unknown language, and the characters fail to awaken in him more than a few vague and indefinite ideas.

How different is the case of the person who is even but imperfectly acquainted with botany! To him a solitary ramble among the green lanes and shadowy woods offers an inexhaustible fund of cheerful, healthful, elevating contemplation. He can read the book that is opened before him, and comprehend much of its language. The simplest flower that springs up beneath the hawthorn hedge suggests to him a train of ideas. Every leaf that issues from nature's press is in his view like the Prophet's roll, printed within and without in characters full of the sublimest significance; every blade of grass is vocal to him, and, awakening the echoes of memory, renews past impressions and past enjoyments. To him there are sermons not only in trees, but in the humblest flower beneath his feet; in the moss that crowns the mouldering wall, the little fern that grows on its sides, or the various coloured lichens that give their peculiar tints to the stones that form it.

These remarks are not less applicable to a ramble by the sea-shore than to a walk among the rustic places of the inland country. In both instances some special and particular knowledge is essential to the pleasure and enjoyment of the observer; and with such particular acquirement the wanderer by the seaside may convert even the murmur of the ocean into an articulate voice, and understand much of what the "wild waves are saying."

No study is better calculated to strengthen our corporeal and mental faculties, or to recruit them when wearied or overtaxed, than that of the Natural History of the Sea-shore. Even the fresh air, the exercise, the freedom from restraint connected with these pursuits, are for a large number of human ills medicines, in the universality of which all physicians are agreed from the days of Hippocrates and Galen to the present hour. And what a solace to mind and body to leave behind the thousand and one "winged cares" which the poet tells us flit about the ceilings of our abodes! What a delight, if they still pursue us as we drive away to the beach, to bid them begone, or, if they succeed in entering the boat with us, to push them over into the bright waves! Nay, the very effort thus to obtain freedom, albeit it may not be entirely successful, is itself conducive in no small degree to mental and corporeal vigour.

Then in the objects themselves which we study how much is there that is wholesome to the moral and intellectual powers as fresh air and exercise to the bodily functions! The various departments of natural history, of which the seaside furnishes illustrations, exhibit innumerable organised structures, singularly beautiful in themselves, and marvellously adapted to places, conditions, and circumstances. It ministers in no small degree to the health and vigour of the mind to examine such structures, and note such adaptations, and suffer them to enforce the lessons they read us as to Creative power, foresight, and beneficence.

It is not necessary for us to inquire as to the manner in which Creative power and wisdom have been exercised. We are not called upon to determine what the method may have been or may still be; whether the great Originator has produced the organisms we admire, directly or indirectly by the action of general laws. Whatever view we may take, the result is the same. We discover substances and elements highly complicated in their relations, resulting in organisms so adapted to the conditions they are placed in, that it is impossible not to admit that the adaptation is designed by the same Agent in which the structure itself originated. Such indications are extremely various and numerous, and to these we invite our reader, to discern with us some of the striking truths of what we venture to denominate Seaside Divinity.

MARITIME GEOLOGY

CHAP. II.

MARITIME GEOLOGY.

Extent, Character, Variety of Aspect of our Sea-shores, and their Relation to Geological Structure.—General View of Geology.—Geological Tour from Cornwall and Devonshire along the Coasts of England and Scotland, exhibiting the General Features of our Sea-shores as regards their Structure.

THE shores of the British Islands, including those of the many smaller isles which form the group, comprehend, when measured along the extremely irregular line of our numerous bays and estuaries, a circuit of several thousands of miles, and exhibit throughout their vast extent the utmost variety of scenery and aspect.

In some instances the shores are tame and uninteresting; but as a general rule they possess great beauty and grandeur. In some parts of the coast the land slopes gently toward the sea, and is either clothed with trees, or consists of rich meadows and cultivated fields, and is terminated by a beach of smooth sand or of pebbles mingled with shells. In others the coast is bounded by precipitous cliffs of great altitude, exposed to the perpetual action of the billows, and presenting features of the wildest and most romantic character. In the one case the wanderer easily gains access to the water's edge, and may enjoy the charms of the seaside

> "in summer eve,
> When the broad shore retiring waters leave,
> And all is calm at sea and still on land."

On the other, all access to the water is impracticable, for it is often of profound depth, and it never leaves the base of the cliffs. But ample amends are made in the sublimity of the scenery, and the extent of the view which from such situations can be obtained.

The variety of features thus presented to us in the scenery of our sea-shores may be traced in a great measure to peculiarities in their geological structure. But there are other respects besides form and outline in which the geology of our shores modify their aspect. The vegetation, both in its amount and its character, depends in a very considerable degree on the nature and properties of the soil; and the soil in its turn is dependent for its quality on the rocks and strata on which it rests; and hence the geology of any particular district is concerned in modifying the character of the vegetation. Thus the tameness or the sublimity of the scenery, and the scantiness or the luxuriance of the terrestrial plants by which the scenery is adorned, may originate in the same cause.

These remarks may to some extent be illustrated even by a very general view of the geology of Britain. The Tertiary formations are for the most part spread along the eastern and south-eastern maritime districts; the formations of the Plutonic rocks and the strata of greatest antiquity occur for the most part on the western coasts. This imparts a corresponding variety to the eastern and western shores. The latter are generally bold and precipitous, the former comparatively tame and low. The natural productions of the soil, too, exhibit a corresponding difference. In the latter they are scanty compared with the luxuriance they exhibit in the former.

To those acquainted in any considerable degree with the variety of aspect presented by our sea-shores, a view of the geological phenomena on which that variety so much depends can hardly fail to prove interesting. We shall, therefore, exhibit to the reader such a sketch as is compatible with the nature of this work, in the form of a Geological Tour along the Coast. It will, however, facilitate our design to take a rapid survey of the chief divisions of geological science.

The solid materials of the globe are by geologists understood to consist of the igneous rocks or those left in their present condition by the action of heat and the aqueous formations, or the strata originating in the action of water. These two great classes comprehend, it need hardly be added, a great number and variety of rocks and strata, more or less distinguished from each other by peculiarities of structure and composition. The "igneous rocks" are of great value in all geological investigations. They are the monuments of vast organic convulsions, caused by stupendous force to which the surface of our planet has been subjected, and they have acted a most important part in causing the diversity of elevation exhibited on the surface of the earth, giving origin to hills and mountains and valleys, with all their variety of scenery; and so causing the conditions necessary to the existence of springs, rivers, and lakes, from which results so much variety and beauty of scenery. But a still higher interest belongs to the study of the stratified formations; for the various organic remains they contain are a record of the past history of the earth, by indicating the character of the plants and animals by which it has been successively inhabited, and by pointing out, in some degree, the nature of the soil, the climate, and in general the physical geography of the earth, in periods incalculably remote from the present time.

One of the most remarkable truths disclosed by geology is, not merely that multitudes of the remains of plants and animals peculiar to former conditions of the earth are preserved in the stratified rocks, but that in many instances these rocks, although of vast depth and extent, are formed almost exclusively of the remains of creatures once endowed with the senses and functions of vitality. This truth, wonderful as it is, is not inconsistent with the wide and all but universal diffusion of life at the present moment; and it proves that in the remotest ages of the earth's history the mysterious principle of vitality was employed by its Divine Originator to minister with a most energetic agency to a great variety and multitude of chemical and organic combinations carried on in the great laboratory of nature.

Races of beings belonging to an epoch of incalculable duration lived and perished, leaving their exuviæ in the solid rock as memorials of their existence. These were succeeded by others of different forms and habits, who also becoming extinct, bequeathed to subsequent times a history of themselves and their age, written, like that of their predecessors, in the durable materials of the globe; they in their turn were succeeded by others of dissimilar forms; these again by others; so that the mutations which geological inquiries disclose may truly be considered as the history of life and its metamorphoses.

Commencing our tour at the Land's End, and proceeding eastwards along the shores of Cornwall and Devonshire, the remarkable circumstance attracts our attention, that the whole of the coast, with certain exceptions, is formed of the old red sandstone, to which the term Devonian strata is applied, but which sparingly occurs in any other district of England, while it constitutes a large portion of the central and northern divisions of Scotland and a considerable portion of Wales. Associated with this prevailing formation we find, moreover, granite rocks, which form the Land's End; serpentine, which constitutes the Lizard; mica and chlorite schists at the promontory of Start Point, and several instances of trap and porphyry occurring at intervals. Proceeding onwards, we discover that the formation of the Palæozoic era of Devonshire is succeeded on the shores of Dorsetshire by the formation of the Secondary era, the oolite and lias, which latter forms the cliffs near Lyme Regis. Along the Hampshire coast formations belonging to the same epoch occur, consisting of the chalk, the wealden, and the oolite, associated in certain places with freshwater and marine tertiary deposits. Advancing towards Brighton, we find the Cretaceous formation, which constitutes the foundation strata of the district, rarely exhibits itself, the shores being for the most part low, and composed of tertiary and alluvial deposits. To the east of Brighton, however, a bold line of chalk cliffs bounds the shore towards the river Ouse, extending to the promontory of Beachy Head, succeeded to the eastwards by the lower series of the Chalk formation, firestone, galt, and greensand, which occur on the southern shores of the Isle of Wight and along some parts of the coast over which we have already passed. Eastwards from Beachy Head, we enter upon the Wealden formation, the range of cliffs which skirt the shore being formed of the Wealden sandstone alternating with clays and shales. From Dover to the N. Foreland, the coast line is formed of chalk cliffs; and at Folkestone and Hythe in particular the lower series of the Cretaceous formation is manifested, the greensand strata being at the base and on a level with as well as reaching beneath the sea, the galt lying over the greensand, the firestone resting on the galt, and over all the lower and upper chalk formations.

Continuing our journey along the Kentish coast, we arrive at the London Clay, a Tertiary deposit of great thickness, being in some instances 600 feet in depth, and covering a very wide area, extending from the eastern shores of Kent to the chalk hills of Wiltshire, Berkshire, Oxfordshire, Buckinghamshire, and Hertfordshire toward the west, and northwards to the extreme limits of Norfolk. This deposit, on which the metropolis of England stands, formed in some remote era the bottom of a gulf of the ocean, and, like the various strata already noticed, constitutes an object of the deepest interest to the geologist, from the abundance of organic remains which it discloses. Of this clay the Isle of Sheppey is entirely composed.

On the northern shores of the county of Norfolk the Cretaceous formation is again manifested, and from this point along the coast of Lincolnshire and beyond the Humber into Holderness the coast line is chiefly made up of low cliffs of gravel, marine detritus, and tertiary deposits. The promontory of Flamborough Head, which we now reach, is formed of chalk, to the north of which the coast boundary is formed of various members of the Oolite and Lias formations. From the river Tees to Tynemouth the trias deposits and the magnesian limestone of the Permian system occur, and beyond this point to Berwick the coast is formed by the Carboniferous system, interrupted at intervals, as at Dunstansborough and Bamborough Castle, by masses of trap rocks.

From the rapid view we have thus taken of the geological features of the southern and eastern coasts of England, it will be observed that it is only toward the extremities of this long line of coast that any instances of the plutonic rocks occur, as in Cornwall, Devonshire, and Northumberland; and that with the few exceptions thus presented by some of the more remarkable headlands on the southern and northern coasts, the entire shores are composed of strata belonging either to the Palæozoic epoch or to the Secondary or Tertiary eras.

Before supposing ourselves to cross the embouchure of the Tweed and continue our expedition, one or two general remarks regarding the geology of Scotland will not be out of place. Geologists, by very distinct natural lines of demarcation, have divided this portion of Britain into three great geological provinces. The Southern province lies between "the borders" and a line running from near St. Abb's Head, in Berwickshire, in a direction S.S.W., to near Girvan, in Ayrshire; the Middle province is comprehended between this latter boundary and a line running also S.S.W., from near Stonehaven, on the east coast, to the middle of the Island of Bute and Cantire on the west; and the Northern province includes the whole region beyond this line. Each of these districts is distinguished by certain general characteristics. The first-mentioned region is that of the formation termed by Werner the Transition rocks, but to which the title of Silurian system is now applied. It consists in a great measure of Grauwacke, limestone, and slate rocks, and in some localities the plutonic or unstratified rocks make their appearance, such as granite, porphyry, and basalt. The Central region, of which the boundaries have been already stated, consists, like the preceding, of formations belonging to the Palæozoic epoch, and chiefly of the Devonian and the Carboniferous formations; the former consisting of the old red sandstone, conglomerates, and other strata of an analogous character; and the latter of layers of ironstone, limestone, and beds of coal. The third, or most Northerly region, comprehending within its limits a space nearly equal to both the divisions already mentioned, is composed for the most part of the metamorphic rocks, known as the Gneiss system, and contains in addition a large development of the old red sandstone strata, as well as numerous instances of the amorphous crystalline rocks, known as the Granitic system, and comprising granite, porphyry, and trap.

A striking dissimilarity prevails between the geology of England and Scotland, not only on account of the large development of the unstratified and plutonic rocks in the latter country, but the almost total absence of the more recent tertiary formations. According to the estimates of geologists, the trap rocks of Scotland occupy about one seventh of the area of the country, whereas in

England they do not comprehend much more than a hundredth part of the area of that country. In Scotland the metamorphic rocks occupy nearly half the surface, whereas in England they are only about a hundredth part; on the other hand, the Oolitic system, and the formations more recent than those of the Carboniferous era, constitute a very insignificant part of Scotland, but extend over two thirds of the area of England. This dissimilarity, extending to the coasts of both divisions of Britain, causes, it is obvious, a corresponding general difference of character on their sea-shores, a difference which becomes very striking if we compare the northern and north-western coasts of Scotland with the southern and eastern shores of England.

But to proceed with our expedition. Beyond Berwick the Scottish coast is in many places very precipitous. The cliffs are, in a few instances, formed of granite, but in general are similar to the strata forming the Lammermuir Hills. Northwards from St. Abb's Head, the sea-shores are skirted by rocks of the Devonian formation, extending to the valley of the Tyne, beyond which groups of trap and porphyry extend along the shores of the Firth of Forth to Aberlady Bay, near which place limestone occurs in immediate proximity to trap rocks, and the coal formation is observed, which extends to within a short distance of Edinburgh, and thence across the whole country to the shores of Ayrshire. The northern shores of the Firth of Forth are in the highest degree interesting to the geologist, exhibiting from

North Queensferry to Fife Ness a great variety of strata alternating with igneous rocks. Northwards along the Forfarshire coast to Stonehaven, the prevailing geological formation is that of the Devonian, appearing as a fine red sandstone, or as a conglomerate intermingled in several instances with trap, gneiss, and other primary rocks. Many parts of the coast are in a high degree bold and romantic. The precipitous cliffs are often from a hundred to nearly two hundred feet in height, and exhibit most picturesque forms. " The incessant lashings of the sea," says Mr. Miller in a very eloquent and graphic passage, " have ground them down into shapes the most fantastic. Huge stacks, that stand up from amid the breakers, are here and there perforated by round heavy-browed arches, and cast the morning shadows inland athwart the cavern-hollowed precipices behind. The never-ceasing echoes reply, in long and gloomy caves, to the wild tones of the sea. Here a bluff promontory projects into the deep green water, and the white foam, in times of tempest, dashes up a hundred feet against its base. There a narrow strip of vegetation, spangled with wild flowers, intervenes between the beach and the foot of the cliffs that sweep along the bottom of some semicircular bay; but we see from the rounded caves by which they are studded, and the polish which has blunted their lower angularities, that at some early period the breakers must have dashed for ages against their bases." *

* The Old Red Sandstone, p. 249.

Between Stonehaven and Aberdeen the seacoast exhibits many interesting geological phenomena; the lofty cliffs, however, which bound the coast, are in many instances so inaccessible as to render an examination of them impracticable. To the north of Aberdeen the coast, for several miles, is formed of a thick mass of drifting sands, forming a group of low irregular hillocks, but beyond this to Peterhead and Fraserburgh gneiss and granite almost exclusively prevail. The coast-line now trends westwards toward the Moray Firth, and exhibits great variety in its geological structure, and forms a most interesting field of scientific inquiry. The geological peculiarities of this portion of the coast would require, if fully described, a very lengthened and elaborate treatise. The shores of the Firths of Moray and Cromarty and the southern shores of Dornoch Firth are composed of the old red sandstone, which, with the exception of the space between Dornoch and Berridale, where rocks of granite, gneiss, oolite, and other formations occur, extends around the whole shores of Caithness. Along the northern coast of Scotland gneiss is the prevailing formation, interrupted toward the west by rocks of quartz and limestone, and the Devonian formation, and at length is terminated by Cape Wrath, a promontory of gneiss and hornblende intersected by granite. Here the surges of the Atlantic are opposed by stupendous cliffs, many of them six hundred feet in height, which, by the action of the waves during a long course of ages, have in many instances been hollowed out into deep caverns, or fashioned into arches and pinnacles, and innumerable grotesque forms, presenting altogether a scene of extraordinary grandeur even in calm weather; but during a storm, when the tremendous billows roll in from the westward, exhibiting a degree of sublimity which it is scarcely possible to conceive.

The vast extent of the western coasts of Scotland renders anything beyond a general description wholly impossible within the limits of this sketch. From Cape Wrath southwards to the great estuary of the Clyde, the coast, with its numerous indentations forming bays and gulfs, or "lochs," which reach far into the land, exhibits a great variety of romantic scenery. The geological formations consist for the most part of rocks of granite, gneiss, trap, porphyry, quartz, and in a few instances of stratified rocks, such as the old red sandstone and clay slate, the former occurring on the shores of Ross-shire, the latter on those of Argyle. On the southern shores of the Firth of Clyde the character of the coast becomes entirely different from that which prevails on the northern or the north-western shores. The aspect is comparatively uniform, with little of the wild and romantic appearance peculiar to the plutonic and metamorphic formations. From about Greenock, conglomerates, and old red sandstone strata reach to Ardrossan, to the south of which place the coal formation occurs, bounded beyond Ayr by the red sandstone. Southwards from Girvan the rocks of the Silurian system occur, and the northern shores of the Solway exhibit the Devonian formation, interrupted at certain districts by granitic rocks.

Continuing our investigation on the English side of the Solway Firth, we find the geological phenomena are those of the Palæozoic epoch, like those of the Southern and Central districts of Scotland, such as the Silurian, Devonian, and Carboniferous systems. Magnesian limestone, to which the term Permian is applied, constitutes the cliffs at Maryport; at Whitehaven and Workington the sea-shores are formed of the Carboniferous strata, the coal mines reaching far under the sea; and at St. Bees the same system is continued covered by the Permian formation. Beyond this point the coal formation is succeeded by the Silurian strata; and upon entering on the coast of Lancashire, marine detritus and alluvium forming the tertiary strata, are discovered. Crossing from Liverpool to Birkenhead, the New Red Sandstone formation called the Trias appears, succeeded to the southwards by the Carboniferous strata. The Welsh coast affords illustrations of the Silurian system, as at the Menai Straits and at Holyhead. At Carnarvon Bay the cliffs are formed of mica and chlorite schists, and in Cardigan Bay the strata consist chiefly of slate associated with the igneous rocks. On the southern shores of Wales the coal measures are again manifested, and on the southern shores of the Severn the coal formation alternates with the Devonian, which is the peculiar characteristic of Devonshire.

The vast extent of sea-shore, the leading geological features of which we have thus pointed out, exhibits the utmost variety of scenery, in numberless instances presenting features of most picturesque beauty, or of the utmost sublimity and grandeur. But perhaps the most striking scenes are those strictly of geological character, and which have had their birth in those agencies which in the course of centuries produce a variety of modifications on almost every sea-shore throughout the globe. Of such modifications many parts of our own shores afford remarkable illustrations.

CHANGES IN OUR SEA-SHORES

CHAP. III.

CHANGES IN OUR SEA-SHORES.

Mutations of the Earth's Surface indicated by Geology.—General View of their Causes.—Alterations which from age to age have occurred in various Parts of the British and Irish Coasts, and their Causes.—Analogous Changes in other Parts of the World.

THE phenomena with which the science of geology is conversant afford unquestionable evidence that in periods long antecedent to that which beheld the present distribution of sea and land, a series of stupendous changes took place on the surface of our globe. Some of these changes may have been effected with comparative rapidity, such as those arising from the elevation of the igneous rocks in a state of fusion; but in general the process of modification must have been slow and gradual so as to extend over many thousands of years. Of this there is incontrovertible evidence in the fact, that all the stratified rocks of whatever kind are of aqueous origin, and were formed by processes which could not be sudden, the disintegration and wearing away of the primary rocks by the action of water, the deposition of the various materials of which they consisted at the bottom of the sea, and their subsequent consolidation either by physical or chemical causes, or by both in combination.

The causes of such modifications have not ceased to operate from the earliest period of the existence of our globe to the present hour, for they depend upon laws originally impressed upon matter by the Great Creator, and not only universal, but unceasing in their action. Many and various as are the vicissitudes to which material substances are liable, the laws by which these vicissitudes occur are not themselves subject to mutation. In this respect those laws partake of the nature of their Mighty Originator, who is "the same yesterday, to-day, and for ever." In the primitive islands and continents which existed in periods incalculably remote from the present epoch, and were afterwards wholly or partially submerged beneath the waters, the combinations produced by the laws of chemistry, and the changes effected by other physical agencies, were no other than those which at the present day take place around us. Heat, light, electricity, together with the chemical ingredients of air and water, produced by their incessant action the same series of combinations as they now effect. The same results as are now observable arose in those remote periods from the mechanical action of material substances. Then as now the waters of the great deep were carried by evaporation into the atmosphere; at an altitude determined by certain laws they became clouds, and fell in snow, hail, or rain upon the mountains, and forming rivers pursued their way to the ocean from which they originally came. The rivers thus formed, even when gentle and silent as the classic Liris, wore away their banks and triturated into sand and pebbles the solid beds over which they rolled. The lakes, too, dashed their waves against their banks, forming beaches more or less extended, while they were themselves either gradually filled up by the substances carried into them by the rivers, or drained by the gradual depression of their outlets. The surges of the ocean also, impelled by the winds, broke against opposing rocks, wearing them down, and then suffering the disintegrated materials to subside to the bottom and form those strata subsequently laid bare; the lightning struck against the cliffs, and hurled them downwards; the rain percolated through their cavities, and exposed them to the powerful action of the oxygen in the air; and the volcano and the earthquake raised new islands from the abysses of the ocean, and caused tracts of land to subside beneath its waters.

The brief span over which human life extends, and the consequent limited range of individual observation, are apt to lead us to suppose that the present state of things is less liable to those modifications which have taken place in former eras of the world's history. But that such a supposition is erroneous, there is abundant evidence to prove. Even during a single lifetime many changes are perceptible. Those places in the smaller lakes at which the rivers which supply them empty themselves, are frequently perceived in the course of a few years to grow shallow and the soil they deposit at last to become sufficiently dry to bear grass and be pastured by cattle. The estuaries of great rivers, by the joint action of the tides and the streams, become soon too shallow for navigation, unless some artificial process be employed to deepen them. Sea-beaches are perceived to undergo great alteration, probably by some unperceived change in the neighbouring headlands; in some cases those which were formed of hard clay becoming covered with sand, shells, and pebbles, and the opposite process occurring. If such modifications have been witnessed in a single lifetime, or if they have been known with certainty to have occurred within a generation or two, or even within the space of a few hundreds of years, it cannot be doubted that the same agencies, acting incessantly for many centuries, nay, many thousands of years, must have produced very great alterations. Geological investigations clearly prove that very great and remarkable mutations have occurred and are still taking place in many parts of our sea-shores. Those mutations afford a subject of study extremely interesting and instructive. We shall advert to some of the most remarkable.

Many very remarkable changes on our shores have been produced by the perpetual action of the waves of the sea. Such changes are frequently to be observed in places where the shores are low and formed of materials easily acted on by the forces of currents and storms. From such agencies even the hardest and most solid rocks undergo in the progress of ages a great alteration. This is more or less perceptible in all those parts of the British Islands where the coast is bounded by precipitous rocks exposed to the fury of the waves. It is remarkably so in the Shetland Islands, which are open to the uncontrolled violence of the Atlantic. Upon these islands the waves of the ocean, during the prevalence of westerly winds and violent storms, break with irresistible force. The spray of the sea, carried upwards by the wind and sinking through the fissures of the rocks, tends to disunite and decompose them, so as to render them more liable to be disrupted by the mechanical force of the waves. In the more solid cliffs composing the coast, the continual action of the water has hollowed out the rocks into deep caves, and in some cases into the forms of arches; in other instances rocks in the form of pinnacles and columns stand in the sea completely separated from the shore by the washing away of the intervening soil. The beaches of some of these islands are also strewed with immense stones, which have been driven forwards by the irresistible power of the waves during the storms of winter. Dr. Hibbert mentions that this is extremely remarkable in the Isle of Stennes, one of the Shetland group, which presents a scene of great desolation. An example of the immense power of the ocean in causing alterations in the appearance of its shores, may be stated in the fact that in 1802 a tabular-shaped mass of rock eight feet square and five feet in thickness was, by the violence of the waves on the coast of that island, removed from its bed and driven along a distance of eighty or ninety feet; and in a storm in 1818, a block of stone seventeen and a half feet broad and two feet in thickness was borne along by the waves a distance of thirty feet, and having broken into pieces, the fragments, many of them of great weight, were driven along still further. In some instances the rocks are formed of materials of various degrees of hardness. Occasionally a broad vein of soft stone occurs surrounded by the hardest granite. In process of time the soft central substance moulders away under the violent action of the sea; and thus caves of great extent are hollowed out, arches are formed, and in many instances promontories or headlands separated from the mainland, and straits with deep water, are formed between the insulated rocks and the land with which they were once connected. The coasts of Scotland and Orkney, and several parts of the mainland of Scotland on the northwest, exhibit many phenomena of this kind.

The process which is thus obvious in places much exposed to the ravages of the waves, is continually carried on, with more or less rapidity, on every sea-shore, causing great alterations in the course of ages. Many instances of this have occurred within comparatively limited periods, in various parts of Britain. In the counties of Inverness, Moray, Forfar, Fife, and others, several parts of the coast have undergone great and remarkable alterations. In Kincardineshire the ledge of rocks which lay between the village of Mathers and the sea was broken through in 1795, the whole village swept away, and its site remained covered by the sea, the shore of which was removed nearly 200 yards inland. At Arbroath gardens and houses have been swept away since the beginning of the present century; and on the southern shores of the Firth of Forth similar occurrences have taken place. A large tract of land, which in 1688 was a common covered with grass, immediately to the east of Leith, is now covered with the tide at high water; and within the last few years the sandstone rocks at Prestonpans, and the soil that covered them, have been so much wasted away by the action of the waves that several small gardens between the houses and the sea-shore have all but disappeared; and within the last two or three years the author perceived what appeared to be parts of stone coffins protruding from the soil, and daily exposed to the action of the waves. The place where these remains appear is part of a garden between the houses of the town and the sea, and is only now a few yards in breadth, the boundary wall and a large portion of the soil having long since disappeared. It was not known to have been a place of sepulture; but, when chosen for that purpose, perhaps two thousand years ago, it may have been several hundred yards from high-water mark. The low sandstone rocks, indeed, which run out in parallel strata seaward, must then have been covered with soil.

In some parts of the ancient village to which we now refer, the washing away of many of the houses is a mere question of time, unless some effectual artificial barrier is opposed to the encroachments of the sea.

On every part of the coast of England similar alterations have been taking place. A variety of instances of very striking changes in the sea-shores of Yorkshire, Lincolnshire, and Norfolk are recorded by geologists. In old maps of the first-mentioned county, spots are mentioned as the sites of towns and villages which are now sand-banks in the sea. The town and harbour of Ravenspur, from which Edward Baliol sailed to invade Scotland in 1332, and where Henry IV. landed in 1399, no longer exists; and in their place are extensive sands, dry only at low water. The ancient towns and villages of Hyde, Auburn, and Harthurn have long since disappeared, and the places where they stood are now covered by the waters. Fears by no means unreasonable are entertained that Spurn Point will at some future time be separated from the mainland and become an island,—a change which will, if it occur, be productive of great devastation from the estuary of the Humber being thus exposed to the ravages of the ocean.

Great changes in process of time have occurred in other portions of the English coast. In the Isle of Sheppey, the church at Minster, now near the shore, was seventy years ago in the middle of the island; and one of the most eminent geologists of the present age asserts that "if the present rate of destruction should continue, we might calculate the period, and that not a very remote one, when the whole island will be annihilated." The church of Reculver, too, affords a remarkable instance to the same effect. A view taken of it so lately as 1781, and published in the "Gentleman's Magazine," represents it as at a considerable distance from the shore; but it now stands close to a precipice, and a few years it is probable will complete its destruction. The church was abandoned in 1804, part of the churchyard and the adjoining houses having been demolished by the sea.

The sea-shores of Lincolnshire have been the scene of very remarkable changes from age to age. Consisting of the deposits of the tertiary formation, and of marine detritus, the shores of Lincolnshire are so low that, as on the Dutch coast, embankments are necessary to keep off the sea. Parts of the fenny tract of land on the coast were in remote ages covered with forests, subsequently inundated, and again reclaimed from the sea. Some of the fens are understood to have been drained and embanked so recently as the time of the Romans, and that after their departure from England the sea again took possession of the land they had cultivated, and covered large tracts of it with beds of silt and marine shells, but that the lands thus lost are once more rendered productive. Independent of such alternations, great devastation has been caused on the coast of Lincolnshire by the inroads of the sea, several large districts having been at different times overwhelmed.

The shores of Norfolk and Suffolk are likewise subject to great changes from the constant assaults of the sea. At Hunstanton, and between Weybourne and Sherringham, the cliffs are constantly undermined by the waves. It is stated by Sir Charles Lyell that in 1805, when the inn at Sherringham was built, it was computed that it would take seventy years for the sea to reach the spot on which the building stands, the distance between it and the sea being fifty yards. But in 1829 only a small plot of ground was left, seventeen yards having been swept away during the preceding five years alone. In the harbour of this same port there was in 1829 a depth of twenty-four feet of water, at a place where only forty-eight years before there stood a cliff fifty feet in height, with houses upon it. The havoc made on the coast of Norfolk has been most formidable. The site of the ancient town of Cromer now forms part of the German Ocean, the inhabitants having gradually been compelled to retreat to their present situation, from which the same process of demolition still threatens to dislodge them. In the winter of 1825, a mass of land of some twelve acres near the lighthouse was engulphed in the sea. The old villages of Shipden, Wimpwell, and Eccles have long ceased to exist, and several manors and parishes have gradually been obliterated, and their sites are now covered with water. In 1605 the inhabitants of the last-mentioned of these towns petitioned James I. for a reduction of their taxes, in consequence of 300 acres of land, and all their houses except fourteen, having been destroyed by the sea. Not half that number of acres now belong to the parish.

Dunwich, on the Suffolk coast, was in former times a large seaport. Near that place two large tracts of land which had been taxed in the time of Edward the Confessor, are referred to in a survey made by William the Conqueror a few years afterwards as having been swept away by the waves. Subsequently a monastery, several churches, the old harbour, four hundred houses at once, roads, town-hall, and various public buildings, are recorded as having perished in succession at different times. In the sixteenth century not a fourth of the original town existed, and the inhabitants continued retreating inland as the sea gained upon them, and still retaining the ancient appellation of their town, although its site had been long obliterated.

As we proceed southwards along the coast of England, we discern that similar alterations have from age to age occurred on the sea-shores. On the coasts of Kent, Sussex, Hampshire, Dorsetshire, and Cornwall, in a great many different places, large tracts of land have been devoured by the ocean, and in others great additions have been made to the shores, probably by the deposition of the materials swept off from other localities. Mention has already been made of the devastations effected by the sea on the coast of the Isle of Sheppey; but in many other parts of Kent the same process has from age to age been going on. Thus at Hythe several encroachments of the sea are recorded; while towards Dungeness the level tract called Romney Marsh has received considerable accessions. To the south of Romney Marsh, the town of Rye was once destroyed by the sea; but by the additions made by the waves, it is now two miles distant from the beach. In the reign of Queen Elizabeth, the town of Brighton was situated on the tract where the chain pier now extends into the sea. In the beginning of last century there still remained under the cliff more than a hundred houses, all of which were swept away from 1703 to 1705; and no traces of the ancient town now remain.

The Isle of Wight affords a remarkable instance of similar changes. Sir Harry Englefield, in his work on that island, states that a great and singular alteration occurred within no very distant period in the shores of the Solent, near Ryde; and that in 1753, the town is said to have been totally inaccessible by sea except at or near high water, as the shore was covered with a vast extent of mud too soft to bear the slightest weight. This mud-bank is now entirely covered with a stratum of fine white sand, smooth and firm enough to bear wheel carriages, and rendering bathing at all times safe and agreeable. This bed of sand now reaches to Binstead, having covered at least two miles of the shore within the last half century; and the inhabitants say it is still extending westwards. To what cause this change is owing it is difficult to guess; but it is an example of the alternation of deposits from the action of the sea, in circumstances apparently unchanged, and which may afford cause for reflection to the geologist.

A great variety of other instances might be mentioned of such alterations on our sea-shores, as occurring from age to age. The western coast is less liable to such alterations, because bounded to so great an extent by rocks, the materials of which offer great resistance to the most violent action of the sea. But on almost all the western coasts, wherever the shores are low or are formed of materials liable to be easily acted on by the waves, great changes have taken place, in some instances extensive tracts having been swallowed up by the waters, and in others great additions by the deposition of the soil being made to the extent of the sea-shore.

But the waters of the ocean and the force of the winds produce other alterations in the aspect of the sea-shore than those now described. In some instances, where the beach is low, the waves cast up mounds of gravel, formed of stones of various kinds, rounded by being constantly rolled upon each other; and these, during the prevalence of storms, and where the shores are exposed to strong currents from either side, are swept along, varying their quantity in different localities as the effects of the impelling forces are modified by the form of the shore itself. In other instances, where the water is comparatively shallow, the waves during the storms of winter drive the sand upon the beach, where it is raised in a bank. This at the recess of the tide becomes partially dried, and during strong winds in summer is carried from the shore for a considerable distance inland, forming mounds of fine sand far beyond the reach of the waters. Some portions of the coasts thus present a remarkable appearance, occasioned by those downs or ranges of low sand-hills, and in some instances fertile tracts of land have thus become covered, to the destruction of vegetation. A remarkable instance may be mentioned as occurring between the towns of Arklow and Wicklow, on the east coast of Ireland. Some years ago the author travelled along a fine road near the sea-shore between these two towns, and on returning a fortnight afterwards, more than half a mile of the road, although at a considerable distance from the sea, had been covered with fine dry sand to the depth of several feet, a storm from the east having taken place during the interval, and drifted the loose sand over the road and the adjoining fields, many of which were entirely covered, so that not a blade of grass could be seen. On the coast of Sligo, a destructive sand inundation took place some years ago, and although in some measure checked, it is still in progress.

On the north coast of Cornwall a similar sand deluge occurred many ages since, completely overwhelming a large tract of once fertile and cultivated land, and forming in its place numerous hills, composed of sand and marine shells, several hundreds of feet above the level of the sea. By the shifting of these sands, the ruins of buildings which once occupied the land have been discovered, and the remains of wells formed by the ancient inhabitants. Among the ruins thus laid bare are those of an ancient chapel, erected, there is every reason to believe, by Piranus or St. Piran, one of the most zealous of the early Christian missionaries in Britain, who in the fourth century fixed his abode in this remote region of England, and devoted his life to the instruction of its rude inhabitants, as Ninian, Kentigern, and Columba did in the western districts of Scotland. On the coast of Norfolk the same cause has produced great devastation; and at Eccles, already mentioned, large mounds of blown sand occupy the places of houses which existed in the beginning of the seventeenth century. About twenty years ago the force of the waves laid open the foundations of one of the houses which had thus been overwhelmed by the sand-flood, the upper part of which appeared to have been pulled down before it was finally overwhelmed. Even the body of the old church of Eccles has been buried under the sand, and nothing now remains but its tower to point out the place where the old inhabitants were wont to assemble for worship, and all around it is completely desolate.

The changes thus effected on various parts of our own sea-shores, by the agency of drifted sand, have also occurred on the shores of France and

Jutland. In Brittany, near St. Pol de Léon, a whole village was so entirely overwhelmed by the sand that no remains of it were visible but the spire of the village church. And on the shores of Jutland large hillocks of sand and sea-shells, intermingled with sea-weed, have been formed by the violence of storms acting on the dry sands.

The alterations thus produced in some districts of our sea-shores are, although on a smaller scale, scarcely less remarkable than those which have been occasioned by the same causes in Egypt, Lybia, and Peru.

In Egypt many of the most fertile plains and valleys which in distant ages teemed with a busy population have been converted into arid wastes, and many of the finest monuments of her ancient grandeur have been overwhelmed by the sands of the desert. On the western shores of the Nile, the sands drifted by the winds have left no lands capable of being cultivated but those which are sheltered by the mountains; and in Upper Egypt whole districts are thus buried, and here and there the ruins of cities and the summits of temples may be seen, which have been thus overwhelmed. Denon observes: "Nothing can be more melancholy than to walk over villages swallowed up by the sand of the desert, to trample under foot their roofs and minarets, and to reflect that yonder were cultivated fields, that there grew trees, that here were the dwellings of men, and that all have now vanished. The sands of the desert were in ancient times remote from Egypt; and the oases, which still appear in the midst of this sterile region on the remains of fertile soils which formerly extended to the Nile." Although the desolation has taken place, it must nevertheless be remembered that the inundations of the Nile are constantly adding to the extent of the alluvial soil, and may, perhaps, be completely counterbalancing the effects produced by the shifting sands.

But in Peru many of the finest maritime plains and valleys are exposed to desolation from the same causes. It appears that the sand-drift has already surmounted the lofty hills which form the boundary of the valley of Lurin, and is flowing down over the cultivated grounds, threatening their total destruction. The same process is taking place on the elevated plain called the Tablada, where the tops of the hills appear like Egyptian oases, the sand falling in overwhelming floods over the valley of Rimac, to the gradual extinction of the sugar plantations of Villa and San Juan.*

Other changes in the character and aspect of our sea-shores may here be referred to as having been produced by strictly geological causes. On a great many districts of our sea-shores, as, for instance, from Brighton to Rottingdean, near Bromley in Kent, and Reading in Berkshire, and various other places on the eastern and western coasts of England, and in a variety of localities

* Blackwood's Magazine, March, 1839.

along the shores of the Firth of Forth in Scotland, are traceable at a distance at certain elevations above the existing margin of the sea, and at various distances from it, deposits of shells and pebbles and sand, which at some far distant period formed the beach washed by the waves of the sea. These phenomena are extremely remarkable, and it is impossible to examine the appearances they present without coming to the conclusion that the coast has risen above its ancient level, and that the waters of the deep have retired from places on which they formerly flowed. Whether the causes which have produced these elevations are still in progress as regards our own shores it is difficult to affirm; but it is certain that within the last few years the sea-shores of various parts of South America have been raised during earthquakes, the relative levels of the sea and land have been greatly altered. Like changes, however, from the raising of the ancient margins of the sea in this country have taken place, it is probable, long antecedent to the period when the human race were called into existence.

Geology, as already observed, points out a series of vast and marvellous changes which have occurred in the physical condition of the globe we inhabit. To these changes our sea-shores have in the progress of ages been themselves subjected, and the agencies by which many of those changes are effected are in active and incessant operation. Stable as we are apt to deem the solid structure of the earth, nevertheless its materials are subject in the course of ages to great mutations, and of this, the changes which occur on our sea-shores afford an example. Such modifications are occasioned by the chemical and physical laws which the All-powerful and infinitely wise Creator of the world has instituted; and the more carefully we investigate, and the more clearly we comprehend, those laws, and the extreme uniformity with which they work out their various and manifold results, the more must we be impressed with a sense of the vastness of that Divine intelligence by which those laws were formed, and by which all the vast complication of results they produce must have been foreseen and intended. Amid the mutations of temporal things, we perceive the invariable character of the laws now referred to, which have acted immutably and incessantly from the earliest birth-time of our planet; and in these laws we recognise their immutable Author, who is without all variableness or shadow of turning.

FOSSILS OF THE SEA-SHORE

FOSSILS OF THE SEA-SHORE.

1, 2. Chain Coral 3. Mushroom Coral 4. The Fossil Flying Fish. 5. A Fossil Fish of Permian Formation.
6. A Fossil Fish of the Devonian Formation. 7. The Herry-bone Fossil Fish. 8. A Fossil Bat.
9. The Great-headed Fossil Lizard. 10 A Trilobite 11. A Small Trilobite. 12 The Lily Encrinite.

(See Chapter 4)

CHAP. IV.

FOSSILS OF THE SEA-SHORE.

General Views.—Fossils of the Palæozoic, the Secondary and the Tertiary Epochs, and various Considerations regarding them.

FROM the geological phenomena presented by our sea-shores as apparent from the preceding sketch, it will be perceived that a very large proportion of the space they include is occupied, not by the Primary or Plutonic Rocks, but by what are called by geologists the Secondary Formations, Tertiary Strata, and Alluvial Deposits. All of these abound in the fossil remains of plants and animals peculiar to the epochs to which they belong. It is requisite therefore in noticing the geology of the sea-shore, that we direct our attention to the remains of organised beings which they contain.

To do this, however, it is not requisite that we proceed to consider the organic remains of the various formations in the miscellaneous order in which they occur to us in a tour along the coast. It will conduce much more to clearness and accuracy if instead of this we adopt the plan of pointing out, independently of their locality, the fossils characteristic of the formations which occur in various parts of the coast. One or two general remarks may, however, be requisite before proceeding to our particular description.

In the Hypogene and Volcanic rocks, and the various groups they comprehend, there are no appearances of organic remains. These rocks include granite, porphyry, basalt, trap, and others which are of a crystalline structure, and evidently appear to have assumed their peculiar forms under the action of intense heat. This circumstance is of itself sufficient to account for the fact that those rocks are entirely destitute of the fossil remains either of plants or animals.

All the other geological formations, comprised under the rocks which are more or less stratified, have the hypogene or primary rocks for their foundation, and in the destruction of which they seem in great measure to have originated, by being deposited in the basins of lakes, bays, and estuaries, and in the profound depths of the ocean. The alluvial deposits, like the stratified rocks, owe their existence to the agency of water, and consist of accumulations of water-worn and drifted materials. All these formations abound in fossil remains peculiar to their respective geological epochs, and in this respect essentially differ from the rocks which form their foundation, and which, as already stated, owe their peculiar structure to the agency of heat.

In taking into view the fossils of our sea-shores, we shall first notice those of the most ancient of the fossiliferous strata, all of which belong to what geologists call the PALÆOZOIC EPOCH. These strata are the Cambrian, the Silurian, the Devonian, the Carboniferous, and the Permian Formations.

These various groups also we shall notice in the order of their antiquity, commencing with the most ancient, and so advancing upwards towards the secondary and tertiary deposits, and observing as we approach the period when man inhabits the earth, the changes which from one epoch to another take place in the character of the living creatures by which the earth is inhabited.

I. We first notice therefore the Silurian formation, which, so far at least as fossils are concerned, may be said to include the Cambrian also. The Silurian, as already described, is largely developed in various parts of England and Scotland, and is in many places bounded by the sea-shores.

The investigations of geologists have not succeeded in bringing to light any vegetable remains in the Silurian system in Europe, with the exception of some imperfect indications of fucoids or marine plants of the simplest character. The lowest Silurian deposits in which those fucoids appear, rest upon the primitive crystalline rocks which contain no fossils, and it has been assumed, therefore, that they indicate the first indications of organic creation. But this view is not held by Lyell, who states in his Travels in America, that, although the Silurian strata in Europe contain no remains of vegetables except the fucoids, the same strata in America exhibit abundant remains of vegetables of the carboniferous type, such as Lepidodendra and ferns. Although the vegetable remains are so few in the Silurian strata in this country, more than 800 species of fossil animals have been discovered, almost exclusively belonging to the Invertebrata, that is to say animals in whose structure the back-bone does not occur. This our readers will observe is what might be expected in the earliest development of animal existence. But the fact that the animals peculiar to the Silurian seas existed in prodigious multitudes is itself evidence that the vegetation must have been proportionately abundant, although consisting, it may be, in great measure, only of the simplest forms of sea-weed; for we must take into view the relation which marine plants bear to marine animals, either as their food, or as the source of the oxygen requisite to their existence. The various remains belonging to the system now referred to may be divided into those of Zoophytes, Molluscs, and Crustaceans.

The ZOOPHYTES comprise various kinds of coral, among which the prevailing forms are those of Catenipora, or chain-coral, and Cyathophyllum, or that of a cup-like figure. These corals appear in immense quantities in the limestone rocks of Dudley. Other zoophytes also occur, such as Graptolites, and various kinds of Crinoidea.

The SILURIAN MOLLUSCA embrace a considerable variety of bivalve shells analogous to those which now swarm in our seas, and thus we perceive that among the first traces of animal life, in the remotest periods of the natural history of our planet, there were many species which still continue to exist. There were also numerous simple univalve mollusca, or Gasteropoda, such as Euomphalus; and many Cephalopoda, such as Orthoceras and Actinoceras. Various examples of Annelida, or animals whose bodies consist of articulated segments or rings likewise occur in the Silurian strata, some of them being naked marine worms, and others those which are covered with shells, of which the Nereis, the Gordius, the Serpula, are instances. Of all these, distinct imprints have been discovered in the limestone rocks of the period referred to.

The CRUSTACEA of the Silurian system include a very remarkable and peculiar race of creatures which are called Trilobites, from the circumstance of their bodies consisting of three lobes or divisions. Of these creatures there are no living representatives: they are entirely restricted to the Palæozoic or most ancient fossiliferous deposits. In these remarkable animals the body is protected by a strong case or shell, composed of numerous ring-shaped segments or arches, and as already stated is divided into three lobes by two longitudinal furrows. The head and the abdomen are, however, enclosed in a single piece of armour. The eyes are large and are found to consist of numerous facets or lenses, and are thus similar in structure to the eyes of several kinds of crustaceans at present existing, as well as those of various insects, such as the house-fly and the dragon-fly. No traces of feet or swimmers have been found, and it has therefore been supposed that these organs must have been of a soft and perishable nature. Trilobites occur in great multitudes in the Dudley limestone. They seem to have varied greatly in form and magnitude. Some of them were of very minute size, others twenty or twenty-four inches in length; some possessed the power of coiling themselves into a ball like the Oniscus or wood-louse; in others this was impossible, the central segments alone being moveable; in some the body was elongated, so as to form a tail of greater or less dimensions, in others it was truncated, without any appearance of a caudal appendage. These remarkable creatures, of which about 250 varieties have been discovered, formed the great mass of the population of the Palæozoic seas. It is impossible not to regard their forms with great interest, inscribed as they are, and with such marvellous accuracy, in the solid rock; for they are the typical hieroglyphics of an epoch, compared with the antiquity of which the remotest period of Egyptian history is as nothing, and they refer us to one of the most august periods in the history of our planet, when the all-creating Spirit first peopled the primitive waters with living forms.

We have already mentioned that the eyes of the Trilobite were similar in structure to those of certain insects and crustaceans at present existing. The discovery of this fact, and some deductions consequent upon it, are among the most marvellous things unfolded to us by geology. The microscope has disclosed to us the structure of an insect's eye, which is one of the most striking miracles of Divine skill which the bodies of living beings exhibit. The human eye, and that of other mammalia, consists of a single optical instrument analogous in its structure to a telescope, or resembling rather a photographic apparatus with its lens, its dark chamber, and the paper on which to receive the reduced image of the object to be observed, answering to similar parts of the eye itself. The eye of an insect, however, consists, not of a single optical instrument thus constructed, but of a series of such instruments, each furnished with its separate lens, pupil, cornea and optic nerve, but all combined together in the one eye. In the common house-fly there are 8,000 such distinct optical instruments in each eye, and nearly 13,000 in the eye of a dragon-fly. Each of these distinct tubes, with its accompanying apparatus of vision, is indicated by one of the facets into which the outward surface of the one compound eye is cut, and the structure is rendered necessary because the eye is motionless and cannot be directed towards its object with the facility in which this can be done by the mammalia. Than this no portion of the structure of an insect exhibits a more remarkable instance at once of creative skill and foresight—skill in the formation of the complicated apparatus itself and its accurate adaptation to the laws of light, and foresight in anticipating and supplying the wants of the creature to whose structure it occurs.

An examination of the eyes of a trilobite proves that they were constructed in the manner now described. The creature has two compound eyes, each of them possessing several hundreds of the separate visual organs already described, but each imperfect on the side opposite to each other, because in that position unnecessary. Dr. Buckland thus expresses himself on the subject:—" We find in the trilobite of those early rocks, the same modifications of the organ of sight as in the living crustaceans. The same kind of instrument was also employed in the intermediate periods of our geological history, when the secondary strata were deposited at the bottom of a sea inhabited by Limuli in those regions of Europe which now form the elevated plains of Central Germany. But these results are not confined to physiology: they prove also the ancient condition of the seas and the atmosphere, and the relation of both these media to light. For in those remote epochs the marine animals are furnished with instruments of vision in which the minute optical adaptations were the same as those which now impart the perception of light to the living crustacea. The mutual relations of light to the eye and of the eye to light were therefore the same at the time when crustaceans first existed at the bottom of the Silurian seas as at the present moment." The conclusion at which Dr. Buckland thus arrives may be less generally expressed thus: At that period in the history of the planet we inhabit, when its waters alone contained living beings, countless ages before the superior races of creatures, or man had himself appeared, the sun-light was as perfect as it now is, the rays of light obeyed the same laws of refraction then as now, and perhaps we may add, when this globe, which is comparatively a small portion of the solar system was in its rudest condition, and those alterations had not yet occurred on its surface requisite to fit it to be the habitation of the human race. The sun, the centre of the system of which it is a part, had already attained a high condition of perfection during an existence it may be of myriads of years antecedent to the time when the all-creating Power called this planet into existence, sent it on its annual course round the sun, and peopled it with its innumerable living forms, and at last placed man upon it endowed with the capacity of admiring the place of his abode, and doing homage to that mighty Artificer whose wisdom and whose power it unfolds.

II. The formation to which we are now to turn is the Devonian, which is second in point of antiquity to the Silurian, and is an assemblage of sandstones, marls, conglomerates, beds of coralline marble and laminated micaceous sandstones: this formation, from the generally dull red colour communicated to some of the strata belonging to it, has been called the Old Red Sandstone. We have already seen in our tour along the sea-shore that it is developed in various parts of the coast, such as Devonshire or Cornwall, Herefordshire, portions of Wales, and various parts of the coast of Scotland. The organic remains of this formation are extremely rich. They contain many peculiar types, and are supposed to form a connecting link between those of the Silurian system, which preceded the Devonian, and the Carboniferous system, which followed it.

Almost the only traces of vegetables found in this system, are, like those of the Silurian, the remains of fucoid plants.

The Zoophytes are numerous, and consist of corals and Crinoidea, comprising a number of kinds; the Mollusca contain many genera and species, such as those of Buccinum, Turbo, Pecten and others; the Cephalopoda are also numerous, embracing such shells as those of Orthoceras, Bellerophon and others.

Among the Crustaceans of this formation are considerable numbers of trilobites, which, as already shown, are embedded in countless myriads in the older strata of the Silurian.

The fishes of this formation, according to Agassiz, amount to at least a hundred species, of which those belonging to British strata are more than sixty in number. Of these the Cephalaspis or buckler-head; the Perichthys or winged-fish; and the Coccosteus or berry-bone, may be mentioned as examples.

III. We now turn to the fossils of the Carboniferous system, so called because it comprises the principal deposits of mineral fuel. This system is next in point of antiquity to the Devonian, which in order of time occupies the interval between the Carboniferous and the Silurian systems. The Carboniferous formation extends, as already stated, to various portions of our sea-shores, as those of South Wales, Lancashire, Northumberland, and various parts of Scotland. This formation consists of the coal measures, deposits of ironstone, millstone grit, and limestone, exhibiting great variety of hue and quality. The organic remains peculiar to it are very numerous, and of great interest.

The fossil plants of this system are extremely characteristic: they constitute the entire mass of those deposits of coal which are of such surpassing value to mankind; they are likewise thickly interspersed throughout the other formations belonging to the carboniferous system, and are, as may be presumed, of great interest to the student of fossil botany. Without discussing the many interesting questions which suggest themselves on the subject of the structure and other peculiarities of the plants of the era to which the coal deposits belong, we can only point out a few examples of those plants. Many of the plants were evidently similar in botanical character to the equisetum or mare's-tail, so common in all our marshes at the present day; but these calamites were of gigantic dimensions; existing plants of this species are little more than a foot and a half in height, and their stems about a quarter of an inch in diameter. The stems of the fossil specimens, on the other hand, are often fourteen inches in diameter, and thirty feet in length. The common fern is also an example of another numerous family of plants which flourished during the carboniferous period. These were Sigillariæ or tree-ferns such as belong at present to the torrid zone. Many of them were from thirty, forty, and sixty feet in height. The leaves of this tribe of plants exhibit great elegance and variety of forms, and are pictured with wonderful accuracy and minuteness in the coal shale. Besides the tree-ferns there were Lepidodendra, or arborescent club-mosses of gigantic dimensions, attaining an altitude of sixty or seventy feet. These cryptogamic plants grew with extreme rapidity and luxuriance in the hot and moist atmosphere of the period to which they belonged, and formed in the mode explained by geologists those immense deposits of coal which belong to the formation now in question.

The animal remains must now be referred to. The Zoophytes and Mollusca exhibit numerous corals and crinoideans, shells of great varieties of form occurring in the limestone strata of the formation. Among the Crustaceans of this period are animals which are referred to the Limulus or king-crab, a genus abundant at present in the Indian seas. We also discover vestiges of the trilobites which belong, as we have seen, to the Silurian waters, but which had become extinct long antecedent to the Carboniferous era. The fossil remains of insects, including various kinds of beetles; fossil scorpions and various fishes, many of them of great magnitude, and some related to lizards in character and form, others to the shark family, and many of them possessed of finely enamelled scales, and having their heads protected by strong and smooth plates of enamel.

IV. The Permian Formation now remains to be noticed as belonging to the Palæozoic system. This formation is the Magnesian Limestone; it occurs in certain portions of our sea-shores, as for example from Tynemouth to Hartlepool, at St. Bees Head, and at Maryport. It is the last, and least ancient of the Palæozoic formations, and is characterised by a peculiar type of organic remains, and by an entire absence of any species of fossil that occurs in the newer strata. Between the period of the Permian formation and the most ancient of the secondary strata, one of the two grand revolutions in the organic world occurred, and hence the fossil remains of the Permian possess great interest, as exhibiting the last and most advanced condition of organic life in the Palæozoic era, and as being separated by a vast and marvellous revolution from the succeeding epoch.

The plants of this formation are such as are common to the coal measures, and the same remark may be made as to a large number of the Radiata, Mollusca, and Articulata. Of the trilobites which swarmed in the Silurian seas, and which occurred to a limited extent in the Carboniferous formation, there are no traces whatever in the Permian.

The fishes of the Permian comprise about fifty species. They all seem to have possessed the peculiar modification of the tail in which the vertebral column is prolonged into the upper lobe of the caudal fins. This remarkable structure of the caudal fin, although apparently universal among the fishes of the Permian group, is found to be of excessive rarity in the fishes of the secondary and tertiary epochs; and at the present day almost the only members of the finny tribe in which it occurs, are the sturgeons and various kinds of sharks, including of course the dog-fish of our own seas. The fishes of the Permian are chiefly ganoid, and are so called from the character of their scales, which are composed of angular plates of horn or bone thickly enamelled. They consist of various kinds, such as Palæoniscus, Platysomus, Ceratodus and others.

The Permian formation affords the earliest certain indications of the existence of reptiles on our globe, although it appears that some slight traces of their existence during the Carboniferous era have been discovered. Fossil lizards, turtles and crocodiles belong to this period; and among the saurians are found the remains of the huge marine lizard called Ichthyosaurus or fish-lizard, the Plesiosaurus, another marine reptile, and the Pterodactyle or winged lizard.

It will thus be perceived that the various formations of the Palæozoic or most ancient strata, are represented more or less abundantly in various parts of our sea-shores.

We now turn to the consideration of the SECONDARY EPOCH, the various formations composing which are more or less extensively represented in various parts of our sea-shores, as, for instance, in parts of Cheshire, Denbighshire and Devonshire. Observing the order already adopted, we shall first consider the lowest and most ancient of the Secondary formations.

I. The Triassic Formation. The name triassic is

derived from the circumstance that this formation exhibits a triple series of limestone, sandstone and variegated marls, and conglomerates, containing peculiar fossils. This formation is the great depository of rock salt.

As to the organic remains the trias presents a remarkable contrast with the formation immediately above in the paucity of such remains. Twenty or thirty kinds of ferns and cone-bearing plants have, however, been attained. The animal remains are numerous and various. They consist of zoophytes and corals, lily encrinites, so called from their resemblance to that flower; fishes of various kinds, reptiles of the lizard and frog tribes, many of them of vast dimensions, and one of them in particular presenting a most unique and marvellous structure, having a pair of huge tusks like the walrus, and thence called Dicynodon or bidental; huge birds likewise appear to have belonged to this formation; their footprints have been discovered distinctly marked, eighteen inches in length by fourteen in breadth, deeply made originally in the mud in which the creature walked. These immense birds appear to have been four or five times larger than an African ostrich, and must have weighed about 600 lbs.

II. The Oolite and Lias formation now claim our notice. These formations, which may be considered as one, occur in some portions of the coasts of Yorkshire and Devonshire, and also in various parts of the Scottish coast.

The fossils of these formations consist of fucoids,

trees allied to pines, and similar to the Araucaria, corals and other zoophytes, nautili, ammonites, belemnites, cuttles, &c.; crustaceans allied to shrimps, lobsters and crabs; various insects and numerous fishes and reptiles.

III. The Wealden formation is next in order, and extends from the interior along the coast of England to the east and west of Hastings, in the county of Sussex. This formation is a series of fluviatile deposits of great thickness and extent, and consists of alternations of clays, limestones, sandstones and sand, with beds of freshwater shells and crustaceans. The fossil remains peculiar to this formation are those of enormous land and aquatic reptiles, and various trees and plants. The Wealden series of deposits afford the most striking evidence of a vast alternation in the relations of land and water having occurred at the remote epoch when they were deposited. All the strata seem to have been deposited by the waters of a great river; the organic remains are chiefly, if not wholly, such as belonged to creatures inhabiting fresh water, and what now forms the south-eastern district of England must at a far distant epoch have been the mouth of an immense river flowing from a vast inland lake, the shores of which were the abode of those prodigious forms of animal life which the strata now disclose. How difficult to realise all this while wandering at the present day along the sea-shores of Sussex! How brief and transitory human life appears when contrasted with the immense series of ages to which these geological changes refer; and how marvellous are those physical laws by which the All-wise Author of Nature carries out the purposes of his creative and providential designs!

One of the most remarkable reptiles of the Wealden is the iguanodon, a lizard of enormous dimensions. The fossil remains of this creature indicate the extraordinary size it attained. The leg and thigh bones prove that the entire length of the limb of a full-grown specimen must have exceeded nine feet, and when covered with muscles and integuments of suitable proportions the limb could not have been less than seven feet in circumference! The body of this gigantic lizard was as large as that of the largest elephant, and its length, if the tail was slender, was probably sixty feet, or if the tail, like that of some lizards, were short, the whole length of the animal must have been at least thirty feet. Besides the iguanodon there were other reptiles of no less magnitude; and fossil remains have been discovered which belonged to reptiles having the power of flying through the air.

The character of the country which these creatures inhabited is remarkably indicated by the fossil remains thus discovered. It does not appear whether it was an island or a continent, but it appears to have been diversified by hills and valleys, rivers and lakes, and possessed a climate much higher in temperature than any part of modern Europe. Palm trees, arborescent ferns, and various kinds of cone-bearing trees formed its groves and forests, and the land was clothed with a large abundance of ferns. Among its herbivorous quadrupeds was the gigantic iguanodon already mentioned; among its carnivora was the megalosaurus and other huge reptiles, and crocodiles and turtles inhabited its rivers, while its waters teemed with mollusca, crustaceans and fishes. The greater part of all the bones which have been discovered appear beyond doubt to have been rolled and broken; the teeth have been detached from their sockets, and all the bones of the extremities and of the vertebræ have been separated, and scattered in confusion. The trees, too, have been torn to pieces, and their branches broken into fragments. This was evidently effected, not by the waves of the ocean, but by the violent currents of rivers. The condition of these fossils is sufficient to prove that they were floated down the rivers with the rafts of trees and other spoils of the land, till, arrested in their course, they sunk to the bottom or became embedded in the soil. The immense extent and vast quantity of the deposits thus accumulated, prove that the river which flowed through the country inhabited by the iguanodon must have been as large in its volume as the Mississippi, and that it had a course not of hundreds, but of thousands of miles. How marvellous are the changes which the science of geology thus indicates as having occurred on the surface of our globe!

IV. The Cretaceous or Chalk formation presents itself to us as the least ancient of the formations of the secondary epoch. It extends over a large district of the interior of England, and reaches to various parts of the coasts of Hampshire, Sussex, Kent, Norfolk and Yorkshire. It consists chiefly of marine strata, comprehending the white limestone called chalk, and various marls, clays, and sandstones.

This formation abounds with the remains of extinct species of zoophytes, molluscs, fishes and reptiles: the characters of the chalk formation are those of a vast oceanic basin, filled up with organic and inorganic debris, the innumerable remains of successive generations of marine animals which lived and died in its waters during periods of incalculable duration.

Having thus briefly reviewed the several formations which belong to the secondary epoch from the most ancient and lowest formation to the least ancient and highest in the series, we are now to consider the fossils of that epoch which intervenes between the secondary and the modern or human epoch.

The TERTIARY EPOCH comprises an extensive series of marine, fluvio-marine and lacustrine deposits, containing the remains of all the existing orders of animals and vegetables associated with those of numerous extinct genera. This formation extends from the interior along the northern coasts of Kent to those of Norfolk, Lincolnshire, and part of Yorkshire, Hampshire and Lancashire. At the time of the great chalk or cretaceous formation, which, as we have seen, is the last and least ancient of the secondary rocks, it would appear that the surface of the earth presented the appearance of great unevenness. On this account what is now the continent of Europe was a group of islands with wide channels and seas lying between them. The tertiary epoch presents us with the geological formations by which many of the deep depressions on the surface were filled up. Thus, London and Paris are situated above the deposits thus formed, the tertiary deposits filling up the basin over which London is built being from 300 to 600 feet in thickness.

The fossils of the tertiary epoch are extremely numerous. The shells alone amount to nearly 3000 kinds. Fishes, reptiles, and birds, occur in it in great number and variety. At this epoch the earth had become the fit abode of creatures superior to the amphibious reptiles which were the principal inhabitants of more ancient formations. Accordingly the remains of the tertiary epoch are those of pachydermata or thick-skinned animals, of which the elephant and the rhinoceros are existing specimens. But many of them were of vast bulk and uncouth shape. The Megatherium was larger than the largest existing species of elephant. The Mylodon was nearly as large as the Hippopotamus. Along the eastern coast of England and off the mouth of the Thames, teeth, tusks, and bones of elephants are often dredged up by the fishermen, which have been washed out of the deposits belonging to the tertiary period. Great numbers of the fossil bones of mammalia have also been discovered at Herne Bay and along the shores of Lincolnshire and Norfolk, as well as other parts of the coast to which the tertiary formation extends.

Such are the various formations belonging to the epochs or periods in the physical history of our planet which preceded the period when the human race became its inhabitants. From the earliest deposits, having for their immediate foundation the primary unstratified rocks, to the human epoch, we discover that an inconceivable multitude of creatures existed, suited with infinite wisdom to the condition of the globe at their respective periods. Vast multitudes of these creatures from age to age became extinct, and were succeeded by others of a higher type as the unnumbered ages passed away. From the first formation of the globe to the completion of the tertiary formation, and the deposit of the bed of clay on which Paris and London stand, everything indicates that, so far as it is possible to judge, hundreds of thousands of years must have elapsed. Imagination is lost in endeavouring to conceive the vastness and the violence of the changes to which the earth has thus been subject, before it became, in the eyes of its mighty Creator, a suitable abode for man. That changes perhaps as marvellous still await the earth it is scarcely possible to doubt; changes in which the destiny of man is involved, and which may be succeeded by an improvement in the condition of the earth and an advancement in the state of the human race, as great and as marvellous as some of those which geology points out as having already occurred. The gradual progress from the lowest to the highest orders of creatures which the investigations of geology establish, may be considered as supporting the hypothesis that such changes as we refer to, and accompanied by still higher advancement, may still constitute a part of the system of the divine administration as regards this portion of the universe.

We shall close the review thus taken of the fossil remains of the various formations with a passage from an eloquent writer, in which he supposes some being of high intelligence from another sphere to describe the series of mutations which have occurred from the period of the Wealden formation to the present time. "Countless ages ere man was created," he might say, " I visited these regions of the earth, and beheld a beautiful country of vast extent, diversified by hill and dale, with its rivulets, streams, and mighty rivers, flowing through fertile plains. Groves of palms and ferns, and forests of coniferous trees, clothed its surface; and I saw monsters, of the reptile tribe, so huge that nothing among the existing races can compare with them, basking on the banks of the rivers, and roaming through its forests; while in its fens and marshes were sporting thousands of crocodiles and turtles. Winged reptiles of strange forms shared with birds the dominion of the air, and the waters teemed with fishes, shells, and crustacea. And after the lapse of many ages I again visited the earth; and the country, with its innumerable dragon-forms, and its tropical forests, all had disappeared, and an ocean had usurped their place. And its waters teemed with nautili, ammonites, and other cephalopoda, of races now extinct; and innumerable fishes and marine reptiles. And thousands of centuries rolled by, and I returned, and lo! the ocean was gone, and dry land had again appeared, and it was covered with groves and forests; but these were wholly different in character from those of the vanished country of the iguanodon. And I beheld quietly browsing, herds of deer of enormous size, and groups of elephants, mastodons, and other herbivorous animals of colossal magnitude. And I saw in its rivers and marshes the hippopotamus, tapir, and rhinoceros; and I heard the roar of the lion and the tiger, and the yell of the hyæna and the bear. And another epoch passed away, and I came again to the scene of my former contemplations; and all the mighty forms which I had left had disappeared; the face of the country no longer presented the same aspect; it was broken into islands, and the bottom of the sea had become dry land, and what before was dry land had sunk beneath the waves. Herds of deer were still to be seen on the plains, with swine and horses and oxen; and bears and wolves in the woods and forests. And I beheld human beings, clad in the skins of animals, and armed with clubs and spears; and they had formed themselves habitations in caves, constructed huts for shelter, and enclosed pastures for cattle, and were endeavouring to cultivate the soil. And a thousand years elapsed, and I revisited the country, and a village had been built on the sea-shore, and its inhabitants supported themselves by fishing, and they had erected a temple on the neighbouring hill, and dedicated it to their patron saint. And the adjacent country was studded with towns and villages; and the downs were covered with flocks and the valleys with herds, and the cornfields and pastures were in a high state of cultivation, denoting an industrious and peaceful community. And lastly, after an interval of many centuries, I arrived once more, and the village was swept away, and its site covered by the waves: but in the valley and on the hills above the cliffs a beautiful city appeared, with its palaces, its temples, and its thousand edifices, and its streets teeming with a busy population in the highest state of civilisation; the resort of the nobles of the land, the residence of the monarch of a mighty empire."

The period referred to in this passage is that which intervenes between the time when the Portland forests were flourishing and the present day. That interval forms but a very small part of the many and vast intervals during which the various formations were deposited which are more ancient than the era of the forests of Portland. And yet it must itself have embraced a period of vast duration.

THE OCEAN

CHAP. V.

THE OCEAN.

Aspect of the Ocean.—Sunrise and Sunset.—Extent.—Relation to Rivers and Lakes.—Medium of Intercourse.—Depth.—Colour.—Saltness.—Circulation in the Ocean.—Coral Reefs, &c.

How magnificent the spectacle which the ocean presents from its shores! Every one who is in any degree capable of creating for himself the "inner world of thought" must acknowledge that no external object is more calculated to elevate the mind, and to fill it with grand and sublime ideas, than the vast and boundless sea. Casting our eyes towards the distant horizon, where sea and sky, air and water, seem to meet and blend together, it is impossible for us, if we are at all alive to ennobling impressions, not to perceive in the boundless and unbroken prospect a striking and sublime image of infinitude.

Let us wander down to the beach before sunrise on a spring or summer morning. There is not a breath of wind stirring. The fishermen's boats anchored a little way from shore lie motionless in the calm water. The shores are deserted. Even their feathered visitants, so busy during the day, have not yet begun their labours. The wavelets, for the tide is full, are gently breaking on the pebbly shore with a soothing murmur, and a narrow fringe of white foam, extending far away on each hand, marks the line where they break upon the shingle. Seated on a rock let us observe the gradual birth of the day.

A long line of light marks the edge of the eastern horizon. The few clouds hanging over it are suffused with a roseate hue suggesting the poet's beautiful idea of the rosy-fingered Eos. Now the colour brightens into a golden tint, the line of light passes into a broad general refulgence, and the sun emerges as if out of the deep. How glorious that long radiant path of light along the surface of the water between the eye and the sun! Now turn toward the shores. How brightly the little billows are glancing as they fall upon the pebbles! How much of all this splendour is due, not merely to the direct rays of light which enter the eye, but to those that are reflected from the water, or refracted as they pass through the clouds and appear on the various tints of gold and purple! While the laws of material nature are adapted to produce these effects, and the eye fitted to perceive them, we must also admit that in the mind to which the scene communicates pleasure, there must likewise be such an adaptation as renders the prospect capable of eliciting the emotions of the soul.

From our western shores the view of the ocean at sunset is no less magnificent, touched although it is with a certain sadness that seems to a thoughtful observer to accompany the waning light of day. Chateaubriand thus eloquently describes a scene not unlike that of sunset from our coasts in midsummer. He is speaking of a voyage along the shores of Virginia, when the crew of his ship were called to evening prayers. " The globe of the sun, whose lustre even then our eyes could scarcely endure, ready to plunge beneath the waves, was discovered through the rigging in the midst of a boundless space. From the motion of the stern of our vessel it appeared as if the radiant orb every moment changed its horizon. A few clouds wandered confusedly in the east, where the moon was slowly rising; the rest of the sky was serene; and towards the north a water-spout forming a glorious triangle with the luminaries of day and night glistening with all the colours of a prism, rose out of the sea like a column of crystal supporting the vault of heaven. He who recognised not in this spectacle the beauty of the Deity was greatly to be pitied. Religious tears involuntarily flowed from my eyes. The consciousness of our insignificance excited by the spectacle of infinity; our songs resounding to a distance over the silent waves; the night approaching with its dangers, and our occupation in supplicating Him whose spirit inclined over the abyss, and who as it were with one hand stayed the sun at the portal of the west, and with the other raised the moon in the eastern hemisphere, and yet lends through immensity an attentive ear to the feeble voice of his creatures. This is a picture which baffles description, and which the whole heart of man is scarcely sufficient to embrace."

One of the first ideas which a contemplation of the ocean originates is that of its vast extent, and a comparison is naturally suggested between the relative extent of sea and land. On examining a map of the world, we observe that from the fortieth degree of south latitude to the Antarctic pole, the earth is almost wholly covered with water. We perceive also that the ocean predominates between the western shores of the New World and the eastern coasts of the Old, containing but a few groups of islands throughout the immense intervening space of water. The proportion of the solid to the fluid surface of the globe is, according to Rigaud, as 100 to 270, in other words nearly three-fourths of the globe are covered with water.

Now these relative proportions of sea and land are no more accidental than the beautiful and highly organised structures of an animal's body, every part of which affords an instance of wise and beneficent design; for it has been clearly established by Humboldt and other distinguished philosophers, that the relation thus subsisting between the solid and fluid parts of the globe exercises a most important influence on the distribution of temperature, the variations of atmospheric pressure, the direction of the winds, and the quantity of moisture contained in the air, with which the development of vegetation is so essentially connected.

Another consideration which suggests itself is

the relation of the ocean to the lakes and rivers of the globe. The waters of the ocean, as already stated, are the source of supply for all the innumerable rivers and lakes in the old and new world. "There is not a fountain," says an eloquent writer, " that gushes in the unfrequented desert, nor a rivulet that flows in the remotest continent, nor a cloud that swims in the highest regions of the firmament, but is fed by this all-replenishing source."

If we regard the continent of South and North America only, with its deep and wide rivers of fresh water and magnificent inland seas,—if we keep in mind that these lakes and rivers are supplied entirely by the evaporation of the sea water, —we cease to wonder that the source of a supply so vast must itself be so inexhaustible. Nor are any of those great rivers greater than is requisite for the requirements of the animal and vegetable world; for, although a large quantity of the water carried down by the rivers finds its way into the sea, it does so only after having been circulated by thousands of brooks and rills, like so many veins and arteries, throughout the valleys and plains, carrying life, freshness, and beauty, to places which must otherwise have been as dry and barren as the deserts of Asia or Africa. The atmosphere may be regarded as the vast distilling apparatus by which the salt waves are converted into pure and fresh water. In evaporation the watery particles alone are raised into the atmosphere, the ingredients previously incorporated with them, and which give them their briny taste, are left behind. Purer than from the finest artificial still, the sea water rises up in the air day and night unceasingly, invisible and impalpable, yet in millions of tons. Even the surface of the ice-covered lake, or the iceberg on the snow-capped mountains, throw forth their contributions to the great aërial reservoir of moisture; for it is remarkable that the surface of the hardest ice, in the coldest weather, evaporates nearly as fast as if it were a movable fluid. It is obvious that the ocean, as the source of the supply of fresh water, is indispensable to the existence of animal and vegetable life. The substance of all vegetables consists to a great extent of water: the same remark is applicable to all animal bodies; the body of man himself, " the measurer of the sea, and the land and the innumerable shores,"* is formed of but little solid matter, a very large proportion of his frame being water more or less modified. But the circumstance that water thus held in solution in the air, is not necessary only for the supply which animals and vegetables demand for their structure, it is requisite even for the respiration of animals (for experiment has shown that an atmosphere absolutely dry is unsuited to breathing,) these considerations alone are sufficient to exhibit the importance of the ocean in the economy of nature.

There is another aspect in which we may regard the ocean. It is the great medium of intercourse

---

* Hor.

between countries remote from each other, the means by which the benefits it confers on all lands as the primary source of rivers are reciprocated between one nation and another.

> "With every wind it wafts large commerce on,
> Joins pole to pole, consociates severed worlds,
> And links in bonds of intercourse and love
> Earth's universal family."

The waters of the ocean indeed unite shore with shore, connecting together the most distant regions of the inhabited world, and rendering every land they wash easy of access. It is evident that if the earth consisted only of dry land, and life could exist under such circumstances, intercourse between remote countries would be impossible; and when we reflect upon the difficulties which travellers find in passing over a few hundred miles in the centre of Africa, or the interior of South America, when there is no transit by water, and that in the latter continent there are, on both sides of the Amazon, thousands of square miles of country through which the most adventurous traveller cannot penetrate, it is not too much to suppose, that, were there neither seas nor rivers, we should have to this day remained in ignorance of all countries at a great distance from our own.

It is plain likewise that as the means of communication between different nations, the ocean must be regarded as the means of a rapid increase in knowledge and civilisation. By its instrumentality the temperate regions of the earth can speedily acquire the richest productions of more favoured climes. Thus, too, we obtain for use in winter the warm furs of the Antarctic seas or of North America. In summer we procure the lighter fabrics produced by warmer climates; for all these commodities we can exchange the productions of our own ingenuity, which could not otherwise be rendered available to distant nations.

Thus the cotton of the West Indies is transported to the looms of Britain, and again in a manufactured state sent to supply the inhabitants of India and China. Thus the riches of the Indies are wafted to our shores, and we are enabled to reciprocate the benefit by a happy and beneficial interchange. One of the most striking illustrations of the importance of the ocean as the medium of communication between remote countries is the recent employment of steam navigation in our intercourse with distant Australia. Over thousands of leagues the steam-ship ploughs her way across the pathless deep, carrying the manufactures of Europe to supply the wants of those far-off colonies, and bringing home their gold and their fleeces in return. But these are by no means the only advantages which the ocean confers by affording the means of intercourse between parts of the earth far removed from each other. In the earliest history of civilised society, many centuries before the discovery of the New World, the Mediterranean and the adjoining seas, although traversed by timid navigators who scarcely dared to venture beyond sight of land, afforded the means by which the advantages of Roman civilisation were carried to the shores of Britain, whose inhabitants were then little removed from the present condition of the rudest aborigines of America; but since the period of the revival of letters and the coeval advancement of science, how unspeakable have been the benefits which Europe has conferred on remote nations by wafting over the deep those stores of knowledge which tend to multiply and strengthen the moral and intellectual bonds that, like the principle of charity, will, it is to be hoped, yet unite the whole brotherhood of mankind!

The Roman poet was so impressed by the idea of the perils of the deep to which, in a short voyage from Athens, his friend Virgil was exposed, that he spoke of the sailor who first trusted his frail bark to the waves, as a man around whose heart was the threefold brass of courage and heroism. What amazement would have filled the mind of that elegant writer, could he have seen the illustration his metaphorical description has obtained in the immense iron steam-ship, with its marvellous machinery, literally surrounding the brave hearts of our countrymen as they venture, not along the shores of sunny Italy, or the once terrible Syrtes, but over seas unknown to the ancient world, where for thousands of miles the waters reach away on every hand.

"Maria undique et undique cœlum!"

What flight of poetry would Horace have attempted in referring to the mighty ship, with her hundreds of passengers, her powerful mechanism, and her vast stores of wealth traversing against wind and tide, not some narrow strait of an inland sea, but the vast ocean that lies between the opposite sides of the earth; and carrying with her knowledge and cultivation, liberty, and the means of human advancement!

The depth of the sea is another question which seldom fails to suggest itself to the minds of the contemplative visitor of its shores. What that depth is, what untold wonders and inexplicable mysteries the abysses of the sea contain, have always afforded a subject of sublime speculation. It is, indeed, scarcely possible to look on the calm surface of the deep, and think of the marvels and the mysteries which lie beneath, without emotions akin to those with which the devout astronomer, in the stillness of the night, contemplates the starry heavens, and thinks of the mysterious worlds they contain, their number, their magnitude, their grandeur, and the questions that suggest themselves as to their probable inhabitants and their physical forms, intellectual powers, their degrees of knowledge, the length of their lives, and the many similar questions that force themselves upon his imagination.

And there is, in fact, much that is analogous in the degree of success which has attended human efforts to penetrate the mysteries of the ocean depths, and to investigate those which belong to the inconceivably remote objects of the firmament. In the former case comparatively shallow places of the ocean have been sounded, and various discoveries made connected with them; in the latter the less remote objects of the heavens have been examined, such as the various planetary bodies of the solar system. But of the profound abysses of the sea little is known, and as to the far distant fixed stars our efforts accomplish little more than to prove how slight is our knowledge of them, and how much we have to learn.

The soundings taken in the Mediterranean prove that sea to be of enormous depth. In the Straits of Gibraltar, where the passage is narrowest, there is a depth of 500 fathoms. Between Gibraltar and Ceuta, Capt. Smyth found a depth of 950 fathoms. At Nice, within a short distance from shore, Saussure found the water to be 2,000 feet deep, and M. Berard, in another place, could not reach the bottom with a line of 6,000 feet. Lyell and others express the opinion that the central abysses of the Mediterranean are at least as deep as the Alps are high; but this is only a conjecture.

Within the last few years great depths, in some parts of the ocean, have been sounded, and specimens of the soil at the bottom have been obtained. By means of a simple line attached to a heavy cannon-ball, Capt. Denham, of H.M. ship "Herald," sounded the South Atlantic Ocean to the depth of 46,000 feet, and Lieut. Parker, of the U.S. frigate "Congress," in the same region let go his plummet, and saw it run out 50,000 feet without apparently touching the bottom. Lieut. Walsh, of the U.S. schooner "Taney," attempted unsuccessfuly to find the bottom of the ocean with a line 34,000 feet long, and Lieut. Berryman reported another unsuccessful effort of the same kind on a sounding line measuring 39,000 feet. In the North Atlantic Ocean the greatest depth to which the sounding line has reached appears to be 25,000 feet. That the greatest depths of the ocean far exceed those measurements there is much reason to suppose, and although Laplace estimated the greatest depth at eleven, and Dr. Whewell at nine, it is probably as much as fourteen or fifteen miles. Whether animal or vegetable life exists at those enormous depths, and under the immense pressure of so great a mass of water, and in the profound darkness which there prevail, it is difficult to say. But as in subterranean waters, under vast pressure, and when no light has access, some species of fishes have been found destitute of eyes, which could be of no use to them, and probably so organised as to sustain the pressure to which they are exposed, living beings may also exist in those unfathomable depths to which the sounding line has never reached.

The colour of the sea is another subject which naturally attracts the attention of the visitor to its shores. That the general hue of its surface varies greatly, as seen from the beach, is well known to every observer. At one time the watery expanse assumes a grey or leaden colour, at another its colour is a light or a dark blue. All these shades of the surface with their modifications are produced by reflection. The surface of the deep reflects the hue of the superincumbent sky, and appears to be of the same colour. Thus, if the day be cloudy and rainy the surface of the sea is more or less of a leaden or grey tinge; if the sky is cloudless or a smart breeze blows to the shore, the waters appear blue, the depth of the colour varying under certain modifications of its causes.

But the sea has other colours besides those occasioned by its reflecting the hues of the sky. It has colour essential to itself. In shallow places along our shores its colour cannot be very accurately observed. In such places it is modified by the reflection of the bottom: if the bottom be, on the one hand of fine white sand, or on the other of dark rocks, the water assumes more or less of the light or a dark hue. It is in the wide ocean that the colour of its waters is best observed. The colour of the sea waters varies in different parts of the ocean from light green to dark blue, independently altogether of atmospheric reflection. The waters of the North Sea and of the Polar regions are light green: those of the regions of the trade wind, and especially of the Indian Ocean, are dark blue. The waters of the great current in the ocean called the Gulf Stream, which flows from the Gulf of Mexico towards the Arctic Seas, are of an indigo blue, and afford a striking contrast with the green of the Atlantic through which they take their course.

The causes of this dissimilarity are not yet fully understood. But probably one of the chief causes is a difference in the chemical constitution of the sea-water in different parts of the ocean, that is to say, a difference in the quantities, and perhaps proportions, of the salts it holds in solution. That some parts of the ocean are salter than other parts is beyond question. Now the salter the sea water, the deeper is its blue, and the greener it is, the less is its saltness. The waters of the Gulf Stream are salter than the ocean through which it flows, and their colour, as above stated, is different, being of an indigo blue. And that this difference in the amount of salts they contain is one of the chief causes of the difference of the colour of the sea-water is further confirmed by the experience of those engaged in the manufacture of salt by evaporation along the shores of Italy and France. The more the sea-water is exposed to evaporation in the vats into which it enters from the sea, the salter it becomes, and it is found that this change in its saltness is accompanied by an alteration in its colour, from the green of its ordinary hue to a gradually deepening shade of blue. The saltness of the ocean-waters, already alluded to, is also a phenomenon which merits the attention of the visitor of the seashore. Several writers, some of them recent, but not well-informed on such matters, follow the old authors who have referred to this peculiarity, by repeating their hypothesis, that the saltness of the water is a provision against the stagnation and putrescence of the ocean. This is altogether erroneous. Neither salt nor fresh water is liable to what is popularly understood by putrescence;

and when this appears to take place in small portions of water of either kind, it is the effect of the decomposition of innumerable animalculæ and minute vegetable substances which multiply and perish in succession, and is not caused by any organic change in the constituents of the fluid itself. But the putrescent condition thus arising is fully provided against in large bodies of water by the relative proportions of vegetable and animal life, a provision which evinces, like innumerable other adaptations of creative power, the most marvellous wisdom and unerring skill and foresight.

If we were thoroughly conversant with all the complicated processes which take place in the system of nature, we should be able doubtless to perceive a variety of reasons rendering it necessary that the waters of the sea should be salt, and not fresh. But, so far as our present knowledge enables us to judge, the sea must have been salt from the earliest period of its creation, when it was inhabited by those creatures whose fossil remains occur in the most ancient strata, and where there was little or no dry land, and therefore neither rivers nor lakes. And this saltness of the sea, as originally constituted, was requisite to the system of circulation which modern investigations have proved to be constantly carried on with a degree of regularity and completeness as wonderful and admirable as the circulation of the blood in the body of an animal.

The currents of the ocean, or its system of circulation, and the saltness of its waters are therefore intimately related. The saltness of the ocean is not the only cause of its currents, it is true; for the difference of temperature in its waters must produce currents, as differences of the same kind in the atmosphere produce winds; yet there is reason to believe that the saltness of the sea materially aids those currents, and thus ministers to a vast and most important part of the economy of creation, and illustrates in a most remarkable manner that divine foresight by which in thousands of instances we find provision is made for conditions and necessities to arise at some long subsequent period. Without entering into this interesting but abstruse subject more minutely than the nature of this work permits some further particulars may here be stated.

It has been already stated that there is some difference in the degree of saltness in the sea in different places. But this is owing to local causes. The general rule is that the constituents of sea water are extremely uniform in their proportions. This is most singularly illustrated by experiment. Thus, for example, in the Red Sea there is no rain, and no rivers empty themselves into it, but the process of evaporation is constantly going on from its surface, by which the fresh water is abstracted and the marine salts are left behind. We should expect, therefore, that the waters of this sea must be salter than that of other parts of the ocean. But the water of the Red Sea is not salter than the ocean near the mouth of the Amazon, a region where the amount of rain is greater than the evaporation; and it is not salter than the Mediterranean, a sea into which a vast number of rivers fall, bringing with them from the countries through which they flow a very large and perpetual supply of salts, sulphates and carbonates of lime, magnesia, soda, potash, and iron, chemical substances which are found in solution in sea-water. Now this equality in saltness is extremely remarkable, and can be accounted for only on the supposition of a system of circulation in the waters of the ocean, and this system we know does subsist.

But the saltness of the sea has a special relation to this system of circulation. In the Red Sea and the Mediterranean there is an undercurrent flowing far below the surface into the Indian Ocean from the former, and into the Atlantic from the latter sea. These under-currents may in a great measure, if not wholly, be attributed to the saltness of their waters. The surface-currents likewise which flow from the ocean into both these inland seas, may be attributed to the same cause.

And this is easily explained. It is well known that in the process of evaporation the vapour of water which is taken up into the air is pure, for the salts of the sea-water are not raised into the atmosphere. Now by the abstraction of the watery particles, the surface-water is rendered salter, and therefore heavier, than the stratum of water immediately below it. It therefore sinks downward and gives place to a layer of water lighter and less salt, on which in its turn the process of evaporation acts, and which again sinks only to give place to another supply. And thus in perpetual succession different layers of surface-water are subjected to the same process, each sinking down afterwards by reason of its increased specific gravity. In the Red Sea and the Mediterranean, which we take as examples, the waters at a great depth are considerably heavier than those at the surface, and by a familiar physical law flow outwards by their own weight in an under-current, while their place is supplied by a surface-current, which, as already stated, flows inward from the ocean. Now in fresh water this system of currents could not occur, because evaporation from the surface of fresh water does not make any change in the specific gravity of the water subjected to the immediate action of the process.

The cause thus explained as regards the two inland seas now referred to is also greatly concerned in the much vaster system of circulation which takes place in the ocean itself; as, for instance, in the under-current of salter and heavier water that flows from the equator toward the poles, and the surface-current of water lighter and less salt that flows in a contrary direction.

But while it is certain that the saltness of the sea in relation to the process of evaporation has much concern in the system of circulation between one part of the ocean and another, other considerations there are which show that the chemical constitution of the sea-water, independently of evaporation, adapts it to this office.

One of the constituent parts of sea-water is a solution of lime. The river or brook to which the visitant of the sea-shore approaches as he wanders along the beach is perpetually engaged, especially if it flows through a country in which limestone abounds, in carrying away to the sea solutions of that substance, which themselves are poured into the channel of the rivers by the rain which percolates through the soil, and dissolves part of the lime it meets with in its course. The solutions which the river thus carries along in its waters are too delicate to be discovered by the sense of taste; nevertheless the aggregate quantity of lime thus poured into the ocean from all the rivers of the earth must be vast.

Now it is from this lime so dissolved and mingled with the sea-water, that in some parts of the ocean, as for instance the Pacific, the prodigious coral reefs are constructed. These reefs form under the waters a solid mountain of stone, often of immense extent. On the coast of New Holland there is one coral reef a thousand miles in extent, and unbroken for a distance of three hundred and fifty miles. In the Pacific there are groups of twelve hundred miles in extent by more than three hundred in breadth. All these vast structures are the work of countless myriads of coral-building polypes (*Madrephylliœa*), and afford one of the many proofs how vast a work may, in the complicated processes of divine providence, be executed by a feeble instrumentality. A little worm which could in a moment be crushed by the finger, and is individually the very type of weakness, can by the multiplication of its numbers, construct a mountain on which the fiercest billows of the ocean spend their fury in vain; on whose shores the proudest ship that ever illustrated human genius may be broken to fragments, and on whose surface plains full of beauty and verdure may appear, and towns and villages the habitation of man be erected.

And how marvellous the thought thus suggested to us! By this means the component parts of the limestone rocks of countries far removed from the sea may be gradually carried thither, and then transported by oceanic currents may be formed into new mountains at the bottom of remote seas, thus giving origin to new countries which in some future geological convulsion may be raised into lands far above the sea level, on whose mountains rains shall fall, and through whose valleys rivers shall flow, again to repeat the process by which the limestone which formed its rocks found its way to the original coral-builders.

And what relation has the coral-building polype to the circulation of the sea? Let us consider this question. Out of the sea-water this little creature has the power,—a power in itself marvellous,—of extracting the lime necessary to the building it is to erect. It secretes this substance, no doubt, for its own individual use; but in so doing it is accomplishing a grand design of Him who originated the economy of the globe we inhabit. It cannot be doubted that the secretion of lime from the sea-water by the act of myriads of polypes at the same instant, must lessen the specific gravity of the water with which they are in contact, and from which they extract one of its constituent parts. Whatever the actual weight of the lime thus secreted may be,—and it may in the construction of one reef alone amount to thousands of pounds in a day,—that weight is so much abstracted from the water, which being thus lighter than the strata of water over it rises upwards to the surface, and is replaced by water heavier, salter, and charged with the lime required by the little reef builder, for the work which he could not carry on if the water he had deprived of its lime remained around him without being replaced by a new supply. Thus the marine insect may have a very important office to perform in the circulation of the ocean waters, and the function the polype thus discharges is not accidental. It is exercised by the design of Him who gave the creature its power to secrete the lime and the instinct with which to labour.

The waters which on becoming heavier, because rendered salter, by evaporation, sink downward, are likewise warmer than those which ascend to supply their place. Thus the circulation of the sea modifies not only its own temperature, but the temperature of the climates of the lands it washes. This effect is produced on a great scale in some parts of the globe; and an illustration of it is presented by our own shores. The western shores of the British islands, and especially the western shores of Ireland and the north-western shores of Scotland, possess a climate greatly milder and moister than the eastern coasts, and it is not to be doubted that this difference is occasioned by the current of the Gulf Stream, which, touching our western shores, imparts to the climate the mildness of its character by diffusing a portion of the caloric brought from warmer latitudes. It is for this reason, for example, that the western shores of Sutherlandshire, although so much further north than other parts of Scotland, possess a climate so soft and genial, and exhibit such early and luxuriant vegetation; and it is for the same reason that the climate of the Orkney and Shetland islands approaches so nearly to that of Torquay. That this circulation of warmth from one part of the globe to another is evidence of a wise design, and that the saltness of the ocean is a part of the instrumentality by which that design is carried out, no intelligent observer can doubt, any more than he can doubt that the design of the fabricator of the eye was that it should be an instrument of vision, or that the wings and limbs of animals should be organs of locomotion.

Independently, however, of its relation to the circulation of the oceanic currents, the composition of the sea-water ought to be regarded in another point of view. In addition to the coral-making polypes who extract the lime it contains for their vast submarine structures, there are countless myriads of creatures inhabiting the deep who employ the same substance to form their own abodes. The structure of a vast number and variety of these creatures is expressly adapted to secrete lime and form it into shells of every form and colour, and in many instances of great magnitude. The external covering of all the crustacea and considerable portions of the internal structure of other marine animals either inhabiting our sea-shores or living in deep water, are formed of lime thus marvellously extracted from the element they inhabit. In all cases where such shelly coverings are found, they are absolutely requisite not only to the enjoyment, but to the very existence, of the creatures whom they enclose. And thus we perceive that the constitution of the sea-water is designed by its Divine originator to minister to the wants of an infinite number and variety of forms, all endowed with the mysterious principle of life, and all possessed of degrees of happiness and modes of enjoyment adapted to their condition.

WINDS AND TIDES

CHAP. VI.

WINDS AND TIDES.

Interest of the Subject.—Air and Water, Ocean and Atmosphere.—Theory of the Tides.—Tidal Phenomena.—Rise of Tide in various parts of the Coast.—The Bore.—Currents of the Sea.—The Winds.

EVERY visitor of our sea-shores ought to be greatly interested in the subject of the winds and tides. Familiarity with such phenomena ought not to render them less worthy of attention than those of a more novel character. It is indeed the province of well-cultivated minds, and such as in any degree possess the quality of genius, to find in things which, because of frequent occurrence, are all but unnoticed by common-place observers, abundant interest and ample supplies of intellectual occupation. Among such as are thus happily gifted we would class those who peruse this book, feeling assured that as they wander by the sea-shore, they will not perceive the periodical ebbing and flowing of the tides, and the varying directions of the breezes that ripple the waters, without considering the causes of those familiar, but at the same time marvellous and beautiful phenomena.

There is no inconsiderable similitude between the sea and the atmosphere. Air and water are both fluids, although in many respects they differ from each other. The vast assemblage of waters which constitute the sea, and the immense extent of air which forms the atmosphere, are both oceans. The marine ocean has its inhabitants, some of which move about on the ground at the bottom, while others swim far above in the midst and at the surface of their watery world; in the aërial ocean these are represented by the animals which move on the ground and those which fly through the air; in the marine ocean there is submarine vegetation of vast luxuriance, answering to the meadows, the fields, the copses and the forests that belong to the aërial ocean; in the former there are currents and tides, represented in the latter by the monsoons and the trade winds, and the land and sea breezes; in both there are storms and calms.

The Roman soldiers, when they first made their way to the shores of the Atlantic, are said to have been filled with astonishment at the regular and periodical ebbing and flowing of the ocean,—a phenomenon unknown to them on the lovely shores of Italy. And but for our familiarity with it, we ourselves should experience the same astonishment on first perceiving so striking a phenomenon.

Do we not call to mind in the well-remembered time of childhood,—happy period passed away!—the ineffable pleasure with which for the first time we trod the beach and picked up the shells and pebbles or ran with youthful glee "along the golden sand?" Do we not picture to ourselves the huge delight with which we saw the flowing tide gradually advance over the far extending and level sands, covering the boulders festooned with algæ that were here and there scattered over it, till at last they were all submerged; and how again we watched with intense interest the ebbing waves as they retreated once more, permitting us with naked feet to ramble over the wet expanse of newly covered sand, to search for some fancied treasure that the sea might have left behind? How pleasant, how charming, were it possible in mature years, to look with the wonder and delight of childhood on those natural phenomena which in the fresh morning of life filled us with those strange emotions with which we behold novel and marvellous things!

The theory of the tides comprehends several problems which are very abstruse, in consequence of the number and variety of circumstances to be taken into account. We require not only to consider the action of the sun and the moon upon the earth and the ocean, but the modifications of this action arising from the position of the earth in relation to the sun and moon, the influence of the diurnal motion of the earth on its axis, as well as its form and density, the figure of continents, the position of islands, the irregularities occasioned by the character of the bottom of the sea, and the laws of motion in fluid bodies and waves. The variety and number of causes and effects thus to be taken into view, render the theory of the tides one of the most complicated subjects in natural science, and has called forth the genius and taxed the powers of the ablest investigators. All that can be done in a work of this kind, is to present a general view of the subject, as plain and lucid as possible without mathematical calculations.

That the ebbing and flowing of the tides depend on solar and lunar influences there can be no doubt, for at every return of new and full moon we have high tides, while at half moon the tides are low. The moon is in a line with the sun both when about to appear as new moon, and when at full moon. At those periods, therefore, the attraction of the moon and the sun upon the earth acts in one and the same direction, and the united influence causes what are called the spring tides. On the other hand, when the moon has completed her first quarter, and her third quarter, her attractive power at those points in her course is exercised at right angles to that of the sun, and thus, by preventing the waters from rising as high as before, the neap or lower tides take place. Nothing can be more obvious, therefore, than the effect of solar and lunar attraction on the phenomena of the tides.

But, along with this general explanation, the motion of the earth on its axis must, as already hinted, be taken into view, and this will be found greatly to influence the tidal phenomena.

Not only does the motion of the earth in its annual orbit, and that of the moon in her monthly course round the earth, produce an alternately diminishing and increasing influence on the tides, but the diurnal revolution of the earth itself exercises a remarkable power. In its daily revolution from west to east it brings every successive hour one meridian after another vertically under the moon, so that the point at which the greatest attractive power of the moon is felt upon the earth, and which is vertically beneath the moon, changes hour after hour as different portions of her surface are presented to the action of her attendant satellite. In consequence of this the attractive power of the moon and the sun is at no time stationary, but is continually moving, as it were, along the earth's surface, changing its position with the apparent place of the bodies by which it is exercised. As the moon therefore moves from east to west, or, to speak more correctly, as the earth revolves in the opposite direction, the waters of the ocean, instead of accumulating in one place, form a tidal wave which follows the course of the moon. This wave, as it moves along the ocean, produces high water on the coasts it visits in its flow; but its force, direction, and height, are more or less modified by circumstances already alluded to, such as the obstacles in its way arising from oceanic currents, irregularities in the figure of the land, the shape, position, and breadth of the channels through which it passes. The broader and deeper the channel, the greater the speed of the tide, and thus the tide-wave traverses thousands of miles of the open ocean in the same space of time it requires to pass through a narrow and shallow channel of comparatively very limited extent.

Without entering into minute details it will be sufficient, in order to illustrate the direction and the rate of progress of the tide, briefly to refer to that which occurs in the Indian or the Atlantic oceans. From the south of New Zealand the tide-wave advances westwards and northwards towards the Cape of Good Hope, at which it arrives in thirteen hours from Van Dieman's Land, at the same time producing high water also along the east coast of Africa, the southern shores of India, and the islands of the Eastern Archipelago. Entering the Atlantic, and moving to the north-west, the wave of high water arrives on the coast of Newfoundland in twelve hours after leaving the Cape of Good Hope. In four hours afterwards it reaches the mouth of the British Channel, where, owing to the nature of the various shores, it is subdivided in its course. One portion passes through the Straits of Dover, another flows up St. George's Channel, a third portion of it passes northwards along the west coasts of Ireland and Scotland, around the Orkneys, and thence southwards till it meets the tide, which, owing to the narrowness of the British Channel, had in the meantime advanced at a comparatively slow rate to the north.

The effect of the double wave thus produced

by the intervention of the British islands, and the comparatively narrow space between England and France, is very remarkable on the Danish shores, where the ebb and flow of the sea ceases to be perceptible, and it is constantly high water.

The height to which the tide flows is various in different parts of the world, and this dissimilarity is chiefly occasioned by the conformation of the coast. In the Mediterranean there is little or no tide, while in some parts of the American coast, as in the Bay of Fundy, the spring tide frequently rises to the extraordinary height of 120 feet, and in Asia, as at the mouth of the Indus, the rise of the tide is 30 feet. Even in Britain there is great difference in the depth of high water at different places. At Chepstow, in the Bristol Channel, the rise of the tide is much higher than in many other places, being from 45 to 60 feet, and, after a strong westerly wind, it is said sometimes to reach 70 feet.

The very striking phenomenon called the Bore cannot be passed over in silence while referring to the subject of the tides. Where an estuary is narrow, and the shore is level to a considerable distance inland, the great body of water produced by the tidal wave being suddenly forced into a confined space, rises to a proportionate height between the opposite shores, and flows onward, partly under the influence of the original impulse acting upon it, and partly by its own gravitation. Into the Bay of Fundy, already mentioned, the "bore" rushes with tremendous force, and with a roaring noise, appearing as it ascends like a cataract pouring down a slope, in the same manner as the rapids of the St. Lawrence. This singular phenomenon takes place likewise in many of the Asiatic rivers. In the Hoogly, or Calcutta River, "the bore," says Rennell, "commences at Hoogly Point, the place where the river first contracts itself, and is perceptible above Hoogly Town, and so quick is its motion that it hardly employs four hours in travelling from one to the other, though the distance is nearly seventy miles. At Calcutta it sometimes occasions an instantaneous rise of six feet, and both here, and at every other part of its track, the boats on its approach immediately quit the shore, and make for safety to the middle of the river. In the channels between the islands at the mouth of the Megna, the height of the bore is said to exceed twelve feet, and is so terrific in its appearance, and dangerous in its consèquences, that no boat will venture to pass at spring tide."* The following is an interesting and graphic account of the same phenomenon, which in China is called the "eagre," as taking place on the Chikiang River, which enters the sea about ten miles below the city of Hang-Chow. "Between the river," says the writer, who was an eye-witness of the occurrence, "and the city walls, which are a mile distant, dense suburbs extend several miles along the banks. As the hour of flood-tide approached, crowds gathered in the streets, running at right

* Rennell, Phil. Trans. 1781.

angles with the Tsien-tang, but at a safe distance. My position was a terrace in front of the Triwave Temple, which afforded a good view of the entire scene. On a sudden all traffic on the thronged mart was suspended; porters cleared the front street of every description of merchandise, boatmen ceased loading and unloading their vessels, and put out into the middle of the stream; so that a few moments sufficed to give a deserted appearance to the busiest part of one of the busiest cities of Asia. The centre of the stream was crowded with craft, from small boats to huge barges, including the gay "flower boats." Loud shouting from the fleet announced the appearance of the flood, which seemed like a glittering white cable stretched athwart the river at its mouth as far down as the eye could reach. Its noise, compared by the Chinese poets to that of thunder, speedily drowned that of the boatmen; and as it advanced with prodigious velocity, it assumed the appearance of an alabaster wall, or rather of a cataract four or five miles across, and about thirty feet high, moving bodily onward. It soon reached the immense assemblage of vessels waiting its approach. Knowing that the bore of the Hoogly, which scarce deserved mention in connection with the one before me, invariably overturned boats that were not skilfully managed, I could not but feel apprehensive for the lives of the floating multitude. As the foaming wall of water dashed impetuously forward, threatening to submerge everything afloat, they were all silenced, and intently occupied in keeping their prows toward the wave; and thus they all vaulted, as it were, to the summit in perfect safety. The spectacle was of the greatest interest when the eagre had passed about half-way among the craft. The boats in front were quietly reposing on the unruffled surface of the stream, others were scaling with the agility of salmon the formidable cascade, while those behind were pitching and heaving in tumultuous confusion on the troubled water. This grand and exciting scene was but of a few moments' duration; it passed up the river in an instant, but with gradually diminishing force, size, and velocity, until at about eighty miles above the city, according to the Chinese accounts, it ceases altogether to be perceptible."*

On our own shores the remarkable phenomenon may be witnessed in more than one instance, and especially in the estuary of the Severn, where the spring tides rush upwards with extraordinary rapidity, and the bore is sometimes nine feet in height. A similar instance occurs in the Solway Firth, where the tidal wave flows into the channel with such velocity that it is said that at a certain part of it, if a man on a swift horse were at the water's edge, the utmost efforts of his steed would be insufficient to enable him to gain the land.

The regular ebb and flow of the ocean waters produce many vastly important effects, although many of their effects in the economy of nature

* North Amer. Jour. of Science.

may be of much higher importance than we are at present aware. Even if we restrict our view of their beneficial results to those which refer to navigation, we may perceive how considerable they are. There are numerous rivers on our coasts, the bars at the entrance of which would be impassable unless during a rise of tide, and many places now used as harbours could not be so employed were the water always to remain at a low level. The currents, moreover, produced by the flow and recess of the tides, are of no small importance to the navigation of estuaries, giving motion to ships when there is no wind.

In speaking of the saltness of the sea-water some reference was incidentally made to the currents of the ocean. A few further remarks on the subject are, however, desirable in this place.

The currents of the ocean differ entirely from the tides, not only in being permanent phenomena, but as arising from causes altogether different. The oceanic currents are very numerous, and it is impossible to contemplate them without perceiving that they constitute a system of circulation carried on in obedience to physical laws, and indicating in a very striking manner the design of the All-Wise.

There are, as already stated, currents which run from the Atlantic into the Mediterranean, and from the Indian Ocean into the Red Sea, and on the principles laid down with great ingenuity by Lieutenant Maury, it may be considered as fully demonstrated that under-currents proceed from those two inland seas outward to the oceans with which they are connected, carrying with them the waters which by the process of evaporation have become salter, and therefore heavier, than those of the ocean; and were this process not to be carried on, it cannot be doubted that the depths of the Mediterranean and the Red Sea would, in process of time, become filled, not only with water saturated with the chemical ingredients of sea-water, but that they would become filled up by deposits of solid crystals of marine salts.

The Indian Ocean and the Pacific have their currents arising from several causes and variously modified, but all obviously subject to physical laws which give regularity to their phenomena, and minister to the great system of circulation in the waters of the ocean.

But the most remarkable of all the ocean currents is the Gulf-stream. This vast flow of waters is more rapid in its course than the Amazon or the Mississippi, and a thousand times greater in its volume than either of these majestic rivers. The Gulf-stream may truly be called one of the most marvellous things in the natural history of the sea. It has its birth in the Mexican Gulf, from which it flows along the shore towards the British islands, the North Sea, and the Frozen Ocean. Our knowledge of the various causes in which this vast current originates, and by which it is modified, is in many respects indefinite, but, according to the views of Maury, two of the principal agents concerned in producing the phenomenon are the increased saltness of its waters, caused by the evaporation necessary to supply the trade-winds with vapour, and the diminished quantity of salt in the northern seas, towards which the Gulf-stream flows. We have already referred to the important influence which this ocean-current has in tempering the climate of those lands toward which it tends. Much highly interesting and minute information on this subject will be found in the various works devoted especially to the physical geography of the sea. But it is not requisite to the plan of this work minutely to discuss a subject which not only demands an elaborate disquisition, but is only indirectly connected with the phenomena which it is our immediate object to illustrate.

The winds or currents of the atmosphere which are now to engage our attention constitute a subject full of interest to those who frequent the beach, and who have opportunities of witnessing the effects which the wind produces upon the ocean. It is a subject also strikingly illustrative of several important physical laws, as well as of the admirable wisdom in which those laws have had their birth. Some general observations on the subject will not be unsuitable before giving our attention to the aërial currents of our sea-shores.

The winds are either constant, or such as blow always in the same direction, periodical, or such as blow six months in one direction and six months in another, or variable, that is to say, such as do not appear to be subject to any general rule. All winds or aërial currents may be said to be caused by something which acts either continuously or at intervals in disturbing the equilibrium of the atmosphere.

Of this the tropical winds afford the most remarkable instances. The trade-winds of the Atlantic are occasioned by the heat of the sun, which, rarefying the air over the African continent, causes it to rise upwards, when its place is immediately supplied by currents of colder air blowing from the north and south. In the Indian Ocean likewise, a similar phenomenon takes place; the air over the vast plains of tropical India becomes heated, and a current blowing from the south to occupy the place of the heated atmosphere causes the periodical winds known as the monsoons. The sea and land breezes which occur during the morning and night in the tropics originate in a similar cause. The sun heats the land, and consequently the air over its surface, which ascending causes a breeze from the cooler atmosphere over the ocean to blow towards the land; but at night, when the land and the air over it have cooled down after sunset, the wind blows from shore to supply the place of the warmer air which then ascends 'from the surface of the sea.

The winds which prevail on the coasts of Britain are extremely variable, and can hardly be reduced to anything like system. But there can be no doubt that they are occasioned by heat and electricity, agents which produce rapid alterations in the equilibrium of the atmosphere. The land and sea breezes already referred to may be frequently perceived on the shores of Britain during the fine weather of summer, and are produced by the same causes which operate on tropical coasts.

The westerly winds which blow upon our shores are much more regular and continuous than any others, and are, as is well known, greatly more genial and healthful. Their causes are similar to those of the trade-winds already adverted to. The heated air over tropical lands rises upwards, as already described, and while its place is taken by cooler currents blowing towards the equator, the warmer air ascending to a great height in the atmosphere spreads itself to the north and south, and as it parts with its superabundant caloric falls again towards the earth, blowing towards our western coasts laden with much of the warmth of tropical lands, and with an abundant supply of oxygen obtained from the luxuriant vegetation of the more favoured climates from which it originally arose.

Thus the ocean and the atmosphere both have their systems of circulation, and those systems produce effects of vast importance in the economy of nature, conducing in a marvellous degree to the vitality and the enjoyment of animated beings. The limits of this work do not permit more than a very general view of those most interesting natural phenomena, but even a general view is sufficient to exhibit the beauty and the efficiency of the laws of physics to which they can be traced, and the beneficence, the wisdom, and the power, in which those laws have their birth. To the continual operation of those laws we may attribute not only those fresh and salubrious breezes which contribute so much to the health and vigour of the inhabitants of our coasts, but those rains which fall upon the land supplying our innumerable brooks, rivers, and lakes; and clothing our hills, plains, and valleys, with luxuriant verdure. In such an agency it is impossible not to perceive an ever recurring evidence of providential design.

MARINE VEGETATION

CHAP. VII.

MARINE VEGETATION.

Analogy between Marine and Terrestrial Vegetation.—Variety of the Algæ.—Marine Botany, its Classification.—Specimens of the three Subdivisions in which our Sea-weeds are comprehended.

THE ocean is not to be regarded merely as a vast kingdom replete with an inexhaustible variety of living forms, but as rivalling the land itself in the profusion of its vegetable productions. The bottom of the sea is in many respects analogous to the surface of the dry land, for it is diversified with level plains, deep valleys, caverns and rocks, hills and mountains, submerged beneath the liquid element, as the plains, valleys, and mountains of the land are covered by the great aërial ocean at the bottom of which we live. And the analogy is no less strict between the vegetable productions of the sea and the land. The general distinction is only such as necessarily obtains from the difference between the circumambient fluids in which they have their abode. Thus the stems of marine plants are slender, because they are sufficiently supported by the dense element in which they grow and do not require to be thick and strong; their roots also are a mere apparatus for attaching them to one spot, for they, unlike most terrestrial plants, gain no sustenance from the root, but from the fluid in which they are immersed.

There is nevertheless no small similitude between the two great classes of vegetable now referred to. Some districts of the bottom of the ocean are covered with vegetation so luxuriant that to such districts we might well apply the term of marine forests. The submarine trees bear in some respects a resemblance to many of the most magnificent trees in an American forest; for although not in any way rivalling them in thickness or in solidity of structure, they are their superiors in altitude. Captain Cook mentions that at Kerguelen Land the sea-weed was of enormous length. In some of the comparatively shallow places the line did not reach the bottom with twenty-five fathoms, and the depth may have been much greater, but the sea-weed grew up in those places from the bottom, not only so as to reach the surface, but spreading over it a profusion of large fronds, and some of the plants were more than sixty fathoms or 360 feet in length.

The geographical range of these immense sea plants extends from the extreme southern islets near Cape Horn to the 43° of latitude, a distance of more than 15 degrees and more than 900 miles, throughout that space affording food and shelter to countless myriads of living creatures of all sizes and varieties. Other subaqueous regions produce other kinds of vegetation differing from the gigantic sea-weeds now mentioned, as the grass of the prairies differs from the trees of the forest. The bottom of the sea in many of the inlets on the Indian coasts is covered with algæ and fuci, as a rich meadow is clothed with grass, and there, at a depth of three or four fathoms, dugongs in immense herds browse like cattle in a meadow. But between the comparatively short marine herbage on which those huge herbivorous animals feed, and the enormous sea-weeds of the southern ocean, there exists a vast number and variety of species, many of those pertaining to tropical seas wholly unknown to the marine botanist.

But it is not our purpose to go in search of marine plants to remote seas and foreign shores. Our own coasts afford many sea-plants; in many instances of much beauty, in some of very considerable value and importance, and in all cases of much interest to the intelligent observer. Before, however, taking notice of a few of these, some general observations may not be out of place.

The growth of marine plants on our shores is, according to the most eminent botanists, limited to certain localities on the coast, and to certain depths of water. Thus some of our sea-weeds have their northern limit on the southern coasts of England; others belong peculiarly to the Scottish coasts and the northern shores of England and Ireland; some, again, have a wider range, extending from the south of England to the north of Ireland and south-west of Scotland, and others even to Orkney and Shetland along the western shores of both islands. As regards depth our marine plants are likewise variously distributed. Some sea-weeds extend to the line of ebb at spring-tides, some belong to an inner line within which they become partially uncovered every ordinary tide; others, again, flourish within the line of the neap-tides, and become entirely uncovered at each recess of the water, and others occupy stations so shallow and near the shore that they are frequently, and for a considerable period at one time, left almost quite dry. It thus appears that there are certain boundaries or limits within which certain kinds of algæ are found to flourish; but, so far as can be ascertained at the depth of fifty fathoms in the British seas, the vegetation is scanty.

The various species of sea-plants on our shores amount to about three hundred and seventy. Some of these are large, some so minute that their structure can be examined only with a microscope. They all exhibit great variety of form. Some are composed of broad, ribbon-like leaves or fronds; some are like long strings of brown cord; others have leaves very similar to those of terrestrial plants; others, again, are like strings of beads, tufts of silk or velvet, network, bunches of slender hairs, tubes of glass filled with colouring matter, or minute trees with spreading branches and numerous slender twigs; in a word, the utmost diversity of form prevails, but in every instance the structure illustrates in a striking manner the admirable skill of the Great Artificer.

All the marine plants are flowerless, and are comprehended in the class Cryptogamia, to which ferns, mosses, lichens, and fungi belong, and they are themselves classified according to the prevailing colour of their seeds.

Thus the term *Melanospermeæ* is given to the series of plants in which the seeds or spores are of a dark colour; *Rhodospermeæ* is the general title of the series in which the seeds are of a red hue; and *Chlorospermeæ* is the name of the series in which the seeds are greenish. One distinction thus supposed to subsist is not sufficiently clear without the consideration of other additional particulars, by which each series may be distinguished from each other; but to describe all such minute particulars would be contrary to the intention of this work.

It is worthy of remark, that of the whole of our marine plants each series now mentioned embraces a different proportion. The first-mentioned series comprehends about one-fifth of the whole number; the second includes three-eighths, and the third contains one-fourth.

Observing the order now stated, we shall suppose the reader to examine a few specimens from each series.

Of the *Melanospermeæ* there are specimens to be found on every sea-shore. One of the most common is the bladder wrack (*Fucus vesiculosus*).

Its colour is dark green, the substance is tough, and the fronds long and narrow, and the air-vessels large, round, and chiefly arranged in pairs, and near the ends of the fronds are vesicles or receptacles, large, swollen, and filled with mucus. This plant is extremely common on all rocky shores.

Another equally common species is the *knotted fucus*. The stem of this plant is divided into branches, which are forked, and the stem is studded at intervals with large air-vessels. The substance is tough and leathery; the colour, olive-green, and where exposed to the air and light, nearly black. This plant frequently reaches six feet in length.

The *Fucus serratus* (or toothed or serrated fucus) is destitute of air-vessels; the receptacles are flat, and placed at the ends of the fronds; the colour is dark olive-green.

The tangle, or sea-girdle (*Laminaria digitata*), is another familiar species. Unlike the species above referred to, which are found between high and low water mark, this plant grows in water of from seven to fifteen fathoms in depth, and is rarely found in places from which the tide recedes. From the roots attached to the rocks shoots up a long stem, the summit of which expands into a broad leaf or frond, divided into a number of irregular strips. This plant is olive-brown in colour.

Another of the same class of plants is the sea-lace (*Chorda filum*). The fronds of this plant are often of great length, extending to twenty and even forty feet, and resembling a cord of leather or gutta-percha. In some parts of the coast, especially of the Orkney Islands, this plant grows in great profusion, forming a sort of marine meadow through which a boat forces its way with some difficulty. The cord or string of which it consists is a hollow tube, divided into chambers filled with air, which renders the whole plant very light, and enables it to float upwards to the top, and along the surface of the water. More than fifty species, all differing more or less from each other, are enumerated by marine botanists as comprehended in the series of the Melanospermeæ.

We shall now notice a few specimens of the Rhodospermeæ. These plants are generally of a rose, purple, or red-brown hue, and many of the varieties, which are numerous, are extremely beautiful, especially those of a pink colour.

> "Their blushes speak
> Of rosy hues that o'er the ocean break
> When cloudy morn is calm; yet fain to weep,
> Because the beautiful are still the frail."

One of the most elegant of these plants is the scarlet plocamium (*Plocamium sanguineum*), with which most visitors of the sea-shore are familiar. It is of a fine pink colour. The fronds are much branched, and are feathery in their structure, the smaller branches being furnished with minute subdivisions like the teeth of a comb;

when dried and expanded on white paper or on the pearly white inner surface of a large shell, this plant is highly pleasing from the delicacy and beauty of its structure.

Probably the delesseria is the most beautiful of all the order to which it belongs. The *Delesseria sanguinea* bears large leaves of extreme delicacy, and in shape resembling those of the red dock, and of a rich rose-red colour, with the margins waved or plaited. This plant is less common than the preceding, and is sometimes found attached by its roots to the larger kinds of algæ as well as to the rocks. Another species of delesseria is the *D. sinuosa* or oak-leaved delesseria. The colour of this plant is claret-red, and it is a remarkably beautiful plant.

The *Nitophyllum*, of which there are likewise several kinds, is a very fine sea-weed. The colour is a rich purple lake in some of the species, which becomes brighter when dried, in others it is deep crimson, and in others a delicate rose-pink. The fronds in this plant are reticulated, membranaceous, and without veins.

Another plant of this class not uncommon is the *Rhodomenia palmata* or dulse. It is of a' fine purplish red colour. The fronds, which grow in tufts, are flat and so divided as to represent in a rude manner the form of the human hand, a circumstance giving origin to the term *palmata*.

The *Chrondus crispus*, or crisped chrondus, is another plant meriting attention. It is frequent on rocky shores, and is found in great abundance on the Devonshire coast as well as on the coast of Ireland. The colour is a purplish green, and it is well known as the Irish moss, which, when boiled, produces a nutritious jelly. Of the class of which we have thus referred to one or two examples there is a large number of species.

It now remains that we notice a few of the series termed *Chlorospermeæ*.

These plants are the least beautiful and interesting of the sea-weeds. The most common of them belong to the order Confervæ. Some of these are to be found on every sea-shore, covering the stones in great profusion, and rendering them very slippery. The *Ulva latissima* or green sloke, the colour of which is a full green, and of which the fronds are broadly egg-shaped or oblong and variously cleft and waved; the *Porphyra laciniata*, or cleft porphyra, laver or sloke, of a rich purple colour, a species sometimes boiled and used at table, and several other species, are comprehended in this class.

Of the three series referred to a large number of species present themselves to the lovers of marine botany, and all of them will be found worthy of notice either from their appearance, their structure, or the purposes to which they are applicable. To some peculiarities in their physiology we shall in a succeeding chapter direct our readers' attention.

PHYSIOLOGY OF MARINE PLANTS

CHAP. VIII.

PHYSIOLOGY OF MARINE PLANTS.

Claims which they have on our Attention.—Fructification.—Peculiarity of their Structure.—Reproduction.—Their remarkable Structure as related to the Element they exist in.—Artificial Uses of Sea-weeds. — Their Relation to Marine Animals, &c.

THE beauty of many of these plants, their importance in the economy of nature, their use in various respects to man himself, are all considerations likely to dispose the intelligent observer to inquire into their structure..

It has been already stated that all the marine plants are comprehended in the class termed Cryptogamia, in which are included ferns, lichens, and other non-flowering terrestrial plants. The fructification of cryptogamic plants differs, as our readers are aware, from that of the class which produce blossoms, and this peculiarity may be readily observed by examining in autumn the back of a fern leaf, or frond on which a multitude of seed-like bodies may be seen grouped together in various forms. These bodies consist of a number of distinct capsules, in which are the germs or spores, analogous to the seeds in flowering plants.

The fructification of marine plants is of this kind. Their reproduction takes place by means of germs or spores which are contained in certain parts of the fronds in appropriate capsules more or less obvious on examination.

The highest forms of marine plants are composed of the same elements as the most simple. They all consist, not of organs related to, and affording nutriment to each other as the root of terrestrial plants does to the branches, but of a series of separate and independent parts. In several marine plants there are various parts analogous to those of land vegetables, such as roots, stems, branches, and leaves. But between these parts of marine plants there is no difference of organisation, all being alike formed of cellular tissue, and each part appearing to have an independent existence, and not to participate in the common vitality of the vegetable.

The manner in which these plants are formed is very simple, and may be easily understood. There is, first, the germ or spore, consisting of a minute isolated cell. This cell, when about to produce a plant, elongates itself and becomes divided in the centre by a septum or cell-wall; thus two cells are formed entirely distinct from each other. The same process of subdivision still continues; the new cell produces by its own elongation and division a third cell; the third gives birth in the same manner to a fourth, and thus either a row or a cluster of cells is speedily formed. In those sea-weeds which are in the form of cords, —such as the *Chorda filum*, already spoken of,— the spores or cells lengthen themselves in one direction, succeeding each other in a line, while in those plants whose parts are broad and extended, the spores or cells multiply laterally as well as longitudinally, and thus the broad frond is formed. Why it is that one species always increases in one direction, and others in a different direction, is one of those mysteries the cause of which eludes our investigations.

It is worthy of remark that the reproductive power of the algæ differs considerably in different kinds. Thus in the ulva already spoken of, known as sloke, whose thin grass green or olive brown and purple fronds abound on some of our shores, every part of the frond is capable of producing cells or spores, and thus the plant is capable of spreading indefinitely on every side. It is otherwise with the algæ of the higher orders, such as the bladder wrack or *Fucus vesiculosus*, and the notched wrack, *F. serratus*; in these it has been discovered that the tissue is less uniform in character than in the simpler forms of marine vegetation, and that some approach is made to that separation of organs perceptible in the higher orders of the Cryptogamia. Unlike the ulva, the fuci now mentioned have their reproductive powers restricted to one part only, the extremity of the fronds. These are found to dilate themselves into receptacles or spore-sacs, beautifully adapted to their office, being furnished with pores through which the germs make their escape when arrived at maturity.

There is another peculiarity in the structure of

sea-weeds extremely worthy of notice, as distinguishing them in a remarkable manner from terrestrial plants, and, at the same time, exhibiting a striking instance of an obviously designed relation of their physiological character to the element in which they exist. To perceive this peculiarity it is requisite to refer to the structure of the higher orders of terrestrial plants. In these the root is not only that which serves to fix them in the soil, but it is the part of the plant which absorbs the moisture requisite to their growth. The power of absorption which the root exercises is very great, some plants being capable of thus taking up in a very short period many times their own weight of water. Thus, for example, in an experiment made with four plants of spearmint grown for fifty-six days in water, it was found that, although they themselves weighed only 403 grains, they absorbed by their roots 54,000 grains of water, a quantity equal to about seven pints. The liquid thus absorbed is transmitted from the root, along with any chemical ingredients it contains, to every part of the plant for the nourishment and growth of its several parts.

Now in the sea-weeds the only function which the roots perform similar to those of land vegetables, is that of fixing the plant to its place. It has no power whatever of transmitting moisture to other parts of the plant, there being no system of vessels for such a purpose, and the cells forming the plant being entirely insulated from each other. Accordingly, while in the majority of terrestrial vegetables the power of absorption is restricted to the root, this power in sea-weed is distributed over every part of the surface, for the obvious reason that it is entirely immersed in the fluid from which its nutriment is extracted. As a consequence, therefore, if a sea-weed be partly raised out of the water, the portions so deprived of their source of nourishment will wither and die from drought, while the portions which continue immersed will continue to thrive, without transmitting any moisture to the part of the plant raised out of the water.

Intimately connected with the subject of the physiology of the algæ is that of the artificial uses to which they are adapted, the peculiar properties they possess, and the purposes which in nature they fulfil.

Many of them are of no inconsiderable importance and value to mankind. All the larger species of fuci already referred to were formerly very largely employed in the manufacture of kelp, an impure carbonate of soda used in soap-making. Chloride of sodium is found in the tissues of marine vegetables, and the carbonate of soda now referred to is produced by the decomposition of this chloride. The chloride is driven off and the carbon and the sodium combine with oxygen, and the chemical result is the carbonate of soda or kelp. The manufacture of this substance, although now in some measure superseded by the introduction of foreign alkali, is still of value. It was at one time extensively carried on at various places along the shores of Britain and Ireland. The sea-ware being collected and dried upon the shore, a simple kiln, five or six feet square, is enclosed with stones, and a fire being made in it, the sea-wrack is reduced to a melted condition. On being allowed to cool it assumes a solid state, not unlike a grey coloured porous clay or stone, and being broken in pieces is ready for the market.

Another important use to which marine vegetables are applied is that of manure in the cultivation of land. Marine plants contain in large quantities those various ingredients, such as phosphates, earthy and alkaline carbonates, that are requisite to enrich the land and render it capable of producing plants of whose composition these ingredients are a part. The sea-ware, therefore, when spread upon the soil and allowed to decompose, constitutes a valuable manure, and being often cast in great quantities upon the shore during storms, affords a rich return to those cultivators of land on the coast who avail themselves of the opportunity of gathering it. The gathering of seaweed for the purpose of manure and for fuel exhibits in the Channel Islands a busy and picturesque scene.

Another use to which some species may be put, is that of supplying food for pigs and cattle, and for this purpose it may at all times 'be applied as well as in times of scarcity. It is applied to this important purpose in the Western Isles, and in several parts of the northern coasts of Europe. The animals fed upon it are said to thrive remarkably well, a result to be anticipated from the chemical constituents of the plant.

It may further be mentioned that from marine plants the chemical substance called iodine is extracted. This substance is of very great value in medical practice, possessing great efficacy in reducing glandular and other tumours. It is said also that the mucilaginous seed vessels of the *Fucus vesiculosus,* when soaked in brandy, may be used with excellent effect as an external application in diseases of the throat, and that the sea-water in which they have been bruised in a considerable quantity, affords a valuable strengthening bath for the limbs of weak and delicate children. A black salt, also possessed of medicinal powers, has also been procured from the same plant.

Thus external appearances are not always to be trusted as evidence of intrinsic worth, and many virtues may lurk under a very plain and unostentatious exterior. Those sea-weeds, thus capable of being put to so many valuable uses, are the least beautiful of all their tribe. But, like some of the most valuable land plants, their sombre and unpretending aspect is made ample amends for by the valuable qualities they possess.

The *Rhodomenia palmata,* already referred to, contains a considerable quantity of saccharine matter, is considered the most nutritious as well as the most agreeable of all the sea-weeds used as food, at least in Europe. It is eaten raw by the natives of the Scottish coasts, and in former times was regularly brought to market in the larger cities.

Even at the present day it may be found for sale in some of the Scottish towns. The name Dulse is derived from the Celtic Duillisk or Dillisk, the name by which the plant is known in Ireland and Scotland, and which signifies a waterleaf.

The crisped chrondus, already referred to, is also of considerable value for domestic and medicinal use. When boiled, it produces a gelatine of very nutritious qualities, which may be used at table in various forms. From its restorative properties, the mucilage may be taken with advantage by those suffering from debility, or from affections of the lungs. Its slight bitterness in taste may be rendered almost imperceptible by the addition of lemon juice or wine.

To this plant is related the species from which the edible birds' nests are formed, which are considered so great a delicacy by the Chinese, and even by our own countrymen who have partaken of them. These nests are brought from certain islands on the Chinese coast, where there are caves in which birds resembling swallows build for themselves these remarkable habitations, employing for the purpose a species of sea-weed, which they subject to the process of maceration before applying it to its purpose.

We have thus seen that sea-weeds are of no inconsiderable value to mankind. But there are other considerations worthy of notice regarding them. The plants of the sea afford shelter and food to countless hosts of animated beings who inhabit the waters, and to whom as well as to man the bountiful Author of every perfect gift opens His hand, and they are filled with good. Man is not the principal beneficiary for whom provision is made in the qualities of marine plants; the humblest of his fellow-creatures share with him the ample supply which divine beneficence has prepared.

But another important truth demands our admiration of the divine wisdom and care by which the processes of physical nature are carried on. It is now fully understood that on the land the great source of oxygen requisite to animal life is the vegetable kingdom; that a continued reciprocation of benefits, so to speak, takes place between animals and plants, the latter consuming the carbon produced by the former, and the former living on the oxygen exhaled by the latter.

The same process is carried on beneath the waters. The marine animals which live upon sea plants also require oxygen, without which their vital functions cannot proceed. This oxygen their organs of respiration separate from the liquid element in which they live. But the sea-water would thus soon cease to be capable of supporting its countless hosts, if some provision were not made for the renewal of the life-sustaining fluid strained from it by the respiration of animals. This renewal, however, is effected by aquatic plants. They are, like land plants, the great source of oxygen; they afford, therefore, food and vital air to the denizens of the deep, from whose decay they in return obtain carbon for their own nourishment. Thus a perpetual circulation takes place, which affords one of the most striking evidences of prospective wisdom that it is possible to conceive.

In reference to the subject of iodine as extracted from marine plants, one remark may here be added. "When it is considered," observes the justly celebrated Liebig, "that sea-water contains less than the one-millionth of its own weight of iodine, and that all combinations of iodine with the metallic bases of alkalies are highly soluble in water, some provision must necessarily be supposed to exist in the organisation of sea-weeds and the different kinds of fuci, by which they are enabled during their life to extract iodine in the form of a soluble salt from sea-water, and to assimilate it in such a manner that it is not again restored to the surrounding medium. These plants are collectors of iodine, just as land plants are of alkalies; and they yield us this element in quantities such as we could not otherwise obtain without the evaporation of whole seas." *

How this process is carried on is not understood, but it cannot fail to add additional interest to the consideration of marine plants, that not only in this respect, but as regards the oxygen they furnish, their structure, simple as it appears, is nevertheless adapted to carry on unceasingly a great system of chemical decomposition for purposes which are all wise and good, although

* Chemistry in its Application to Agriculture and Physiology, p. 83.

we understand but few of them, and are unable to perceive all the ends they are intended to effect.

We behold enough, however, to incite us to know more, and above all to teach us to adore that mighty Being who has not only arrayed in all their beauty the lilies of the field, but has conferred such qualities and functions on the plants that adorn the fields of the great deep, as tend to evince at once His beneficence in providing for the wants of the millions that wander "through the paths of the sea;" and the exuberance of His skill and power in dispersing at the same moment in inexhaustible profusion and luxuriance forms of vegetable life which flourish in consummate grace and beauty, although far removed from human eye amid the abysses of the ocean.

MARITIME PLANTS

CHAP. IX.

MARITIME PLANTS.

Seaside Flowers.—Interest attached to them.—Vegetation of Seaside less luxuriant than in Inland Places.—Sea-side Grasses —Sea-side flowering Plants.—Examples of various Species.

MANY a charm, besides its geological features, its rocks festooned with algæ, its beach of smooth sand or of intermingled shells and pebbles, does the seaside present to its contemplative visitor. It exhibits to him a class of objects very pleasant at once to the mind that thinks of them and the eye that perceives them, in the flowers and plants peculiar to the sea-shore or its vicinity. To such plants and flowers the title of maritime is given. They delight to dwell, as a general rule, out of the reach of the waves, but still almost always near enough to the sea to be sprinkled with its spray during a storm; and had they but organs of hearing they must always hear the voice of the waves either murmuring on the beach in the soft west winds, or thundering on the shore in a tempest.

And truly most agreeable to the mind and the eye are those maritime plants, for they possess much of the beauty derived from form, from colour, or from adaptation of character and quality to the place of their abode, and they suggest moreover to those who are able to perceive typical resemblances, not a few emblematic lessons regarding virtues of great store in the business of human life. Some of them dwell in solitary spots rarely seen or visited, wasting whatever sweetness they possess, not indeed upon the desert air, but upon the wild sea breezes; and so afford emblems of modest and retiring virtue which courts no approval from without, and is amply contented with its own rewards. Others there are that select their abode in places so arid as hardly to afford them any kind of nutriment, nay, scarcely any footing by which to resist being torn up by the fierce winds, and yet in places so unpromising and unproductive, thriving and flourishing, and opening their blossoms gratefully to the summer sun, and so exhibiting types of humble and contented poverty, and thus having more beauty than many a plant nurtured by a sedulous gardener in the warmth and luxury of a hothouse: others again there are which seem to derive no nourishment whatever from the dry sands or the hard rocks on which they grow, whose roots seem to serve no other purpose than to fix them to one place, and whose thick, succulent leaves derive the moisture that fills them from the air, and so afford emblems of those who by ingenuity, industry and toil know how to make the most of untoward conditions, and how to prosper where others less energetic must perish. Then, once more, these various plants are hardy in the extreme; the cutting east winds injure them not; the storm or the ocean spray does them little harm; and so they are all more or less suggestive of that mental vigour, that strength of character, and those sterling virtues of courage and self-dependence, which enable the brave to smile at the frowns of fortune, and by the force of perseverance to be superior to adversity. If there be sermons in stones; if we discover theology in the strata of the sea-shores; we may also discover divinity in the flowers and plants that make their dwelling by the wild sea waves.

As a general rule, vegetation at the sea-shores does not exhibit the luxuriance by which it is characterised in situations at a distance from the sea. In many parts of the coast, and especially on the eastern coast, trees will not grow unless in sheltered situations, and those which do take root seldom attain to the size they exhibit in inland localities. They appear to increase slowly, and to have a stunted aspect; the principal branches, it is remarkable, grow chiefly from the side of the trunk, which is toward the land, towards which all the branches appear to be directed. This is probably caused by the violence with which the wind blows on an unsheltered shore, and by the saline quality of the air when impregnated by the spray, which in high winds is carried like small rain over the adjacent land, and sometimes in storms to an immense distance. Proximity to the sea, therefore, is unfavourable to the growth and development of plants belonging to inland situations; but, as already observed, there are plants and flowers which flourish in no locality so well as on the sea-shores, for which they are peculiarly adapted. Their fitness for the localities in which they thus flourish affords one of the many proofs which the various departments of nature exhibit of the express purpose and design of the all-wise Creator.

The numerous family of British grasses comprehends more than a hundred and twenty species, and of these about twenty belong exclusively to the sea-shores, some making their habitation in rocky and stony places, others in salt marshes and in muddy soil, and others growing in the sand. Those making their abode in the sand are considerably more numerous' than all the rest. It will be sufficient to enumerate a few of those most likely to come under the notice of the visitor of the seaside.

The seaside Catstail-grass (*Phleum arenarium*) is a short grass about six inches in height, which flowers in July, and grows in the sand. The beard grass (*Polypogon littoralis*), which flourishes in salt marshes is about a foot in height, the straws are branched, the leaves are rough on both sides, and the panicle or cluster of flowers is of a purplish colour. The Dog's-tooth grass (*Cynodon dactylon*), like the last, is found on the southern shores of England, but grows in sand; the grey hair-grass (*Aira canescens*), found chiefly on the sandy shores of Suffolk and Norfolk, is about six inches high, and possesses a panicle of numerous small flowers, variegated with purple, green, and white. The Sea-reed, Mat-grass, or Sea-bent (*Arundo arenaria*) is common on various parts of our sandy shores, and easily recognised; the straw is stiff, and of a greenish yellow colour. The root of this species of grass is creeping, and often twenty feet in length, and being very tough, and sending forth numerous fibres, it serves the valuable purpose of binding the loose sand, and preventing its being blown away during high winds. On the coast of Norfolk, between Hunstanton and Weybourne, low hills or "dunes" of blown sand are found along the shore, some of which are fifty or sixty feet in height. They are composed of dry sand, but they are bound into a compact mass by the long creeping roots of this useful species of grass. It has been planted for the same purpose on the shores of some of the islands of the Hebrides, and there are several parts of the Irish coast on which it might be encouraged with great advantage. The *Arundo arenaria* has also been employed in various useful manufactures; it is not only well adapted to make door-mats and floor brushes, but it forms ropes of considerable strength, and is employed in making sacks for holding grain, and hats for summer use. For these purposes it is the peculiar toughness of the straw which renders it available. In addition to these there are two species of Glyceria or Sweet-grass peculiar to sandy places on the sea-shore; the fescue grass (*Festuca uniglumis*), remarkable for its being single-husked, and which also affects the sand; the Sea Hard-grass (*Rottbollia incurvata*) flourishing in salt marshes; the upright sea-lyme-grass, with straws three or four feet high, leaves hard and stiff, and remarkable for having thorny points; the sea-barley or squirrel-tail grass, and some species of sea-wheat-grass (*Triticum junceum* and *Triticum loliaceum*), all of which make their abode on the sand. The study of these various seaside grasses affords much interest; but it is requisite to employ for this purpose the aid of a botanical treatise, by which the minute peculiarities of each species are specially described.

Interesting, however, as the study of the seaside grasses may be, they attract less attention than those plants which bear coloured flowers, some of which among those which flourish on the coast possess no inconsiderable beauty.

One of the most beautiful of those seaside flowering plants is the sea-bindwood, of which the scientific name is *Convolvulus soldanella*. Like the bent, it is very useful in retaining the sand, which without such numerous fibres as it throws out might be easily blown away. The characteristics of this plant render it easily to be recognised. The root is creeping, the stems about two feet in length, the leaves kidney-shaped and somewhat thick and succulent, the flower-stalks, like the two other species of convolvulus which are found in inland localities, bearing a single flower, which is large and of a purplish-pink colour, with pale yellow plaits.

Another flower which is found in gravelly places on the sea-shores in the north of England, in

Ireland, and in Scotland, is the sea gromwell or sea bugloss, known to botanists as the *Lithospermum maritimum*. The leaves of this pretty plant are, like many others belonging to the sea-shore, somewhat fleshy or succulent, egg-shaped, sprinkled with callous dots; the stems are numerous, and from one to two feet long, the flowers in leafy clusters, and of a beautiful purple.

The Dwarf Branched-centaury (*Erythræa pulchella*) is another beautiful plant of the sandy sea-shore. The stem of this plant is sometimes much branched, sometimes simple, and only from one to three inches in height, the leaves egg-shaped, the flowers, which spring from the fork of the stem, are slender, and are of a fine pink colour, and are often found in some situations in such profusion as to produce a most agreeable impression upon the eye. Another species (*Erythræa littoralis*), minute like the preceding, and perhaps a mere variety of the same species, and with rose-coloured flowers in dense clusters, is found in the same situations as the preceding.

The Sea Eryngo (*Eryngium maritimum*) is another gay and beautiful plant, the characters of which are easily perceived. The stem is about a foot high, round and branched; the root-leaves are roundish, plaited, and thorny, like the holly; the heads of flowers, which are stalked and numerous, are of a bright blue; the leaves are of a bluish green.

Contrasted with the eryngo is the Yellow Horned Poppy (*Glaucium luteum*) and the Scarlet

Horned Poppy (*Glaucium phœniceum*), both inhabitants of the sea-shore. The latter is rare, but the former by no means uncommon. It derives its name from the glaucous colour or bloom which every part of the plant exhibits, and may be readily recognised. The root-leaves are numerous, stalked and hairy, the stem-leaves embrace the stem, and are waved, rough, and deeply cut, and from these arise the flower stalks, bearing large bright yellow flowers, which falling off are each succeeded by a pod shaped like a horn, and nearly a foot in length.

The Sea-pink, Sea-gilliflower, or Thrift (*Statice armeria*), is a familiar plant, and produces a great profusion of pink blossoms, which in the months of July and August, when they are in full bloom, have an extremely gay appearance. There are three other species of this plant, which differ in some respects from the preceding, and which bear spikes of blue, and of purplish blue flowers. One of these is called the Sea-lavender (*Statice limonium*); another is the Upright-spiked Thrift (*S. spathulata*); and the third is the Matted Thrift (*S. reticulata*).

The Sea-Rocket (*Cakile maritima*) is a plant which grows in sand and is common. It is about a foot in height, the stem is much branched, the leaves, which are scattered, are fleshy, and pinnatifid, that is to say, cut transversely into oblong segments, something like the oakleaf, the flowers large, growing in dense clusters, and of a lilac colour.

The Great Sea-Stock (*Matthiola sinuata*) occurs in some localities, but is less frequent than the preceding, although a genuine plant of the seashore. The stem grows to the height of two feet, the leaves are downy, obtuse at the ends, sinuate, but those of the branches undivided. The whole plant is covered with dense starry hairs and short prickles, and the flowers are purple.

Two species of Sandwort (*Arenaria*) invite the attention of those who visit the localities where they flourish, and which, as the name indicates, grow in the sand. The one is *A. peploides*; its leaves are egg-shaped, acute, and fleshy, and its flowers white and inconspicuous. The other (*A. marina*), which has semi-cylindrical leaves, has rather large flowers of a pale purple; both plants are fleshy and succulent in their structure, and are associated by botanists in the order to which pinks and carnations belong.

The Sea Stork's-bill (*Erodium maritimum*) is another plant common on the sandy shores of various parts of the south of England; its leaves are simple, heart-shaped, crenate or notched in their margins, and rough, the stems depressed and hairy, the flowers small and of a pale red.

Taking up their abode in gravelly and sandy places on the sea-shores there are likewise several plants of the vetch family, one characteristic of which is the pod more or less similar to that of the pea. The Sea Pea (*Pisum maritimum*), with a procumbent stem, bearing alternate pinnated leaves and branched tendrils, and stalks with numerous flowers, purple and veined with crimson; the Smooth-podded Sea Vetch (*Vicia lævigata*), with pale blue or whitish blossoms; the Purple Milk-Vetch (*Astragalus hypoglottis*), with stems two or three feet long, and pale yellow flowers in egg-shaped spikes, supported by short axillar stalks; and the Kidney-vetch or. Ladies'-fingers (*Anthyllis vulneraria*), the stems of which are about a foot high, and the corolla yellow and sometimes white, — a plant which, unlike the preceding, grows in dry pastures near the sea.

Several species of clover (*Trifolium*) are also peculiar to the coast. On the south-eastern shores of Britain and other districts, is found the Suffocated Trefoil (*T. suffocatum*), so called from the circumstance that the whole plant is generally buried in the sand,—bearing heads of flowers of a pale rose colour; the Teasel-headed Trefoil (*T. maritimum*), which flourishes in the same localities as the preceding plant, has flowers of a pale red in heads of an oval shape.

The Sea Cotton-weed (*Diotis maritima*) is an easily recognised plant belonging to the southern coasts of England. The stems, which are about a foot in height and branched, bear lance-shaped leaves, the blossoms are yellow, and the whole plant white and cottony. Then there are many others which we shall only very briefly mention. The Sand Strap-wort (*Corrigiola littoralis*), with lance-shaped, linear, glaucous leaves, and terminal clusters of numerous white flowers; the Sea Plantain (*Plantago maritima*) and the Buckshorn

Plantain (*P. coronopus*); several varieties of rushes, especially the *Juncus acutus,* and *J. maritimus;* the Sea Feverfew, with its large flowers, which have a very convex yellow central disk and white rays; the Sea Beet (*Beta maritima*), the flowers of which are green; several species of Orache (*Atriplex*); the Sand Mustard, (*Sinapis muralis*), with greenish yellow flowers; the Sea Radish (*Raphanus maritimus*), with flowers large and of a pale yellow; the purple Broom-rape (*Orobanche cœrulea*), with its funnel-shaped greyish-purple corolla; the broad-leaved Pepperwort (*Lepidium latifolium*), with its compound clusters of numerous very small white blossoms; in addition to which, among the less conspicuous seaside plants, there are two or three kinds of Scurvy-grass (*Cochlearia*), with white flowers; the Hare's-ear (*Erysimum orientale*), with its cream-coloured flowers, in loose clusters; the Sea Chamomile (*Anthemis maritima*), and several species of spurge (*Euphorbia*), all which have their own peculiar claims on those who cultivate the botany of the sea-side.

With the exception of a few that inhabit gravelly places and in dry mud, all the plants now enumerated grow in the sand. We shall now direct our attention to those which flourish in salt marshes, or in muddy places in the vicinity of the sea.

Among the plants most characteristic of marshes of which the water and the soil are largely impregnated with salt, is the common Jointed Glasswort, Saltwort, or Marsh Samphire (*Salicornea herbacea*). It is a small herb, about a foot high, the stem is erect, herbaceous, fleshy, cylindrical, and divided into joints, the leaves are like scales, which proceed from the joints, at which point also three minute flowers on the two opposite sides of the stem are produced. This plant makes a good pickle. It is also eaten by cattle. There are two other species of saltwort found in the same localities.

The Water-Parsnep (*Sium verticillatum*) also occupies the salt marsh. This plant has leaflets in whorls, that is to say, growing in a circle around the stem and of a hair-like form. It produces numerous white flowers on terminal umbels, or flower-stalks arising from a common centre.

The slender hare's-ear (*Bupleurum tenuissimum*), a plant from three to twelve inches high, with lance-shaped leaves, and yellowish flowers, few in number and, like the last, in umbels; the Sea Sulphur-wort or Hog's-fennel (*Peucedanum officinale*), has a stem about three feet in height, leaves deeply divided, and bears yellow flowers; the Mud-rush (*Juncus cœnosus*); the smooth Sea-heath, with its flesh-coloured flowers; the parsley Water-Dropwort, (*Œnanthe pimpinelloides*), bearing flesh-coloured flowers; the Least Lettuce (*Lactuca saligna*), with pale yellow flowers; the Star-wort (*Aster tripolium*), with its large purple flowers with yellow disks; all belong to the salt marsh. To these we may add the Bartsia (*B. viscosa*), with its yellow corolla stained with purple; the beautiful little plant called the Sea Milk-wort or Black Saltwort (*Glaux maritima*), which bears flesh-coloured flowers, and is found, not in salt marshes strictly so called, but in muddy places along the shore, and is very common in many parts of the coast; and the Sea Campion or Catchfly (*Silène maritima*), with its inflated bladdery calyx, of a purplish colour, beautifully reticulated, and its white petals.

There are two plants to which we would solicit the reader's special attention, on account of the remarkable evidence they afford of the effects which may be produced on members of the vegetable kingdom by cultivation. The first to be noticed is the Sea Cabbage, (*Brassica oleracea*). This plant is from one to two feet in height; the leaves are glaucous, waved, lobed, and smooth; the flowers are large and pale yellow; the plant is a biennial and grows on maritime cliffs, and is very abundant along the chalky cliffs of the English coast. Looking at this plant in its native condition, no one could possibly imagine that by the care and skill of the gardener, it could be made in the course of time to assume the extraordinary appearance of the ponderous drumhead cabbage of the kitchen garden, or the character of the cauliflower or brocoli. Yet such a metamorphosis is actually effected. In its natural state the stem of the wild cabbage is slender and its leaves are small. Under the influence of cultivation the stem becomes thick and fleshy, and the leaves become succulent, and so numerous and closely packed on the internal stem that they have no room to expand, but form into a compact and solid body, from the internal portions of which the sunlight being wholly excluded so that they are perfectly colourless, as well as much more delicate and tender than the external green leaves. So extraordinary is the alteration thus made that, although the plant in its wild condition may not weigh more than a few ounces, it is forced to shape itself into a solid sphere several feet in circumference, and weighing perhaps thirty pounds.

The other plant to which we made reference is the Sea-Kale (*Crambe maritima*). The leaves of this plant are roundish, sinuated, toothed, and of a glaucous hue, and leathery; the stems are about two feet in height, branched and spreading; the flowers are large and white, in terminal clusters. It flourishes, like the sea cabbage, in the south of England, and in various parts of the Irish coast. This plant undergoes under a similar process a transformation almost as remarkable as that of the brassica, and by being placed in rich although light soil, and blanched by being carefully covered from the sunlight, it produces the delicate sea-kale of the kitchen garden.

These two instances now given are among the most remarkable effects produced by human ingenuity on the natural characters of plants. Along with many hundreds of examples to the same purpose, although not more remarkable, they afford evidence of a peculiarity in which may be traced the purpose and design of creative foresight. The members of the vegetable kingdom are endowed with a power of accommodating or adapting themselves to circumstances and localities, and vicissitudes of soil and climate; a power which it may easily be conceived is necessary to the preservation of the species, and perhaps we may add, without being far from the truth, in order that they may minister in an improved, or at least a more useful and available form, to the wants of man, somewhat in the same way in which various animals which have been domesticated are rendered useful by their acquired habits and instincts. It is important also to notice, on this very interesting subject, that the same creative power which gave to the vegetable kingdom this peculiar adaptability, has also marked out a limit to it, as in the case of the animal creation; so that the cabbage, the cauliflower, the brocoli, and the seakale of the kitchen garden, if left by the gardener to grow wild, will not continue to exhibit the monstrous forms into which they have been driven, but will return to the simple and natural conditions which they display in their native abodes.

In addition to the numerous plants and flowers above referred to, there are others of larger dimensions which add in no small degree to the amenity of the sea-shores where they occur. A few of these we shall now mention.

The Tree Mallow (*Lavatera arborea*) grows in rocky places, attains the altitude of from six to ten feet, and produces large flowers, the petals of which are purplish rose-colour, darker on the base than elsewhere; the Tamarisk (*Tamarisk gallica*), a small shrub with minute scattered leaves and beautiful clusters of reddish, flesh-coloured, or white flowers, is found in rocky places, and chiefly on the southern coast of Britain; and the common sallow thorn, a bushy shrub five or six feet in height, with green flowers and orange-coloured berries, whose native places are the rocks and cliffs of our eastern shores, and various species of the Rock Rose (*Helianthemum*), which produce in rapid succession during summer thin white or yellow flowers which are so frail as scarcely to last a day. Then there is the Red-fruited Dwarf Rose (*Rosa rubella*), about three feet high, bearing white flowers tinged with pink, and bright scarlet fruit, which grows in the sand in several parts of the eastern coast; and the silky sand willow, a shrub about four or five feet high, which makes its abode on the sea-shore among loose sand.

We have hitherto confined our enumeration strictly to those flowers and plants which belong to the sea-shore, and either occupy the rocks, or grow in sand and gravel, or in marshes, or in muddy places. This plan was indispensable, because in the "debateable ground" which is neither sea-coast nor inland, as well as in sheltered fields and meadows, or along the shores of estuaries not much exposed to violent tempests, and too narrow to allow the waves to rise so high as to scatter their salt spray to great distances, numerous flowers and shrubs flourish which strictly belong to the country; and to do more than refer to these would be to pass beyond the limits assigned to a book which treats of the productions of the sea-shore. Without going beyond those limits, we have pointed out a large number of plants and flowers, many of them of much beauty, and all of them of much interest to the student of nature, and the characters of all of which may be easily discovered by the aid of a botanical treatise, if our brief description shall be insufficient. Every part of the coast has its peculiar features and productions; and whether the sea-shore be bounded by rocks and cliffs, or consists of level sands, the investigation of the botany of the particular districts can hardly fail to have many claims for the eye, and to suggest many lessons to the mind, of the contemplative observer.

PHYSIOLOGY OF MARITIME PLANTS

CHAP. X.

PHYSIOLOGY OF MARITIME PLANTS.

Adaptation of their Structure to their Places of Abode.—Special Instances of this Adaptation.—Analogy between Marine and Maritime Plants.—Functions of Roots.—Adaptation of Leaves to their Office, &c.

In our enumeration of littoral plants and flowers, it was unavoidable to take into view among those lovely denizens of the sea-shore some occasionally found inhabiting places far removed from the beach. Such plants do not differ in their general structure from the ordinary botanical specimens found in inland districts. It is therefore unnecessary to speak of their physiology. It is our province chiefly to describe objects peculiar to those localities, the natural productions of which it is our object to illustrate. With reference to the subject of physiology, we shall therefore restrict our observations to plants strictly belonging to the sea-shore.

The chief object which attracts our attention in considering the physiology of littoral plants, is the series of admirable adaptations in their structure, fitting them in a special manner for the places of their abode.

Such is the rich profusion with which the hand of Creative Power has scattered over the earth the various plants comprehended in what is called the vegetable kingdom; and such are the beautiful and beneficial adaptations of the parts of plants to each other, or of the whole plant to the place it is to occupy, that there is scarcely any portion of the earth's surface, however apparently unfavourable, where some form of vegetable life may not be found.

Thus it is not only in the soil which has been rendered rich and fertile by the decay of successive generations of vegetable substances that plants chiefly flourish. In such soil, indeed, the higher orders of plants are to be found, because all the conditions are favourable to their luxuriant development.

But vegetation proceeds in situations the most unpropitious. The coral island in the midst of the ocean, on which there does not exist a particle of soil, and which has been but recently raised above the level of the sea, soon becomes covered with verdure. The surface of the hard rock, on which no soil could find a resting-place, becomes covered with many-coloured lichens, which season after season flourish and cast their germs; the castle wall, between the crevices of which nothing but the hardest lime is to be discovered, affords a resting-place to the moss or the fern.

Even the extremes of heat, cold, and drought, are not incompatible with vegetation. A hot spring in the Manilla Islands, the water of which raises the thermometer to 187°, is not too hot for plants to flourish in it. In the boiling springs of

Iceland, in which an egg can be cooked in four minutes, a species of plant is known to flourish; and in the mud of a hot spring in the Island of Amsterdam, the heat of which is considerably beyond the boiling-point, a kind of liverwort grows. On the other hand, in the realms of perpetual frost, the snow, which scarcely yields to the influence of the solar rays in midsummer, is often reddened for miles by the profuse growth of the minute cryptogamic plant known as "red snow," and the lichen, which forms the food of the reindeer, grows in great luxuriance entirely buried under the snow. In like manner, in situations where in general these roots can find no moisture whatever, numerous races of plants thrive with apparently as much luxuriance as " willows by the watercourses." In all such instances it is obvious there must be a designed correspondence and adaptation of the plant and its organisation to the conditions under which it is to exist.

These observations obtain a striking illustration from the physiology of sea-shore plants, strictly so called. Some of them make their abode on shores and rocks, in gravel, or in the sand. In such instances there is either no soil whatever, or the soil contains no moisture, and is destitute of the chemical properties which belong to the ground in inland situations. For such peculiarities of condition there must be an express provision in the organisation of the plant, otherwise it could not subsist.

Without referring to those plants which, although found near the sea-shore, do not differ in their physiological structure from those occupying inland situations, we shall notice those only which are specially adapted to such localities. The house-leek, which belongs to the order Crassulaceæ, so called because of their thick, succulent leaves, may be considered as a type of those we now refer to. All such plants flourish in places which would be fatal to those differently organised. They can occupy the driest situations, where not a particle of grass, and not even moss, can grow, such as naked rocks, old walls, hot, dry sands exposed alternately to the fiercest rays of the sun and the heaviest night-dews. They represent in the temperate regions of the earth the cactus, and other succulent plants of tropical countries, the structure of which enables them to flourish in similar circumstances.

One of the most familiar examples of the kind of plants now referred to is the Sedum or stonecrop, several varieties of which exist in Britain, and flourish in the dry sand of the sea-shore.

We have already stated that the function performed by roots of the algæ or sea-weeds, seems chiefly, if not altogether, to be that of fixing the plants to one place. The same remark may almost be made as to the roots of the succulent plants of the sea-shore. The places in which they grow afford so very small a quantity of moisture, except during rains or when the spray of the waves reaches them during a storm, that in general the root, even were its powers of absorption as great as those of inland plants, could not furnish to the stem, the leaves, and the flowers a supply of moisture equal to the great demand arising from a situation not only extremely dry, but exposed to the greatest heat of the sun. Two objects, therefore, require to be effected, both of them apparently indispensable to the very existence of the plant: one of these is the power of obtaining moisture otherwise than by the root; the other is the means of preventing the evaporation or loss of the moisture when so obtained. To perceive how this object is accomplished, it is requisite to consider the structure and functions of leaves in general, and those of succulent plants, such as we now speak of, in particular.

The functions of the leaves of plants are precisely similar to those of the gills of fishes and the lungs of land animals. The gills and lungs of animals expose over a wide surface the venous blood to the action of the oxygen contained in water or in air; by this means the blood, which during the process of circulation had parted with some of its most important constituents, is again rendered fit for the purposes of imparting vigour and health and continuing the growth and life of the animal. Unless the vital fluid be thus continually supplied with these qualities, obtained by respiration, the animal necessarily ceases to exist; if the supply be deficient it ceases to possess health. This great rule is often exemplified by members of the human family. The fresh breezes of the sea-shore, laden with vital oxygen from the tropics, are often known to restore to the cheek of the invalid the bloom of health, lost amidst the defective ventilation of the busy factory or the impure atmosphere of the crowded city.

The fluid taken up by the roots of plants or absorbed by their leaves is as unfit to nourish or promote growth, till exposed to the influence of the atmosphere, as the blood of animals before it is supplied with oxygen. The leaves are the lungs or gills by which vegetables breathe. They are the organs in which the crude juices of the plant are elaborated by exposure to atmospheric influences, and so rendered capable of ministering to the health, the growth, and the life of the plant.

An examination of the leaf proves how admirably it is adapted to the office it is intended to perform. It consists of an extension of the skin or cuticle of the plant into a flat expanded surface, supported by a skeleton prolonged from the wood of the stem or branch. Between the upper and under cuticle of the leaf is a soft green tissue, which on being examined by the microscope is found to consist of distinct cells packed together more closely near the upper surface than the lower, where there appear to be many cavities and spaces between them.

The cuticle is furnished with what botanists call stomata or mouths. These are apertures or pores of an oval and sometimes circular form, bounded by two kidney-shaped cells containing green matter, by the expansion and contraction of which cells the aperture is diminished and increased. These stomata are always placed over the spaces between the cells of tissue, and so minute and numerous are they that in some leaves 70,000 occur in a square inch of cuticle; the longest are about the $\frac{1}{500}$ of an inch in length, and the least are not the $\frac{1}{3000}$. Their office is to allow of the passage of watery vapour and gases from the soft tissues of the leaf, and to permit the access of the sunlight and atmosphere and their chemical influences to the sap or juice, in order to its being converted into a substance adapted to the nourishment of the plant. The exhalation from the leaves of inland plants is so great and rapid that, if planted for experiment sake in the dry hot sand in which any sea-shore plants thrive, they must speedily wither and dry up. If, therefore, there were no modification of structure in the leaves of the plants now in question, they could not even for a few hours exist in the situations in which we find them.

Let us take, therefore, the sedum and the samphire with their fleshy and succulent leaves as special examples of the adaptation now in view, and exhibited in many other strictly sea-shore plants. In such plants the leaves possess a very high power of absorbing moisture from the surrounding air compared with those of other plants. In this respect they are similar to the cactus and other succulent plants of the tropics which collect their stores of moisture almost wholly from the atmosphere. The power of thus absorbing moisture is singularly adapted to the locality in which the sea-shore plants flourish, for, although the soil or sand in which they are fixed is dry and hot, the air is loaded with moisture, the process of evaporation from the surface of the sea being carried on with the greatest rapidity during the heat.

But the power of absorbing fluid from the air is not the only peculiarity of the succulent plants of the sea-shore. They are in a remarkable degree exposed to the influence of heat and drought, and they must perish unless some provision exists in their structure to check the exhalation which otherwise would take place with great rapidity from the leaves. The cuticle, therefore, is much firmer in its texture, and much thicker, than in plants occupying situations in which the root can obtain an abundant supply of moisture. Moreover, in succulent plants the stomata are comparatively so few in number that sometimes they appear to be wholly absent; and as it is by these stomata that air enters the leaves and carries off, as if by evaporation, their fluid contents, the deficiency of those orifices along with the thickness of the cuticle itself, render these plants capable of retaining their moisture, producing their blossoms, and completing their fructification, under circumstances which even in a few hours would be fatal to other races of vegetables.

This is but one out of the innumerable instances

of express adaptation to special circumstances which the physiology of plants affords. But it is impossible not to perceive that it is a very striking instance, inasmuch as without it there could be no vegetation in places such as rocks, where there is no soil, and in arid sands affording little or nothing of the moisture ordinarily required for luxuriant vegetation. It is impossible, therefore, not to regard the physiological structure of the succulent plants of the sea-shore as an evidence of design on the part of that Being whose will it is that the earth should nowhere be wholly destitute of vegetable productions, and by whose intention accordingly the capability of existing and flourishing in their particular locality is specially provided in the structure of the plants now referred to.

CLASSIFICATION

CHAP. XI.

CLASSIFICATION.

Number and Variety of Organic Forms.—Generalisation.—Classification of the Animal Kingdom.

IMPERFECTLY as we are able to investigate the zoology of the ocean, and although by far the greater part of the vast expanse beneath the surface of which the various objects of our research have their abode is unknown and unexplored, there is abundant reason to believe that the subaqueous realms are much richer in the number and variety of the organic forms that inhabit them, than the terrestrial portions of the globe.

Speaking of the myriads of living creatures whose existence is connected with one species of sea-weed found in the southern ocean, Darwin makes the following remarks:—" The number of living creatures of all orders whose existence depends on that of the kelp is wonderful. A great volume might be written describing the inhabitants of one of those beds of sea-weed. Almost every leaf, excepting those that float on the surface, is so thickly encrusted with corallines as to be of a white colour. We find exquisitely delicate structures, some inhabited by simple hydro-like polypi; others by more organised kinds, and beautiful compound Ascidiæ. On the flat surfaces of the leaves various patelliform shells, Trochi, uncovered Molluscs, and Bivalves are attached. Innumerable Crustacea frequent every part of the plant. On shaking the great entangled roots, a pile of small fish, shells, cuttle-fish, crabs of all orders, sea-eggs, star-fish, beautiful Holothuria,—some taking the external form of the nudibranch Molluscs,—Planariæ, and crawling nereidous animals of a multitude of forms all fall out together. I can only compare those great aquatic forests of the southern hemisphere with the terrestrial ones in the tropical regions. Yet if the latter should be destroyed in any country, I do not believe nearly so many species of animals would perish, as under similar circumstances would happen with the kelp."

"In the oceanic depths," says Humboldt, "far exceeding the height of the loftiest mountain chains, every stratum of water is animated with polygastric sea-worms, Cyclidiæ and Ophrydinæ. The waters swarm with countless hosts of small luminiferous animalcules, mammaria of the order Acalephæ, Crustacea, Peridinea, and circling Nereides, which when attracted to the surface by peculiar meteorological conditions convert every wave into a foaming band of flashing light."

If we reflect upon the almost infinite numbers and variety of marine animals from those of microscopic size to the largest of the crustacea, and if to these we add the countless myriads of various fishes, and especially the gregarious tribes, we can hardly fail to admit the accuracy of the comparison made in the quaint words of Spenser:—

> "Oh! what an endlesse worke have I in hand,
> To count the sea's abundant progeny!
> Whose fruitfulle seede farre passeth those in land,
> And also those which wonne in the azure sky,
> For much more eath to tell the starres on hy,
> Albe they endlesse seeme in estimation
> Then to recount the Sea's posterity;
> So fertile be the flouds in generation,
> So huge their numbers, and so numberless their nation."

The organisation of these various animated beings so exactly adapted to their condition, the habits and instincts they possess, the supply of food for their vast and never-ceasing demands, the kind and degree of enjoyment of which they are capable, all afford subjects of the most instructive contemplation, illustrating in a striking manner not only the wisdom and the power of the great Source of Existence, but the beneficence by which those attributes are directed.

The living beings from which such lessons are derivable present themselves to our observation in a miscellaneous manner; it ought nevertheless to be our object to study them with some attention to system and order. And the reason of this may be found in the constitution of the mind itself, and not in any arbitrary mode of classification adopted by naturalists. The power of generalisation is possessed and exercised even in early youth, and independently of instruction. The child classifies as if by intuition objects which seem to it to possess some one quality in common. The principle is indispensable to the acquirement of knowledge; and in adopting what at first sight appears to be a system of artificial classification, the philosophic naturalist is merely giving effect to the tendency of the human mind as manifested even in childhood. The application of scientific terms not only to the classes and orders into which living beings are subdivided, but even to the individual animals themselves, is certainly a considerable difficulty in the way of those unacquainted with the ancient languages from which those terms are taken. Such terms, however, are extremely convenient, and may perhaps be said to be indispensable to a system of classification.

We are now to suppose the reader to enter on the study of some of the animated beings of which the sea-shore furnishes specimens, and although they present themselves to him in a miscellaneous manner, he will find it highly conducive to his purpose to study them in somewhat of the order in which they are placed by naturalists. The scientific phraseology need not occasion any alarm. It may be to some extent laid aside, and can always be explained.

Thus our reader may be presumed to classify all the living forms that come under his notice in one or other of the four great groups into which the illustrious Cuvier and others who have followed him have divided the whole animal kingdom.

The FIRST of these four groups comprehends all animals that have backbones or vertebræ, and which are hence called the Vertebrata.

The SECOND group comprehends all those animals which have soft bodies, and are therefore called the Mollusca.

The THIRD group includes those animals that are jointed, and which are therefore termed the Articulata.

The FOURTH group contains all those that are rayed, and are therefore called the Radiata.

The reader may further be presumed to begin with the lowest of these four great divisions, and thence to advance upwards in the scale. This is the best mode of advancing to the consideration of the higher ranks of organised beings. We shall therefore presume our reader to adopt this course, and to observe also the subdivisions of the groups brought under his attention, so far at least as the natural objects which the sea-shore presents to him shall enable him to do so.

RADIATA, OR RAYED ANIMALS—
ZOOPHYTES

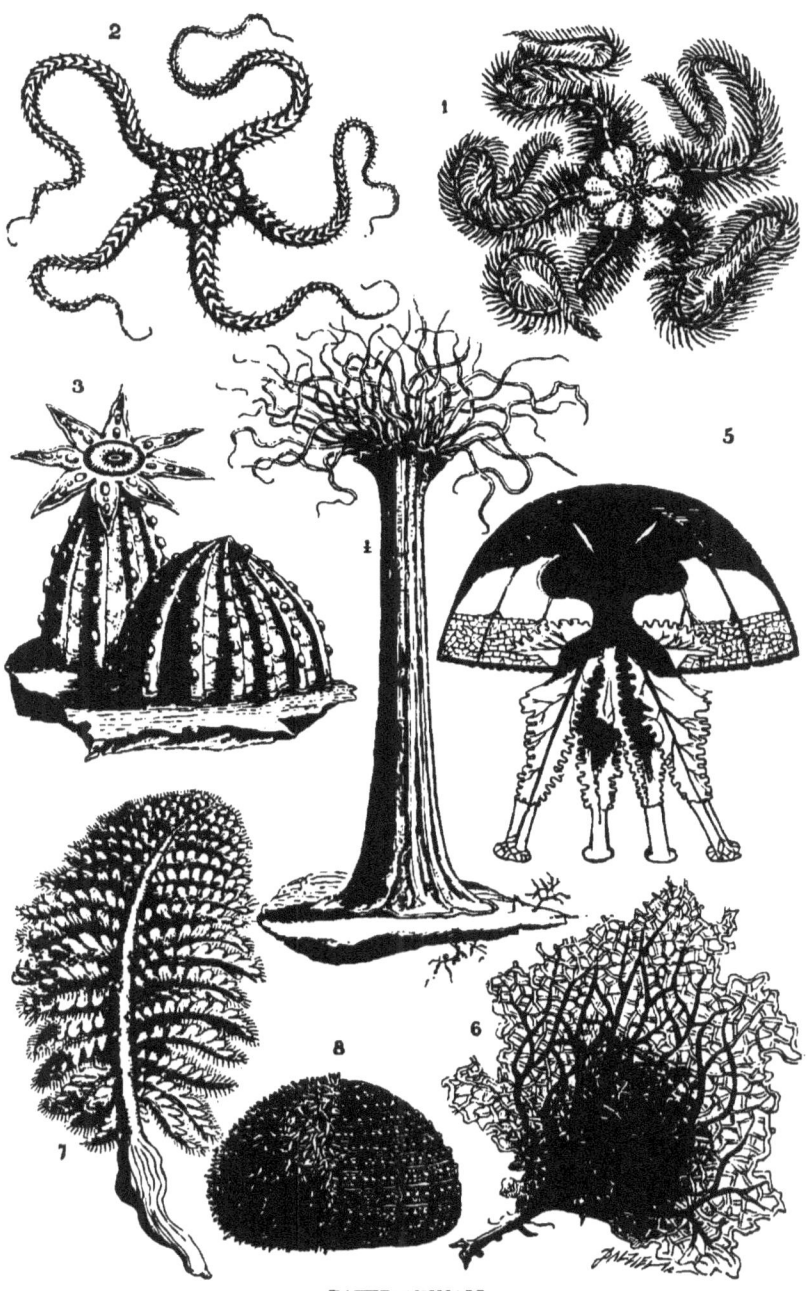

RAYED ANIMALS.

1. The Sand Star.   2. The Brittle Star.   3. Gemmed Sea-Anemone.   4. The Medusa Sea-Anemone.
5. A Jelly Fish.   . The Sea-Fan.   7. The Sea-Pen.   8. The Sea-Urchin.

(See Chapters 12 13 14 and 15.)

CHAP. XII.

RADIATA, OR RAYED ANIMALS — ZOOPHYTES.

Various Species of Zoophytes.—Tubularia.—Sertularia.—Sea-pen.—Sea-fan.—Actiniæ, "Sea Anemones," &c.

LET us restrict our attention to such specimens of the great sub-kingdom of the Radiata as our visit to the sea-shore affords us an opportunity of examining, keeping in view the subdivision of the Radiata into the four great classes into which scientific men have included them.

Here is a little rock pool. It contains sea-water clear and pure, left by the last tide. Its sides are festooned with sea-weeds, and the bottom of it, on which those little crabs are moving about, is composed of fine sand. Let us take up a little of this sand and subject it to our microscope, which although a pocket instrument possesses no inconsiderable power.

The sand is itself an interesting object when magnified; but we perceive mingled with it a multitude of extremely minute shells. Some of them are broken, but many of those which are complete are extremely elegant in their forms. These minute but beautiful shells belong to a tribe of microscopic creatures called Foraminifera.

These little creatures belong to the class Infusoria; they are found to exist in inconceivable multitudes and in great variety in the open ocean far from land, and even in the cold waters of the Polar seas.

An hour or two spent in dredging for specimens in the deep water off the shore often supplies many members of the great sub-kingdom we are now speaking of. Examples of the class Zoophytes may thus be frequently obtained.

Among these are the *Tubularia* and *Sertularia,* which comprehend a great many varieties of species. Some of these may be found in such a rock-pool as we have been visiting or attached to sea-weeds near low-water mark. The *Coryne Pusilla* is an object which ordinary industry may discover on almost any shore. It is a very remarkable zoophyte, or animal-plant, as the term means. It is found attached to stones and sea-weeds, and resembles a plant with its stem and branches. The ends of the branches are terminated by the heads of the zoophyte, which are fleshy and of a reddish colour and covered with short and thick tentacula.

The Sertularia are also zoophytes. The specimen we pick up on some sea-weeds at low-water mark is a very common but elegant species. It is called *Sertularia filicula;* it resembles a fern in shape, having a middle stem from which pinnated branches, (like the fronds of some species of fern,) proceed. These, and others of the same genera, are compound and formed of a vast multitude of individuals, a single specimen sometimes containing five or six thousand individual polypes, and some of the species, known as *Sertularia argentea*, being formed of eighty or ninety thousand, all united together by the medullary substance or fibre contained in the branches. Numerous specimens of this kind are often found fixed upon a single sea-weed, which would thus afford an abode to a population greatly more numerous than the most populous city in the world.

The Sea Pen is by no means a rare object on many of our coasts. It belongs to the family of polypes, and is compound, consisting of numerous individuals united. The *Pennatula phosphorea* may often be met with, and is extremely remarkable. It is three or four inches in length, of a purplish red colour, and fleshy in substance, and like a pen naked at one extremity and feathered on the other, with closely-set pinnæ, on the edges of which are the cells of the polypes. The body of the common stalk and branches, or pinnæ, is calcareous, and thus possesses the requisite degree of strength. The sea pen is phosphorescent, and when irritated or injured or thrown into fresh water the polypes shed a brilliant light.

The Sea Fans are of the same order. The *Gorgonia flabellum* is a well-known West Indian species, called Venus's fan, but it has occasionally been found apparently cast ashore on the British coasts. One of the British species of sea fans is common on the shores of Devonshire, and is

o

called *Gorgonia verrucosa*. This species is from six to twelve inches in height, and much branched. On the surface of these branches, which are calcareous, like other corals, is a flesh-coloured crust, which is the living membrane in which the individual polypes reside. A careful examination with a microscope of these creatures will amply repay the observer; and, independently of the structure of the whole, or of the individual polypes that compose it, not the least marvellous is the faculty they possess of secreting from the surrounding water the lime requisite to the structure of their common abode—a faculty not the less wonderful although shared by them with a great multitude of other inhabitants of the sea.

Specimens of another order of zoophytes present themselves to us on every rocky shore, belonging to the order Helianthoida, so called because of their resemblance to the sunflower. These are what are known as *Actiniæ*, or, in popular language, sea-anemones. They have fleshy bodies, of various hues and sizes, are attached to one spot, and the tentacles which surround their mouths when expanded give them a striking resemblance to flowers. When the tide has receded, they may be seen attached to the sides of the rocks, beneath the overhanging seaweed. Their appearance when thus discovered is by no means attractive. They resemble small hemispheres, or cones, in the centre of which is an orifice closed up, something like the mouth of a bag when tightly drawn together by the string.

Those of a red colour are very similar to a piece of raw flesh, and, on being touched, the resemblance is still more striking, on account of the tough muscular sensation they convey. Very different does the sea-anemone appear when the tide is in; it then puts on all its charms: and if the sea is clear and tranquil, and not too deep, may be seen in great perfection, expanding under the influence of the water, as the flower unfolds its petals to the sun. The cone-shaped mass of inert matter is now full of life and activity; the tentaculæ, before concealed within the body of the animal, are now extended, reminding the beholder, by their form and colour, of some gay denizen of the garden; so much so, that where many of these creatures are found together, they resemble the parterre adorned with many-coloured blossoms.

About twenty varieties of *Actiniæ* common to our shores are already known to the naturalist, and beyond doubt many others yet remain to reward his researches. The specific names of many of these are the same as the flowers they are supposed to resemble, while others have appellations derived from some peculiarity of form or of colour. Thus we have the cereus, the daisy, the pink, the aster, the sunflower, the auricula, the gemmacea, and others named after their discoverers, or the particular locality they inhabit.

The *Actinia mesembryanthemum*, so called from the resemblance of its extended tentacula to the starry petals of its floral namesake, is one of the most common. It is not so beautiful as many of its fellow ocean-flowers; its stalk or body, instead of the graceful bell-shape and brilliant appearance which distinguish many other species, is of uniform thickness, smooth, and of a dull crimson colour; the edge of its disk is surrounded by a single row of tubercles, and the tentacula are numerous and slender.

This very common species is far surpassed in beauty by many other less known denizens of our sea-shores. A few of these will be here described, although no language can do justice to the beauty of these singular creatures, when seen to advantage in their native element.

The *Cereus*, frequently found on the Welsh coast, and also on the south-western shores of England, has its body marked with longitudinal furrows, or sulci. Its summit, when expanded, is furnished with slender tentacula, from a hundred and twenty to two hundred in number; the body is of a pale chestnut colour, the tentacula of a sea-green, varied with purple.

The *daisy* anemone (*Actinia bellis*) is a remarkably beautiful species, also found on the south-western shores of England, and also in other localities. A cylindrical stalk from one to three inches in length, and of a fine red colour, supports the disk or body. When expanded, it exhibits a radiated surface or disk much larger, in comparison with the size of the body, than that of any other varieties. The surface of this disk is covered by several hundred tentacula disposed in separate circles round the centre, from the outside of the disk to near its centre. These tentacula point outwards to the circumference of the circle, with the exception of those forming the inner ring, which are elevated more or less from the plane of the disk. These numerous feelers exhibit great variety of hue. In some they are dark brown, yellowish, ornamented with white spots, while the disk itself is tinted with grey, lilac, white, and is sometimes dark brown with scarlet lines diverging from the centre. This species is exceedingly like a beautiful flower.

Another remarkable kind is the *Actinia gemmacea*. It derives its name from the circumstance that it has its stalk or body marked with tubercles like gems, reaching from the base to the top. When contracted, it assumes the form of a bell with the mouth downwards, and the gem-like rows of tubercles converge in an elegant manner from the base to the closed aperture of the mouth. The body is of a beautiful rose colour. The rows of tubercles are alternately white and grey, the disk when expanded is variegated with different hues, green, white, scarlet, black, while the tentacles are of a fine blue colour and add much to the beauty of this " gem of the sea." The actiniæ, although almost invariably found attached by their bases to the rocks, are understood by naturalists to be able to remove from one station to another. Their food consists of aquatic animals of all kinds; they swallow crabs and shell-fish, the hard and indigestible parts of which they afterwards disgorge.

Sea anemones, like other members of the zoophyte family, possess remarkable powers of bearing mutilation. If the tentacula are cut off, others speedily take their place. If the body of the animal be cut into two parts lengthwise, each part will become perfect, and two separate actinias will be the result. Even if all the original animal be destroyed except a minute fragment of the base, this fragment will be sufficient to originate a new and perfect specimen.

A very singular instance is related by an excellent naturalist of the marvellous manner in which this creature is enabled to accommodate itself to circumstances of the most apparently untoward character. "I had once brought to me a specimen of the *Actinia gemmacea* that might have been originally two inches in diameter, and that had somehow contrived to swallow a shell of *Pecten maximus,* the common scallop, of the size of an ordinary saucer. The shell fixed within the stomach was so placed as to divide it completely into two parts, so that the body, stretched tensely over, had become thin and flattened like a pancake. All communication between the inferior portion of the stomach and the mouth was of course prevented; yet, instead of emaciating and dying of atrophy, the animal had availed itself of what had undoubtedly been a very untoward accident, to increase its enjoyments and its chances of double fare. A new mouth, furnished with new rows of numerous tentacula, was opened up on what had been the base, and led to the under stomach!"

Specimens of the coral-building polypes of the tropical seas have sometimes been found in deep water off the shores of the British islands. They belong to the same order as the sea-anemones we have been referring to, but to a different family. The structures which these creatures rear in the Pacific are of amazing extent. One of the coral reefs off the eastern coast of New Holland is 1000 miles in length, and there are groups of coral islands extending more than 1200 miles with a breadth of 300 or 400. These are entirely constructed by those minute but indefatigable labourers, and afford one out of many other proofs of the magnitude of the effects which by the arrangements of Divine Providence are produced in the natural world by agents individually feeble in the extreme, but possessing marvellous power when united in great numbers. The organisation of those apparently insignificant beings, and the instinct with which they are endowed, adapt them to perform, with a precision never exceeded by the most skilful chemist, one of the grandest operations of nature's laboratory. The currents of the ocean bring to them in the sea-water a solution of carbonate of lime, washed by the rains and carried by the rivers of remote continents into the sea. This lime those little chemists separate from the sea-water, and form into a symmetrical structure as compact and solid as marble. Myriads of them thus labouring without a moment's intermission day and night and year after year, are able to transform the dissolved lime contained in the waters of the deep into solid mountains on which the utmost force of the billows is spent in vain, and which perhaps, in some future geological epoch, will form the foundations of new continents and new islands, in which all the richest charms of natural scenery will be exhibited, and where future cities may arise inhabited by man in his highest condition of civilisation.

RAYED ANIMALS — SEA NETTLES

CHAP. XIII.

RAYED ANIMALS — SEA NETTLES.

Structure and Organisation.—Variety of Species.—Differences in Form, Colour, Modes of Locomotion.—Luminous Properties.—Reproduction, &c.

MORE marvels than the most active and acute naturalist can ever fully investigate, are profusely scattered around us in the comparatively shallow waters of our sea-coasts. At every reflux of the tide, creatures are to be found whose structure, habits and instincts, richly reward the utmost patience of the investigator, and yield lessons as to the great Fountain of Life calculated to fill the soul with love and praise, and tending to impress the mind with the great philosophic truth, that, viewed aright, no creature is " common or unclean ; " and that even those which seem to the ignorant and superficial of uncouth and forbidding aspect, may, in a scientific and religious point of view, be truly termed beautiful, because giving birth to sentiments of beauty in the reflecting beholder.

The tide has now receded, and a long reach of shore is uncovered. We pick our steps along those slippery stones covered with green *Confervæ*, towards the rocks now laid bare. We venture to feel assured that something shall be found to justify our laudation of a sea-beach ramble. The bard of Avon sings of "books in the running brooks," and "sermons in stones:" we doubt not that we shall discover many goodly volumes even in the little pools left by the receding waters; and although we shall not look for homilies *in* the stones, since we are not now to discuss the subject of mineralogy, we shall obtain *under* them many a text for seaside divinity. We are not disappointed! Here, hopelessly entangled among the still dripping seaweed, is one of the largest of those strange creatures which naturalists term Acalephæ, — the Greek word for nettles, — a title they have merited from the power of stinging they possess.

It is impossible to contemplate these creatures without surprise. Their bodies are frail in the extreme. They appear to be no more than a mass of jelly. Yet that jelly is animated. The sacred and mysterious principle of life is contained in it, and gives motion, and no doubt a kind of perception, to the simple structure.

And the structure is indeed marvellously simple. A large jelly-fish weighing two pounds when recently taken from the water will be represented, when the fluid parts are allowed to drain off, as Professor Owen remarks, " by a thin film or membrane not exceeding thirty grains in weight." The structure of a body exhibiting apparently so little complexity baffles the skill of the anatomist, but even it, if fully understood, would evince the marvellous skill and wisdom from which organised beings proceed, as fully as the structure of bodies greatly more complex. The property of emitting light which many of the acalephæ possess—the power of stinging seated even in the finest of their thread-like tentacula, and the wonderful digestive powers by which their stomachs quickly dissolve fish and even crustacea,—all afford matter of surprise, and when the simplicity of their structure is considered furnish problems, both in chemistry and anatomy, which it requires the highest skill to examine and the greatest genius to solve. On this subject an excellent writer thus expresses himself:—" Our admiration of the various functions performed by the acalephæ is much increased when we reflect upon the extremely small quantity of solid matter which enters into their composition. This fact admits of easy illustration. On one occasion I took a dead cydippe, and placing it on a piece of glass exposed it to the sun. As the moisture evaporated the different parts appeared as if confusedly painted on the glass, and when it was become perfectly dry, a touch removed the only vestiges of what had been so lately a graceful and animated being."

Although the mode by which the organisation of the jelly-fish enables it to perform the functions now referred to is in a great measure mysterious, yet that organisation itself is in some degree understood. It appears that the body of the animal is composed of large cells, accurately put together, and filled with a transparent fluid, and that these cells are arranged in a peculiar manner in the various families and genera into which these animals are subdivided. Thus they are either four in number, or some multiple of four, and are placed in a certain relation to the centre of the creature's body in which they are arranged. Considerable variety, too, exists in the organ in these animals for the reception and assimilation of food. In some the arms which hang down from the central disk have at their extremities a multitude of pores. These are the mouths by which animalculæ or the juices of decayed animal substances are imbibed. In another species the food, consisting of fishes and crustacea, is received into a single mouth furnished with four lips.

Those visitors of the sea-shore who indulge in the pleasures of boating must frequently have observed and admired the frail but beautiful creatures we are speaking of, and beheld with delight their graceful movements as they impelled themselves through the water, by the alternate contraction and expansion of their umbrella-like bodies: now mounting through the clear water to the surface, now descending slowly downwards to the depths below, though at first sight their apparent want of power seems to make them the sport of every wave and current.

The order of the Acalephæ comprehends a great variety of species in addition to those already pointed out. Some are so minute as to be invisible to the naked eye, and can only be seen by the aid of the microscope; others have a diameter of two or three feet. The forms of some are hemispherical, of others orbicular. Some are seen adorned with long tentacula, which stream behind them in the water; others again have no such appendages. Their mode of locomotion is also various. By means of contracting its disk, one species propels itself through the water; by aid of small paddles placed on the circumference of the disk, another species urges its way onward. They differ also in colour. Some are singularly beautiful, exhibiting those symmetrical patterns produced by the kaleidoscope; some are brown in the centre, with sixteen lines pointing like radii to the circumference; some have a light purple cross in the middle, between each bar of which is a horseshoe mark of a similar, though much deeper, hue, and from the circumference diverge rays of the same tint, but lighter than the rest. Others again have a white cross, with a black spot on each of its arms, and others have a disk almost as translucent as the water in which they float, but in its centre is a bright crimson spot, like a piece of cornelian encased in crystal. The hues of others are still more beautiful, though they are extremely minute. Of one of these last, whose tints are white and crimson, the late ever-to-be-lamented Professor Forbes thus elegantly speaks:—" There is not a medusa in all the ocean which can match for beauty with the minute creature now before us, though its smallness is such that a split pea would overtop it; yet small though it be, it has shape, colour, and substance, so disposed that as yet no explorer of the sea has met with another like it. It is gorgeous enough to be the diadem of sea fairies, and sufficiently graceful to be the nightcap of the tiniest and prettiest of mermaidens."

These singular and interesting creatures are to be found in immense multitudes floating in all our seas. Some of them, as already stated, have the power of stinging when handled. This property, however, belongs only to a few of those that inhabit our coasts. The medusa most remarkable for the possession of this power, this weapon of defence, is the *Cyanea capillata*, or hairy cyanea. Contact with it produces a burning sensation, similar to that caused by the sting of the common nettle. And the swimmer knows this to his cost when he chances to come in contact with the long tentacula of this creature, as it marks his body with long red lines, like the cut of a thin whip, causing considerable pain and feverishness.

The cyanea is a very common species, and must have been seen by all frequenters of the coast, either lying helpless on the beach, or floating at sea. Its disk is of a brown colour, with the edge festooned with an immense number of tentacula of various lengths, that extend behind it as it flaps along beneath the surface. The name Crineta, perhaps, might be appropriately applied to it, from its resemblance to a comet with its streaming tail, which the old Greek astronomers distinguished by that title.

The acalephæ, as already mentioned, have the power of emitting light. In the seas of warmer latitudes this power produces an effect so striking that the most eloquent description is insufficient to do justice to it. So innumerable are these medusæ in tropical waters, that the points of light they emit illuminate the whole surface of the midnight deep. Under such circumstances the scene from on board ship has a magical effect. As the vessel urges her way through the waters where these *sea lamps* hang suspended, the consequent agitation of the waters excites their illuminating powers into greater activity, and she is surrounded not only with innumerable sparks of phosphorescent fire, but broad flashes of light run along the top of every surge that strikes her sides, while globes of fire are seen just below the surface, produced by the larger jelly-fish. If during a dark night one could descend a few fathoms below the surface, the appearance on looking upwards would be beautiful in the extreme, presenting, in the orbs of greater or lesser magnitude scintillating in countless galaxies overhead, much the aspect of the heavens on a starry night, fretted with golden fires.

In our own seas similar phenomena occur, though much less brilliant in character. And few occupations are more delightful to the naturalist in rowing along some romantic shore, than to watch in the deepening twilight the phosphorescent radiance of the larger acalephæ, as the boat glides silently past them, and to admire the shower of sparks that fall from the oars at every stroke, produced by the microscopic animals of the same kind.

The order of acalephæ now referred to, are distinguished from others by their mode of swimming. This they effect, as has been stated, by the sudden contraction of their mushroom-shaped bodies, which thus strike the water with their under parts, and propel themselves forward. This movement, easily perceptible in smooth water, has a sort of resemblance to the action of breathing performed by the lungs, and from this fancied similarity to the heavings of the chest, the general name of *Pulmonigrade* is applied to the whole of this order of jelly-fish.

Another order is known by the name *Ciliograde*, because they progress, not by alternate contraction and expansion, but by means of the cilia that fringe their bodies. These minute and innumerable cilia or hairs strike the water like a set of paddles, ranged in rows along the outside of the living machine; and thus propel it through the deep.

One of the members of this class, of most fascinating aspect, is known to naturalists by the name Beroë, and the name is absurd enough; for what resemblance is there between this beautiful and symmetrical creature and the decrepid old woman whom Juno impersonated in her interview with Semele?

The Beroë is from half an inch to about an inch in length; its body is pellucid; in shape it is like a nutmeg. Its body is subdivided by eight equidistant bands or ridges, much in the same way that a terrestrial globe is subdivided by the lines from south to north marking the longitude. Depending from the body are two tentacula, five or six inches in length, and furnished with a number of slender fibres like tendrils, all of which this fairy-like creature can at will draw up within its body. With these long tentacula it either secures its prey, or attaches itself to some point of support.

The locomotive machinery of this little medusa is even still more worthy of admiration than its singular beauty. A minute examination of the bands or ridges already mentioned exhibits the extraordinary fact, that on the surface of each of them are a multitude of flat plates, formed by hairs or cilia, with their edges placed together like the plume of a feather. These paddles the Beroë puts in motion, and the power is sufficient to propel its orbicular body through the yielding water. But what is still more noteworthy, not only can the Beroë thus move forward, but by reversing the motion of these living paddles, it can move backwards, and by using those on one side only, it can turn round. " Man justly boasts his steamboat," says Professor Jones, " and with pride points to those paddle-wheels with which he walks upon the waves. The paddle-wheels are here more perfect far than ever were contrived by human ingenuity, for all the cumbrous engineering required by man to urge their movements is not needed; each float self-moving keeping time with all the rest."

This wonderful creature, endowed with so marvellous and complicated a mechanism, is nevertheless amazingly simple in structure, so far as appearance would lead us to suppose; it is so translucent, that during day it is visible only by the iridescent hues shot forth from its paddles as they strike the water, and in darkness it shines with a blue phosphoric light, reminding one of a bubble inhabited by some sea-fairy, whose diadem glows through the fragile covering in which she is encased.

Another species of the medusa derives its title (*Physograde*) from the circumstance that it moves by means of a kind of air bladder with which it is furnished, and by inflating which it can also rise to the surface. The well-known Physalia, or Portuguese man-of-war, is an example of this order, and can hardly be considered one of our native species, although occasionally found on the shores of the South of England and Ireland.

The *Cirrhigrade,* of which the Velella is an example, is another species of the jelly-fish.

The Velella sails on the surface of the sea, and may be found in multitudes on our south-western shores during summer and autumn. It has a flattish oblong body, which, although membranous and fleshy, is transparent, and is tinged with dark blue spots. It is distinguished from any of the preceding species by the possession of a sort of skeleton or framework, also transparent, and of a horny texture furnished with a plate, which, when the animal comes to the surface, serves as a sail, by which it is wafted onward. And more wonderful still, by means of long blue appendages which hang downwards from its body, this animated skiff can row itself onward, in the absence of a breeze, or steer when going before the wind.

Until very recently the mode in which the young of the acalephæ are produced was wholly unknown, although much curiosity was naturally felt on such an interesting subject. Discoveries, however, have been within the last few years made by several distinguished naturalists, which greatly add to the interest with which they are regarded.

It appears that the medusa gives birth to a multitude of minute bodies, gelatinous like itself, and in shape somewhat oval, like the seeds or sporules of some of the sea-weeds, and clothed with cilia, or hairs, that by their vibration propel them through the water. These buds, as they have been appropriately called, after a little while, fix themselves to some stationary object, and soon undergo a rapid transformation. The body, instead of retaining its oval form, becomes elongated, growing like a plant from the point by which it is attached, increasing in width at its upper extremity. In this upper extremity a mouth is soon formed, surrounded by four prominences that soon become long tentacula, like those of the sea anemones. When this process has reached a certain stage of maturity, the young medusæ begin to be formed. Their earliest appearance is detected in the series of cups into which the stalk is divided. These cups are placed one within another, and have their edges divided into lobes. At length, in each of these cups an independent life is developed. The upper one separates from the rest, and immediately begins to swim about by means of the alternate contraction and dilation peculiar to the parent medusa. The second hemisphere soon follows the first, like ripe fruit from the stem on which it grew. And so the process goes on. In succession the juvenile jelly-fishes set forth on their voyage through the waters, as soap bubbles blown from a pipe wander through the air.

However various in size and in other respects the acalephæ are, they are all in the highest degree worthy of admiration. Not to speak of other peculiarities, how astonishing is it to find in creatures not exceeding the size of a pea, and as pellucid and apparently as simple in structure as the soap-bubble, apparatus perfectly adapted to purposes of locomotion, and evading in subtilty of structure our acutest scrutiny. Referring to those beautiful and delicate organisms the poet justly exclaims,

> "Figured by hand divine, there's not a gem
> Wrought by man's art to be compared with them,
> Soft, brilliant, tender through the wave they glow,
> And make the moonbeam brighter where they flow."

On the subject of the luminosity of the sea, Professor Rymer Jones thus eloquently expresses himself, speaking of the phenomenon as witnessed by himself in the Mediterranean:—" The light is not constant, but only emitted when agitation of any kind disturbs the microscopic medusæ which crowd the surface of the ocean; a passing breeze, as it sweeps over the tranquil bosom of the sea, will call from the waves a flash of brilliancy which may be traced for miles; the wake of a ship is marked by a long track of splendour; the oars of your boat are raised dripping with living diamonds; and if a little of the water be taken up in the palm of the hand and gently agitated luminous points are perceptibly diffused through it, which emanate from innumerable little acalephæ, scarcely perceptible without the assistance of a microscope. All, however, are not equally minute; the Beroës, in which the cilia would seem to be vividly phosphorescent, are of considerable size, and the *Cestum Veneris*, as it glides along, has the appearance of an undulating ribbon of flame several feet in length. Many of the larger forms shine with such dazzling brightness that they have been described by navigators as resembling ' white-hot shot,' visible at some depth beneath the surface."

RAYED ANIMALS — STAR-FISHES

CHAP. XIV.

RAYED ANIMALS—STAR-FISHES.

Crinoideæ of Primæval Seas.—Different Families of the Star-fishes—Their Structure, &c.—Ophiuridæ.—Feather-star.—Sun-star.—Brittle-star, &c.

ALL the animated beings we suppose that our readers have hitherto examined belong, let us remind them, to the great sub-kingdom of radiated animals. There is, however, another order of creatures belonging to the same group examples of which may be discovered on every shore. These are the star-fishes, known to naturalists as the *Echinodermata,* a division comprehending all those rayed animals which are enveloped in a covering either hard or rough or beset with prickles, like the hedgehog, a peculiarity from which the general title of the order is derived, *echinus* being the Greek word for hedgehog, and *derma* meaning in the same language a covering.

The star-fish differs in a striking manner from those gelatinous radiaries already noticed, not only in the hardness of the integument with which it is invested, but in the extreme complexity of its structure. The various species of star-fishes likewise differ widely from each other. Thus, the star-fish and the urchin belong to the same order; but nothing can be more remarkable than their external dissimilarity.

The whole order has been subdivided by naturalists into six families, some specimens of which we shall suppose to fall under our readers' observation.

In the first of these six families are comprehended those fossils so well known to geologists as *Crinoideæ*, a term signifying *likeness to a lily*. These animals were the inhabitants of the primæval seas. They consisted of a stalk, by which they were attached, like other zoophytes, or like marine plants, to a particular spot, on the extremity of which stalk was the body of the animal, formed, like the common star-fish, of arms or rays diverging from a centre. The jointed stalk by which the lily-shaped body was supported consisted, like the back-bone of a fish, of a large number of pieces perforated in the centre. These pieces, separated from each other, may frequently be picked up among the shingle on the beach. In ancient times they were often formed into rosaries by being strung upon a thread by means of the perforation in the centre, and in the north of England they are still known as St. Cuthbert's beads, after the name of the venerable Abbot of Lindisfarne. Sir Walter Scott thus refers to the ancient tradition to which those parts of the crinoidea owe their name: —

> "But fain St. Hilda's nuns would learn
> If on a rock by Lindisfarn
> Saint Cuthbert sits and toils to frame
> The sea-born beads that bear his name;
> Such tales had Whitby's fishers told,
> And said they might his shape behold,
>   And hear his anvil sound:
> A deadened clang,—a huge dim form,
> Seen but and heard when gathering storm
>   And night were closing round;
> But this, as tale of idle fame,
> The nuns of Lindisfarn disclaim."

The multitudes of Crinoideæ which inhabited the primitive ocean exceed all conception. The immense deposits of what is called encrinital marble which are found in some districts of England, are formed almost entirely by their remains.

The second family of the star-fishes is that of the Ophiuridæ. These are distinguished by their circular bodies, and five long and very slender legs.

The third family are the Asteriadæ, or true star-fishes.

The fourth family is that of the Echinidæ, or sea-urchins.

The fifth are the Holothuridæ.

The sixth are named the Siphunculidæ. These in external appearance resemble worms, but their natural history has not been fully investigated.

The families now enumerated include a great variety of species, a special description of which would occupy a large space, but a few of the more interesting varieties may be described.

Let us suppose then that the reader has

secured a specimen or two of each of these great families of the *Echinodermata*, and that he is desirous to examine their structure, we can assure him that his labour will be amply repaid by the results of such investigation.

Let him first examine his specimen of the *Asteriadæ*, by the aid of the description now to be given of these peculiar inhabitants of the seashore.

The star-fishes then or *Asteriadæ* (*aster*, a star), have their bodies divided generally into five lobes or rays, more or less elongated. In some cases the rays form the points of five angles, into which the body is divided. The upper surface of these rays is protected by a very thin skin, which seems to the touch as if filled with a soft pulpy substance. The lower surface, however, is much more complex in structure. From the centre to the point of each ray runs a groove or channel, lined on each side by two walls of shelly matter, which form part of the skeleton of the little animals. In each of these channels are a multitude of suckers. These suckers are placed on the ends of transparent footstalks; they serve the double purpose of *hand* and *foot*, enabling the star-fish to move from place to place, seize upon its food, or to attach itself to one spot. Each of these feet, thus terminated by a sucker, issues from a hole in the groove already spoken of. Each foot is formed by a tube filled with liquid, which is injected into it from a gland at its base by means of muscular pressure. When this pressure is withdrawn, the liquid retreats into the gland, and the feet collapse. Thus by this simple and effective mechanical arrangement the star-fish can either retract or extend his feet at will. Individually the suckers exert little power, but their collective force is fully adequate to all the animal's requirements.

The *Ophiuridæ* (*ophis*, a serpent, and *oura*, a tail) are very common along our sea coasts. This generic term by which they are known, a name assigned them by the celebrated naturalist, Professor Edward Forbes, accurately describes their general form. Their bodies, small and round, are furnished with fine, long, and slender arms. These arms, instead of the sluggish movement of the ordinary star-fish, are endowed with great activity, and move and twist about with great rapidity, and, by their resemblance to the tails of small serpents, suggest the name by which they are distinguished. The celerity of motion possessed by these arms furnishes the creature with power to crawl with considerable rapidity.

Another beautiful variety is the *Comatula* or feather star. It possesses much elegance of form and beauty of colour. Its body is of small size, covered with jointed filaments. Fine, long, and slender arms, feathered along their sides and furnished with claws, enable it to adhere to rocks or seaweed with great force. Its internal structure is most elaborate and wonderful, and cannot be well described without recourse to very minute de-tail; in fact, it must be seen, as no description can do justice to the marvellous mechanism of its organs of locomotion, respiration, and deglutition. The student will recognise it by its fine rose colour, sometimes variegated with bands of crimson and yellow.

Another beautiful species of these interesting animals is the Sun-Star. It is so called because the disk is surrounded by twelve broad rays. In colour the sun star is variable. Sometimes the whole body is red; sometimes, also, it is purple; sometimes the centre is red and the rays white.

Several of these remarkable creatures now described are further distinguished by the possession of a most singular power—the power of self-destruction; for on being removed from their natural element they fall to pieces: they are hence called " brittle stars." Whether this peculiarity is the result of voluntary action, or the natural effect of exposure to the air or to touch, it seems difficult to determine, although in some instances it looks like an act of will on the creature's part.

Let us hear what Professor Edward Forbes says on this point. Having taken a fine specimen of the Lingthorn (*Luidia fragilissima*), a star-fish measuring some two feet across, he gives the following humorous account of its suicidal propensities:—"Never having seen one before, and quite unconscious of its suicidal powers, I spread it out on a rowing bench, the better to admire its form and colours. On attempting to remove it for preservation, I found only an assemblage of rejected members. My conservative endeavours were all neutralised by its destructive exertions; and it is now badly represented in my cabinet by an armless disk and a diskless arm. Next time I went to dredge on the same spot, determined not to be cheated out of a specimen such a way a second time, I brought with me a bucket of cold fresh water, to which article sea-fishes have a great antipathy. As I expected, a luidia came up in the dredge, a most gorgeous specimen. As it does not generally break up before it is raised above the surface of the sea, cautiously and anxiously I sank my bucket to a level with the dredge's mouth, and proceeded in the most gentle manner to introduce luidia to the purer element. Whether the cold air was too much for him, or the sight of the bucket too terrific, I know not, but in a moment he proceeded to dissolve his corporation, and at every mesh of the dredge his fragments were seen escaping. In despair I grasped at the largest, and brought up the extremity of an arm, with its terminating eye, the spinous eyelid of which opened and closed with something exceedingly like a wink of derision."

Before quitting the subject of star-fishes, a highly interesting fact in the natural history of the *Cribella oculata* common on almost every seashore, must be noticed,—its maternal solicitude. The young of the star-fish are produced from ova, and the *cribella* by bending its arms forms its body into a concave figure and hatches the eggs in the hollow thus made. During this process, which it is said requires eleven successive days, the mother star-fish remains in this recurved and contracted form necessary to her purpose, and in that attitude cannot obtain any nourishment. This singular circumstance affords one of the many proofs which have been discovered that parental instincts are not confined to the higher orders of animated beings, but are shared with them by the humblest creatures, to whom for wise ends the Great Parent of all has permitted the exercise of parental solicitude.

Another observation we would make before passing on, is one suggested by the statement made by Professor Forbes of the voluntary dismemberment of the luidia, on the subject of pain as endured by the humbler orders of creatures.

Various species of Crustaceans, such as crabs and lobsters, possess the power of dismemberment, and share it not only with the "brittle stars," but with many other creatures both terrestrial and aquatic. These and a great many analogous phenomena seem to afford very conclusive evidence that in a numerous class of animated creatures, bodily injury is not accompanied by what we call pain, as is the case in the higher order of animals.

If this be so, and there is little reason to doubt it, the fact presents us with a very beautiful and striking illustration of the beneficent wisdom of that Great Being "whose tender mercies are over all his works." Pain is to man an admonitary intimation of physical injury received or threatened; it is a provision absolutely essential to his security, since, without this warning, he might sustain irreparable damage without being aware of it. It is a warning, too, strictly consistent with man's intellectual superiority, and furnishes a powerful stimulus to the exercise of prudence, caution, foresight, as the means of escaping it, while it acts likewise as an impulse to his skill and ingenuity in remedying those evils by which it is occasioned. Bodily pain would be a very gratuitous and an almost unnecessary infliction, if man were not highly endowed with intellectual powers, by the exercise of which physical evils may be avoided or obviated; or if the very effort to avoid these evils did not tend directly to administer to the strength and the activity of his mental powers. We may truly observe that among the means devised by supreme wisdom for human advancement, both in a moral and intellectual point of view, pain, employing the term in its widest sense, is one of the most appropriate as well as efficient. But in the case of the lower animals, to what purpose could pain tend, if accompanying bodily injury? It is indeed inconceivable that infinite goodness and wisdom should in vain, or to little purpose, expose a vast multitude of helpless creatures to physical agony.

There is therefore reason to believe that in proportion as the lower orders of animated creatures are exposed to injury they are free from those sufferings which injuries produce in those of higher organisation, and in this respect there is reason to perceive an evidence of the same benignity which so great a variety of other considerations tend to favour.

RAYED ANIMALS—SEA URCHINS

CHAP. XV.

RAYED ANIMALS — SEA-URCHINS.

Antiquity of the Race.—Egg-urchin.—Complexity of Structure.—Method of Enlargement.—Mechanism of Spines, of Mouth, &c.

IT has been already stated that the fourth family of the Echinodermata is that of the Echinidæ or sea-urchins. Although this creature differs in appearance so completely from the star-fish, an investigation of its structure places it unquestionably in the same order.

The urchin belongs to a race whose pedigree extends far into the ages of hoar antiquity, having existed thousands of years before man became a denizen of this terraqueous globe. The species now existing indeed are not found in a fossil state, save in very recent deposits; but their ancestors flourished in prodigious multitudes during the secondary and tertiary epochs, and are found imbedded in the oolite and chalk formations, some shaped like helmets, some elliptical in form, some turbinated, and others heart-shaped like those of the present day. The urchin is therefore an object of interest to the geologist as well as to the student of natural history.

Let us suppose the student to obtain a specimen of the egg-urchin (*Echinus sphæra*), a species which may often be found beneath the seaweeds that cover the rocks on our sea-shores. The shell, it will be seen, is globular, but somewhat compressed, much like the orange in shape. Its structure is most interesting. This is adapted to suit the growth of the animal within. The shell, in fact, grows with the growth of the dweller within, and it does so because, unlike the lobster or crab, the urchin does not cast its shell. Now this necessity for the increase of the size of the house with the growth of the tenant is provided for by an arrangement wonderfully complex and beautiful. The shell is formed in the first place of hundreds of minute portions, for were the panoply to consist of one piece, it would not admit of increase or growth in every direction. But, as it has been said, the sphere consists of hundreds of minute segments of a pentagonal shape. These are fitted together like the stones of an arch or dome. On the inside of these segments, and also between their edges, is the mantle, a thin delicate membrane. It is the office of this membrane to enlarge the sea-urchin's house whenever he feels himself *pressed* for room. And how does the mantle do this? Simply by secreting carbonate of lime, and thereby adding to the thickness and the superficial size of each individual segment of which the shell is composed. It is in this way that the shells of all bivalves and molluscs are increased in size. Accordingly the number and form of the divisions of which the shell consists, are the same both in the full-grown urchin and in the young animal; they differ only in size. By this beautiful provision the sphere is gradually enlarged, without any alteration of its form or of the relative position and size of its various parts. How admirable this arrangement! How completely adapted to the end in view! Were we to suppose there existed a necessity for a certain bridge gradually to increase in size up to a particular point, we could imagine no other available plan than this. Either the whole structure must be taken to pieces and built with stones either larger or more numerous, or the stones originally employed must increase in breadth and length by the addition of new matter at their sides and ends — a process, however, far beyond the limits of human contrivance.

Other parts of this creature's structure are no less striking and interesting than those now described. If the shell be denuded of the spines, it will appear to be from top to bottom marked out by five double rows of small holes into ten spaces shaped somewhat like the gores into which paper is cut in forming a balloon. Each of these spaces is studded with rows of minute hemispheres. These little points, which seem when the shell is divested of its spines to be merely ornamental, are a portion of a piece of mechanism truly admirable. It is to one of these that each of the spines is fixed when the animal is alive. Each spine is furnished with a socket, into which the little point or prominence fits, so that the spine revolves upon it precisely in the manner of what is called by engineers a universal joint, — a kind of mechanism exemplified in the shoulder joint of the human frame, with this difference, that in the human arm the convex part of the apparatus revolves in the socket, whereas, in the case now referred to, the spine with the socket revolves upon the stationary convexity or point.

The spines thus adjusted are put in motion by a set of appropriate muscles, acted on by nerves obeying the instincts of the animal. From each of the holes already mentioned issues a sucker, by which the urchin either attaches itself to one place or changes its position. Among the spines are likewise numbers of minute pincers, called by naturalists *pedicellariæ*, consisting of a stalk with a knob at the end furnished with three hard teeth, some obtuse and others elongated. The use of these pincers does not appear to have been ascertained; but whatever be the special use for which they are intended, they are beyond doubt, like all the understood portions of the complex structure, adapted with inimitable skill to the purpose intended.

If, again, we examine the mouth of the urchin, we shall find its mechanism to be extremely complex. It is scarcely possible, indeed, to convey a suitable notion of it without pointing out its parts in a living specimen; but sufficient may be said to incite the reader to examine for himself. The teeth or jaws consist of five pieces of triangular shape, fitting together into the form of a cone in the centre of which is an additional tooth. This cone occupies the middle of the orifice in the base of the shell, and the teeth or jaws of which it consists are attached to the arches around the orifice, by means of powerful muscles, and are furnished with others enabling them to work upon each other so as to triturate and grind the substances on which the animal preys. To this purpose the jaws are so perfectly adapted that very hard substances exposed to their action are speedily reduced to a pulp.

The elaborate and complex mechanism which is presented to us in the structure of the sea-urchin, cannot be perceived by the intelligent and candid observer without those convictions which consummate excellence in the adaptation of animal mechanism rarely fails to originate. "In a moderate sized urchin," observes Professor Forbes, "I reckoned sixty-two rows of pores in each of the ten avenues. Now as there are three pairs of pores in each row, their number multiplied by six and again by ten, would give the great number of three thousand seven hundred and twenty pores; but as each sucker occupies a pair of pores, the number of suckers would be half that amount, or eighteen hundred and sixty. The structure of the egg-urchin is not less complicated in other parts. There are above three hundred plates of one kind, and nearly as many of another all dovetailing together with the greatest nicety and regularity, bearing on their surfaces above four thousand spines, each spine perfect in itself, and of a complicated structure and having a free movement on its socket. Truly the skill of the great Architect of nature is not less displayed in the construction of a sea-urchin than in the building of a world!"

ARTICULATA, OR JOINTED ANIMALS—
MARINE WORMS, ETC.

JOINTED ANIMALS.—SOFT-BODIED ANIMALS.

1. Hermit Crab. 2. Spider Crab. 3. Cockle. 4. Cuttle Fish. 5. Eggs of Cuttle Fish.

(See Chapters 17, 18, and 19.)

CHAP. XVI.

ARTICULATA, OR JOINTED ANIMALS—MARINE WORMS, ETC.

Their Structure.—Tubicolæ and Serpulæ, &c.—Nereis, Seamouse.

We have supposed our admirers of the sea-shore and its productions to classify the objects of their attention, in other words, to observe them not in a miscellaneous manner, but in the order prescribed by natural history, this being for a variety of reasons the most advantageous.

According to this plan we presume our readers to have discovered various specimens of the lowest rank of animated beings, which, as already stated, are grouped together in the great sub-kingdom of the Radiata, and proceeding with this plan of observation, we now arrive at another great subdivision, called the Articulata.

The Articulata, or Articulated Animals, are so called from the Latin word signifying a *joint*, and they are therefore jointed animals, as distinguished from those which are called Radiata, as being constructed in rays, in the manner already described. It is by no means easy in all cases for an observer not already instructed upon the subject, to ascertain on what principles the term "jointed" is applicable to all the creatures so called. As a general rule, however, the distinction is sufficiently obvious. But in their internal structure the articulata differ widely from all the members of the group to which reference has already been made. Their nervous system is not, as in the radiaries, placed in the centre, from which it extends in rays or branches, but it consists of a brain from which a thread of the nervous matter extends along the body, having at certain distances along the thread nervous centres, called ganglions or knots, from which proceed the nerves which supply the limbs or other extremities. The articulata are arranged in five different classes, each comprehending animals distinguished by some general character.

The first of these classes to which we shall suppose our attention to be directed is that of the Annellata. The animals comprised in this class are very numerous, and various specimens may be discovered with a little industry on almost every sandy sea-shore at low water. The whole class may be considered as represented by the common leech or the earth-worm, the bodies of which creatures are formed of numerous rings, a circumstance which gives origin to the generic term, derived from the Latin word *annellus*, signifying a little ring.

A very common, but, when carefully examined, a very interesting example of the animals of this class is the lug, a large worm inhabiting the sand and much employed as a bait by fishermen.

The place where this worm may be found is easily known by a small heap of sand, somewhat like a worm in shape, lying on the surface, within eight or ten inches from which is a circular depression frequently filled with water. The latter is the place at which the lug protrudes its mouth, and the former the point at which its tail is extended to the surface, and between which two points it can be obtained by digging to the depth of eight or ten inches.

On examining this annelid it will be found that the upper extremity of the body is of considerable thickness, and the lower end so much thinner as to exhibit the appearance of a tail. On opposite sides of the body rows of tufts of a dark crimson colour will be found. These tufts are the lungs or respiratory organs of the worm, through which its blood circulates, and undergoing the same process as the blood of fishes when passing through the gills, becomes suited to the purposes of vitality. All the worms inhabiting the sand form a tribe called Arenicolæ.

Another tribe of marine worms are those which inhabit tubes, and are from this circumstance called Tubicolæ. The tubes they inhabit are constructed by themselves, either from particles of sand joined together by some species of cement with which they are provided, or consisting of lime secreted for the purpose by some process similar to that by which the shells of various crustaceans are formed.

The Serpulæ, of which there are several

varieties, are found upon shells, stones, or broken glass and pottery, which have been long immersed in the water. On these the tube-worms form their abodes, consisting of a vermiform encrustation of carbonate of lime, firmly attached to the surface of the hard body with which it is connected, and presenting a variety of fantastic convolutions. There are, however, several distinct species of serpula. Some are very minute, some form their shelly tubes in a spiral manner, others twist them into a great variety of convolutions. In others again the tubes are lime-coloured, in others perfectly transparent; in some they are round, some wrinkled and angular. Some of the serpulæ are evidently gregarious, a large number of them occupying the surface of the same shell or stone, while, on the other hand, we find a large species which is solitary occupying the surface of one shell, and living without any companion.

The serpulæ differ from the lug already spoken of in the peculiar modification of their breathing apparatus, which consists of a fan-shaped body extremely graceful in its form and brilliant in its colouring, which the worm, in order to breathe, protrudes from the end of its tube-shaped domicile. By obtaining some of the serpulæ alive and placing them in sea-water, the process of respiration may be easily perceived. At the mouth end of the tube is a door, the mechanism of which is singularly admirable. This door, when the whole of the animal is immersed in water, is opened, and the inhabitant slowly protrudes the upper part of its body, from which soon afterwards it spreads out its two fan-shaped branchiæ or respiratory organs, the purple or scarlet hues, the form, and the motions of which are extremely interesting. The habitations of the other species of tube-worms referred to, are frequently found in vast quantities lying upon the dry beach, or half buried in the wet sand, and these consist of thin semi-transparent tubes, formed, as already stated, of particles of sand, but not attached, as those just described, to the surface of stones or other hard substances.

The Nereis is another marine worm of which there are several varieties, some of which may attract the attention of the visitor of the sea-shore. Some of these worms are extremely small, but, like some other very minute creatures, they possess the faculty of emitting light, and are able to illuminate the midnight waters with marvellous splendour. It is in a great measure to these diminutive annelids that the brilliancy is owing which is perceptible on the agitation of the water.

Another species is of much greater length, but not possessed of the power of producing light. It is about four inches in length, and of a bluish-green colour, semi-pellucid, and formed of about 184 distinct segments. It is frequently found in the sand at low water. Another species is a foot in length, and as thick as a goose quill; the tail is orange colour, and the rest of the body exhibits a beautiful iridescence. There are several other varieties of this worm. These and some other kinds are found under stones when the tide has retired.

Instead of being sedentary and attached to one place, they move from place to place with great rapidity along the bottom of the water. The movements of these worms are extremely active and graceful. They are all greedily sought after by all kinds of fishes, to whom their naked bodies furnish an easy repast; but their movements are so rapid that they readily make their escape by hiding beneath the fronds of seaweed or between the stones.

Before quitting the numerous family of marine worms, one may be mentioned which is not uncommon on the coast of Devonshire, and also in some localities on the west coast of England. It is the largest example of the Gordius or hairworm. It grows to the extraordinary length of thirty feet, and possesses the singular power of contracting and expanding itself at will, one of eight feet in length being found to contract itself to one-eighth of its extent. The colour of this remarkable annelid is dusky brown with a tinge of green. Those of the largest size are taken by dredging in deep water, and are found inhabiting old bivalve shells.

Belonging to the tribe we are now referring to is the sea-mouse, or Aphrodite, a creature of which several varieties may be discovered on the shore after the tide has ebbed, and especially after a storm. The largest and most common is the *Aphrodita aculeata.* Although belonging to the family of worms, this creature altogether differs from its relatives in its shape. Instead of being thread-shaped or elongated, its body is oval, and about three or four inches in length, and from an inch and a half to two inches broad. Its back is clothed with silky hairs of a rich metallic lustre, and exhibiting several of the colours of the rainbow. Along its sides are bundles of bristles attached to muscular points which the creature can move at will, and which serve as organs of motion, either in swimming or crawling along the bottom. The splendour of the colours which adorn this creature is not inferior to that of the feathers of the humming bird, although its habitation is the mud at the bottom of the sea. The structure of the humblest organised being is sufficient to excite the sentiment of beauty in any intelligent observer, even in the total absence of mere brilliancy of external colouring. All the marine worms afford marvellous evidences of the same divine skill in which the most complicated organisms have originated.

ARTICULATA, OR JOINTED ANIMALS—
CIRRIPEDA

CHAP. XVII.

ARTICULATA, OR JOINTED ANIMALS—CIRRIPEDA.

"Curl-footed" Animals.—Balanus or Acorn-shell.—Barnacles. — Pentalismus anatifera. — Popular Error. — Young of the Barnacle Shell, &c.

PASSING from the numerous family of marine worms which, as already stated, constitute the class called the Annellata, we suppose the visitor of the beach to proceed to examine the class which naturalists have named Cirripeda (or curl-footed).

Examples of the Cirripeda may be found on every sea-shore. The stones and rocks covered at high water, but left bare when the tide has ebbed, are often found entirely covered with the most common species. Shells which have been long immersed in the water, limpets, oysters, whelks, are also frequently found more or less occupied by them.

The animal now referred to is known as the Balanus or acorn-shell. Our readers will easily recognise it by a brief description. Each shell is composed of several pieces, so placed together as to form a cone, the broadest part of which is attached to the rock or shell which forms its abode. Of these acorn-shells there are several varieties. The size of some is from about a quarter to six-eighths of an inch at the base, and from a quarter to half an inch in height. Others are considerably larger, being an inch and a half in diameter at the base, and from half an inch to an inch and a quarter in height. These shells on superficial examination appear as if formed of one piece. But this is not the case. They are, as already stated, composed of several pieces, and this circumstance is of the greatest importance, being absolutely necessary as a provision for the growth of the animal. This circumstance caused them formerly to be classed with the multivalve shells, and the animal was classed with shell-fish or mollusca. But their structure is now better understood, and the acorn-shells and barnacles form a small class with characteristic peculiarities of their own, although allied to the crustacea.

Like the various kinds of actiniæ and other marine animals, the inhabitants of these acorn-shells are entirely inactive when no longer covered with water. But as soon as the tide rises they project from the opening in the upper part of the shells the apparatus from which their name curl-footed is derived. This has a striking resemblance to a plume of feathers, the motions of which are extremely regular and graceful. This apparatus is adapted at once to the respiration and the nutrition of the animal, and its structure, adapted to these purposes, affords a striking evidence of that marvellous skill which has been employed in the adaptation even of the humblest living creatures to their mode of life and the exigencies of their condition. The manner in which the little inhabitant of the acorn-shell extends its organs, by which it breathes as well as obtains food, may be easily observed. Let our visitor of the beach carry home with him a shell or piece of stone to which some of them are attached, and in depositing it in sea-water the balani will be seen in a few minutes expanding their apparatus, and gently moving it in the still water.

In the same class with those now referred to are the Barnacles. One of these, which is called *Pentelasmis anatifera*, is very common in some parts of the southern coasts of England and Ireland, where it is found in great numbers attached to drift wood. The bottoms of ships are sometimes covered with them. The shell of this cirripod is whitish, flattened at the sides, and opening down the edges by a slit. It is composed of five distinct pieces, united together by a membrane, and the whole is attached to a flexible stalk several inches in length, of a fleshy or rather tendinous character. The feathered apparatus or cirri, by which, like the acorn-shell already described, the animal breathes, have been supposed to be the rudimentary feathers of a future bird to be excluded from the shell when arrived at a sufficient state of maturity.

This popular error is of considerable antiquity, and still prevails in many of those parts of the sea-coast in which the barnacle is found. Gerard, a naturalist who flourished at the close of the sixteenth century, and whose authority in his own day stood very high, not only repeats this fable as an ascertained truth in natural history, but enters into a detailed account of the metamorphosis by which the cirripod is changed into a bird. The following is a passage from his "Herbal" on the subject, part of which has been frequently quoted by modern writers on natural history :— "What our eyes have seene and hands have touched we shall declare. There is a small island in Lancashire called the Pile of Foulders, wherein are found the broken pieces of old and bruised ships, some whereof have been cast thither by shipwracke, and also the trunks and bodies with the branches of old and rotten trees, cast up there likewise; whereon is found a certaine spuma or froth that in tyme breedeth into certaine shels, in shape like those of the muskle, but sharper pointed, and of a whitish colour, wherein is contained a thing in form like a lace of silke finely woven as it were together, of a whitish colour, one end whereof is fastened into the inside of the shel, even as the fish of oisters and muskles are; the other end is made fast into the belly of a rude masse or lumpe, which in tyme commeth to the shape and forme of a birde: when it is perfectly formed the shell gapeth open, and the first thing that appeareth is the aforesaide lace or string; next come the legs of the birde hanging out, and as it groweth greater it openeth the shel by degrees, till at length it is all come forth, and hangeth onlie by the bill : at short space after it commeth to full maturitie, and falleth into the sea, where it gathereth feathers, and groweth to a fowle bigger than a mallarde and lesser than a goose, having blacke leggs and bill or beake, and feathers black and white, spotted in such a manner as is our mag-pie, called in some places a Pie-Annet, which the people of Lancashire call by no other name than a tree-goose: which place aforesaide and all those parts adjoining do so much abound therewith that one of the best is bought for three pence. For the truth hereof, if any doubt, may it please them to repaire to me, and I shall satisfie them by the testimonie of goode witnesses."

This fabulous history of the origin of the bird so well known as the barnacle was by our ancestors held to be perfectly correct, and it still maintains its footing among those inhabitants of our sea-shore from whose minds modern and more accurate ideas have not yet expelled the errors of former ages. But natural history exhibits many phenomena greatly more marvellous than any that originate in the imagination of a credulous naturalist. In this respect the remark applied to the department of literature occupied by the novelist, that truth is stranger than fiction, is equally applicable to natural history. And as regards the creature now referred to, the metamorphosis it undergoes prior to assuming its condition in the shell as above described, is fully as wonderful as that which it has been fancied to undergo subsequently. Prior to entering upon a condition which is permanent and not subject to any further change—the young of the acorn-shells, and likewise those of the barnacles, have been discovered by Mr. J. V. Thomson, Mr. Owen, and other naturalists, to be minute creatures of an oval form, furnished with six pairs of legs, terminated by hairs, and capable of impelling them with great rapidity through the water, by acting in concert with each other, like oars all pulled at the same moment. After passing some time wandering hither and thither through their native element, these singular creatures select the place of their future permanent abode, and attaching themselves to it, begin immediately to assume the form of an acorn-shell or a barnacle, as the case may be; their organs of locomotion, and even of sight, cease to exist, and they henceforth depend for their food on what happens to come in their way, having no longer any power to pursue their prey.

Such alterations of condition and form are precisely the opposite of that which occurs in the instance of the jelly-fish already spoken of. These in their earlier stages of growth are attached to a stalk, and are successively thrown off like living buds, to wander through the watery plains; while the others, free to rove in their youth, become fixed to one locality, where they attain maturity. How marvellous the variety of those works which proclaim the wisdom of the mighty Creator!

ARTICULATA — CRABS

CHAP. XVIII.

ARTICULATA — CRABS.

Structure. — Spider-Crab and various other Species. — Pagurus, Habits and Structure, &c. — Zoea.

WHEN the aged priest of Apollo found his prayers for the liberation of his fair daughter rejected by Agamemnon, he betook himself, the poet tells us, to the shores of the loud resounding sea, and seeking an unfrequented place poured forth his supplications to the Silver Bow-bearer. And truly no locality is more suited to devotion, whether in grief or gladness, than the shores of the great deep. Nowhere do we find so much to awaken those sublime emotions which are so closely allied to all true devotion.

And it may be affirmed that of all men the diligent student of nature is best able to decipher and understand the language with which the sea-shore addresses both the intellectual and the moral faculties and powers of the soul. What a world of wonders does not the sea-shore unfold to him, all but invisible although they be to other and common eyes! Even if he confine himself to an examination of the structure, the forms, the habits of the Crustacea alone, what a fund of strange and interesting knowledge awaits him; and what undeniable evidences of careful adaptation and of express design on the part of the great Author of life, whose tender care has been bestowed alike on the most minute as well as the greatest of His creatures! Of all this the observations we have already made afford ample confirmation.

Let us wander away along this patch of sand, on which there has not been impressed the mark of a footstep since the tide left it white and smooth, with clean-washed pebbles and shells scattered over its surface, and here and there a piece of olive or pink seaweed. We shall make our way to those distant rocks, now uncovered, from whose sides hang a profusion of the dark olive-green seaweed, along the fronds of which are bladders, dear to our boyhood, because cut off and dried they produce prodigious explosions when cast into the fire. Around those rocks there are pools of water, bright and clear as if from a spring, and in those pools, sheltered by the overhanging seaweeds, or hidden in holes under the rock itself, may be found numerous living beings, marvellous and beautiful in structure in the eyes of those who regard them with true wisdom.

Here is a pool which probably will repay an investigation. It is a foot or so in depth at the base of the large stone which juts into it as a miniature peninsula. We lift up the green seawrack by which the sides of the stone are festooned, and which are still wet, for the tide has but recently receded. Lo! here are limpets and mussels attached to the stone beneath the algæ, and in the water, but half concealed beneath the overhanging fronds, a large crab of the edible species usually brought to market, another kind usually found in rock pools, and two or three hermit-crabs, whose claws are protruded from the mouths of the shells in which they have taken up their abode. Then there are several shrimps, which, terrified by our visit, have darted off, and are busily engaged burying themselves in the sand, on which their semi-transparent bodies would be almost effectually concealed without the process of sinking into the surface. Leaving such of the molluscs as we thus discover to be studied on some future ramble, we shall pay our respects to our hermit and his relations.

According to the most eminent naturalists, the essential character of the class Crustacea is the combination of branchiæ, or breathing apparatus, with jointed limbs and distinct sexes. "The name of this class refers," as Professor Owen observes, "to the modification of the external tegument by which it acquires due hardness for protecting the rock-dwelling marine species from the concussion of the surrounding elements, from the attacks of enemies, and likewise for forming the levers and points of resistance in the act of supporting the body and moving along the firm ground. In the crab and lobster tribes the internal layer of the integument is hardened by the addition of earthy particles, consisting of the carbonate with a small proportion of the phosphate of lime."

The Crustacea are to be found in every part of the ocean, but in the tropical seas they attain their greatest size, and are frequently possessed of most brilliant colours. The excellent naturalist who accompanied the expedition of the "Samarang" to Borneo, speaks with the liveliest rapture of the beauty of colouring which some large crabs exhibited, which he perceived on rocks in the deep water, but of which, from their singular activity, he found it impossible to procure any specimens. The variety of form which the class exhibits is very remarkable. Unhappily, however, we cannot expect on visiting the beach to be so fortunate as to pick up a specimen of more than a very few of the many species by which even our own seas are frequented. Such as we discover will nevertheless be sufficient as an example of their various relations in the class to which they pertain.

The crabs we have supposed ourselves to find in the pool are worthy of careful attention. The large one is a specimen of the *Cancer Pagurus*, and so well known from the excellence of its edible qualities, as well as from its size and its smooth claws, with black tips, that little special description of its outward aspect is requisite. This crab is found on all our rocky coasts, and in the south of England is sometimes taken of the weight of nine, ten, and even fourteen pounds. The other is a specimen of the common crab, *C. mœnas*, a small species found on any coast, and whose abode is in the rocks near the shore, where it lurks beneath the seaweed. It likewise buries itself in the sand.

These are but two from among a large number of species belonging to the coasts of Britain and Ireland, some of which are very remarkable.

One of the most singular species is the Spider-crab, of which there are several kinds. The body of this crab is triangular or heart-shaped, and the legs of great length, so that it is able to elevate its body very much in the same manner as some of the long-legged spiders, to which it bears no inconsiderable resemblance. One of the commonest of these spider-crabs,— to which naturalists have given the name of *Stenorhyncus phalangium*,— is obtained by dredging on scallop and oyster banks. Its body is an inch in length, triangular, spiny, and the legs are four times the length of the body, and covered with rough hairs. This creature is not possessed of the nimbleness so frequent among its various connections; it is sluggish and feeble, and its shell is often found covered with a growth of seaweed and zoophytes. A very singular case of this kind is related by an excellent writer in the " Annals of Natural History." He states that a spider-crab, the breadth of whose shell was only two inches and a quarter, had an oyster of three inches in diameter firmly attached to his back; and that this oyster was encrusted with large acorn-shells, so that it must have been of considerable age. All this weight the spider-crab carried about with him from place to place, unable to shake off the incubus which adhered to his back, with a tenacity greater than that with which the old man of the sea clung to Sindbad's neck, and we may suppose that the unfortunate spider-crab's feeble limbs were often wearied out by the burden they were thus compelled to sustain.

Another remarkable species is the Spinous crab, not uncommon on many parts of the shores of Britain, one of the family of the *Maiadæ*, which bears a considerable resemblance to the spider-crabs already spoken of. Its body is oval and convex; it possesses in front two stout horns, and the whole surface is covered with spines and tubercles of various sizes. The Masked-crab is another singular species, deriving its name from the circumstance that the depressions and protuberances on its shell are so arranged as to present some resemblance to the human face. The Wrinkled-crab is another species, the shell of which is corrugated transversely, and the Velvet-crab has a coat of fine hairs covering his shell. The smallest of all the crab family is the Pea-crab, *Pinnotheres pisum*, of which there are several varieties. They form a very interesting group, not only on account of their diminutive size, but their habits. These little crustaceans are only about a quarter of an inch across their shells, which are rounded and convex, and of a delicate texture of a brownish colour.

The most singular circumstance regarding these minute crabs is that they take up their abode in the large bivalve shells, not after the shell has been deserted, but during the life of its occupant. The pinna and other mussels, and the cockle, are the favourite dwelling-places of the pea-crab. The species called *Pinnotheres veterum*, takes up its residence in the shell of the pinna only,— a bivalve so large as to measure sometimes three feet in length, and deriving its appellation from the resemblance it was supposed to possess to the *pinnæ* or plumes worn by the Roman soldiers. This habit of the pea-crab was known to the naturalists of classic times, who fancied that the crab discharged the office of intimating to the pinna the moment when, by suddenly closing its shells, it might seize upon some unwary fish that might serve for its food. For this reason this minute member of the crab family was called *Pinnophylax*, or the pinna's keeper. To this fable the Greek poet Oppian refers in the following lines:—

> "In clouded deeps below the *Pinna* hides,
> And through the silent paths obscurely glides;
> A stupid wretch, and void of thoughtful care,
> He forms no bait, nor lays the tempting snare;
> But the dull sluggard boasts a Crab his friend,
> Whose busy eyes the coming prey attend.
> One room contains them, and the partners dwell
> Beneath the concave of one sloping shell;
> Deep in the watery waste the comrades rove,
> And mutual interest binds their constant love:
> That wiser friend the lucky juncture tells
> When in the circuit of his gaping shells
> Fish wandering enter; then the bearded guide
> Warns the dull mate, and pricks his tender side;
> He knows the hint, nor at the treatment grieves,
> But hugs the advantage, and the pain forgives.

His closing cells the *Pinna* sudden joins,
And 'twixt the pressing sides the prey confines:
Thus fed by mutual aid, the friendly pair
Divide their gains, and all the plunder share."

Modern observation has discovered that there is no ground for the statement thus made by the ancient poet; and the pea-crab, so far from discharging the functions referred to, is understood to enter the shells of the bivalves for self-protection.

The hermit-crab next claims our notice. There are several in the pool we are examining; one of these occupies the shell of a whelk, and is of a large size. Others are small, and have taken up their abode in shells not much larger than the common periwinkle.

The hermit-crab (*Pagurus Bernhardus*) is an interesting little creature, both in its structure and habits. It seems to constitute a sort of intermediate link between the crab and the lobster, and is in consequence of its similarity to the lobster, as regards the length of its body, comprehended in the order to which the lobster belongs. The very singular peculiarity of the hermit-crab is that, although its tail is prolonged like that of the lobster, it is wholly destitute of the hard, defensive covering in which the tail of the lobster is encased, and by which the anterior portion of its own body and its claws are enclosed. Surrounded as he is with many and various enemies, and especially by those of his own relations of the crab and lobster families, the naked and exposed condition of so essential a part of the hermit's person would be speedily fatal to him, as the sharp pincers of his rapacious foes would quickly deprive him of his tail, a part of his body greatly more important to him than the caudal appendage of a terrestrial animal. An instinct, however, is given to this otherwise helpless animal, which compensates for the apparent defect in its structure. Exposed to the imminent peril of having the posterior part of his body tampered with by the unscrupulous claws of his congeners, he ensures its safety by appropriating some shell suited to his own dimensions, into the spiral chambers of which he extends his unprotected part, and is at once in security, carrying about his abode with him with as much convenience as if it originally formed a part of his organisation. Deserted shells of very small size are suited to the hermit in his juvenile condition; but, as he increases in bulk, being unable, like the original owner of the house, to increase its dimensions with his own developement, he is obliged to seek a new domicile with ampler accommodation; and at length, on arriving at maturity, he finds it requisite to appropriate the shell of the whelk. It is, however, extremely probable that the hermit does not always content himself with shells which have been abandoned by their true owners, but that he resorts to the most violent proceedings in order to eject the owner and gain possession of his abode. This is rendered almost certain by the perfect freshness of many of the shells in which he is found. To effect this nefarious purpose, the hermit probably seizes some unsuspecting mollusc, as it is grazing on the fronds of the seaweed, and, lacerating it with his powerful claws, drags it from its abode, and, after devouring it, takes quiet and undisputed possession of the vacant shell. The stealthy manner in which the creature moves about, would enable it easily to surprise its victim, who, if possessed of any instinctive fear of such a foe, might be easily deceived by the hermit's outward similarity to one of its own harmless race. Thus the hermit-crab, while acting on its own instinct, accomplishes, along with other voracious inhabitants of the waters, the object of keeping in check the increase of the tribe of molluscs, and so preserving the balance so marvellously maintained between various species in the animal kingdom, and which in so striking a manner bears testimony to the intention of the Great Artificer.

Among the many evidences of divine foresight and intention of which marine animals afford examples, the most striking and instructive, as well as beautiful, are those which are afforded by a combination of instinct and organisation adapted to each other. Of this kind of evidence the hermit-crab affords an admirable instance.

On the one hand, the singular instinct by which it seizes upon the shell of a species entirely different from itself is not accidental; it is not forced upon it by the notion of self-preservation, in consequence of its exposed condition; but, like all instincts, is an original impulse, a tendency forming part of its constitution. On the other hand, the structure of the uncovered portion of its body is such as to prove beyond question that it is expressly adapted to the act to which it is instinctively impelled. The tail or hinder part of its body is not merely capable of assuming a spiral form, so as to fit itself into the chambers of the shell, but it is terminated by certain hard, movable pieces, worked by a powerful muscle, by which it can easily fix its tail in the interior of the shell and draw itself into its retreat at will. The instinct could not have given origin to the structure, nor could the structure have suggested or inspired the instinct which the little creature acts upon long before it has had either the experience of its danger or of the facility its structure affords for the end in view. We must regard this adaptation as a beautiful and striking evidence of the intention of Him to whose divine skill and purpose alone we can attribute at once the structure and the instinct of living beings and such adaptations as that to which we now refer.

One of the most marvellous things in the history of the crab is the strange metamorphosis it undergoes before assuming its permanent form. It was long believed by naturalists that the young of the crab, on being excluded from the ova, presented a minute but perfect resemblance to the species they belong to; and this belief gained support from the circumstance that vast numbers of very minute crabs are frequently to be found on the sea-shores. This opinion, however, has been found erroneous; but the change of form which the creature undergoes is so remarkable that, were it not established upon unquestionable evidence, it could not be credited.

Certain minute creatures to which the name Zoea was formerly applied, and which were supposed to form a distinct tribe of crustaceous animals, have been discovered to be the young of crabs. But nothing can be more dissimilar from the form and habits of the crab than that of the diminutive zoea.

When the crab is first hatched and escapes from the egg, its appearance is in the highest degree grotesque. Its head is shaped like a Russian helmet, with a long spike projecting from the top of it. In the front of this singularly formed head are the antennæ and a long beak, together with a pair of huge eyes, not raised on supports as in the full-grown crab, and beneath are four pair of legs, with hairs at their extremities, and a long, jointed tail. Thus furnished, the little creature is capable of swimming with rapidity through the water, and in this respect differs entirely from its parents, who, instead of sporting through the waves, live only at the bottom of the sea. After remaining in this shape a certain length of time, the zoea undergoes its first change, and approaches in some degree its permanent form; the eyes become elevated on stalks; the claws appear; but the tail is not yet laid aside, and the creature still continues to swim through the water. The next stage completes the progressive metamorphosis, and the form of the crab is in all respects assumed; the power of swimming is laid aside, and the little crustacean, although scarcely yet the eighth of an inch in size, relinquishes its mode of life, and its habit of living near the surface, for a very different state amidst the rocks and seaweed at the bottom.

Strange as these successive alterations of form and habits are, they are not more so than those of other creatures with which we are more familiar, as, for example, the mutation of the caterpillar into a butterfly. But the result appears very different. The caterpillar advances from its condition to one not only displaying more complexity of structure, but habits of vastly increased activity, with power to range through the bright sunshine, amidst the perfume of many-coloured flowers, and amidst those sounds of joy of which its senses beyond doubt have a perception. But how different is the result as regards the zoea! Although its organs and faculties are much more perfect when it assumes its permanent condition, the scene of its future existence presents no analogy with that to which the caterpillar is advanced. The waves, bright with sunshine, are no longer the scene of its activity; it sinks to the bottom, and the perfect condition of its habits and organs consigns it to a state of comparative darkness and inactivity.

In this, as in all such instances however, we behold an evidence of the inexhaustible variety which the animal kingdom exhibits, and in which, how different soever the results may be, we may trace the same ever-prevailing design of infinite skill and goodness adapting the creature to its place in creation, and conferring on it, whatever its condition be, appropriate means of enjoying its existence and accomplishing the end for which it was called into being.

ARTICULATA — LOBSTERS, ETC.

CHAP. XIX.

ARTICULATA—LOBSTERS, ETC.

The Shrimp. — The Common Lobster. — Various Species. — Structure and Habits, &c.

WE are now to look at another order of crustaceans in which the prolongation of the animal's body into a tail distinguishes it from all the various species of crabs. Our rock pool which has already afforded us specimens of other crustaceans also contains a few shrimps, one of the most familiar examples of the order referred to. There are, however, a large number of species included in the order to which the lobster belongs, but it is, of course, impossible to mention more than a very few of the most familiar.

The shrimp (*Crangon vulgaris*) is a well-known inhabitant of our sea-shores, frequenting some sandy beaches in vast multitudes. The prawn (*Palæmon serratus*), which is a shrimp of large size differing in some minute particulars from the common shrimp, is likewise found on many of our shores among loose stones, and what is remarkable it is sometimes taken at sea on the surface of the water when there has been a depth of more than thirty fathoms.

The young of the shrimp or prawn are often

found in myriads on the beach close to the margin of the sea. These, during the ebb, each receding wave leaves for a while uncovered, when they may be seen leaping as they endeavour to find their way to their native element, which threatens to leave them high and dry upon the sand. Dr. Paley, speaking of the happiness which such creatures probably experience, thus describes the movements of the young shrimp, and deduces from them a lesson of Divine goodness:—"Walking by the sea-side on a calm evening upon a sandy shore and with an ebbing tide, I have frequently remarked the appearance of a dark cloud, or rather very thick mist hanging over the edge of the water, to the height, perhaps, of half a yard, and the breadth of two or three yards, stretching along the coast, as far as the eye could reach, and always retiring with the water. When this cloud came to be examined, it proved to be nothing else than so much space filled with young shrimps in the act of bounding into the air from the shallow margin of the water, or from the wet sand. If any motion of a minute animal could express delight, it was this; if they had meant to make signs of their happiness, they could not have done it more intelligibly. Suppose then, what I have no doubt of, each individual of this number to be in a state of positive enjoyment, what a sum, collectively, of gratification and pleasure, have we before our view!"

Besides the common lobster (*Homarus vulgaris*) there are several varieties of this crustacean, all of which differ more or less from the species with which we are most familiar. In the common lobster the body and thorax are smooth, the antennæ long, the claws and fangs large; one of them, which is greater than the other, has the inside of the pincers tuberculated; the other, which is less in size, is not tuberculated, but serrated on the inner edge.

Another kind, called the Long-clawed lobster, differs in a remarkable degree from the common species. The body is smooth, indeed, like the preceding, but in front of the thorax there are three sharp, slender spines, the legs are weak and bristly, and the antennæ slender. In this species the body and tail are about five inches long, but the long slender claws and fangs are six inches and a half in length.

In the Norway lobster there are other peculiarities. The snout is long and spiny, the body is marked with three ridges, the claws are long and angular, having spines along the angles, the legs are slender, and, what is remarkable, they are furnished with pincers.

The Spiny lobster differs from all the preceding species in several particulars. It has a broad front armed with two large spines, and between them a smaller as guard to the eyes which are prominent; the body and thorax are all covered with spines, the claws very small and short, and the fangs small, single, and hinged, the legs slender and smooth, and the tail longer than in the common lobster.

Another remarkable species is the Plaited

lobster, which is only about six inches in length. The snout is of a pyramidal form and spiny, and the thorax, body, and tail, elegantly plaited; the claws long, spiny, and tuberculated. This species is extremely active, and, when taken, slaps its tail with much violence and noise. All these different kinds are found in many parts of our rocky coasts and are sometimes taken by the hand, sometimes by means of traps or pots, and sometimes with nets.

The common lobster being the best known example of the family to which it belongs a more particular account of it will most gratify the reader.

The habitation of this species is the clearest water at the base of rocks overhanging the sea. Places of this description are frequent in many parts of the coast. The western and northern shores of Scotland abound in places where lobsters are found in great numbers, many of which are of great size. Various parts of the English coast, and many localities on the shores of the sister island, are frequented by this crustacean.

Lobsters are extremely prolific; more than 12,000 eggs have been counted under the tail of one hen lobster. They begin to breed in spring and continue doing so the greater part of summer depositing their ova in the sand where they are hatched.

In addition to the power of creeping along the bottom, and rising gracefully over the sunken rocks and the sea-weed, the lobster possesses the power of darting or shooting with great rapidity through the water. This act is performed by means of the tail, the broad plates at the end of which put in motion by the powerful muscle connecting them with the anterior part of the body, strike the water with immense force, enabling the lobster to project itself many feet. One of the most singular feats performed by the creature is that of throwing itself, apparently with one stroke of its tail, directly into its hole, from a distance, it is said, of twenty or thirty feet.

In all the crustacea, crabs as well as lobsters, the shelly armour which they wear being inelastic and incapable of accommodating itself to the increased size of the animal, an admirable provision is made by which, from time to time, the covering can be thrown off, and its place supplied by a new suit perfectly adapted to the convenience of the possessor. But for this provision the animal upon increasing in size must inevitably perish.

Crabs and lobsters are said to cast their shells once a year, and the facility with which this apparently impossible process is performed is truly marvellous. At first sight it would appear as impossible for the animal to extricate itself from its unyielding envelope as it would have been for a soldier, in the days when complete suits of armour were worn, to find his way out of his steel clothing without opening the joints and separating the pieces composing it. Impossible as the process appears, however, the crab and lobster are gifted by the express design of the All-wise Creator with the power of performing it with perfect facility.

We are indebted to the celebrated naturalist, Reaumur, for an account of the manner in which the cray-fish or fresh-water lobster throws off its shell prior to obtaining a new suit of armour. The animal retires to its hole so as to be free from danger and interruption, and remains for several days without food. During the period it is probable it becomes more or less attenuated while a new skin is in the act of forming under the shell. Observing that a cray-fish was about to moult, Reaumur carefully observed the method in which the action was performed. The animal commenced by rubbing his feet together and struggling violently, as if by its contortions to loosen the shell. It then appeared to distend its body, upon which the first segment of the shell of the abdomen separated from that of the thorax, the membrane which united these portions of the crust then burst asunder, and the new body appeared beneath. After resting awhile, the cray-fish repeated the process till all the pieces of the armour were separated and cast off, and so completely that in the exuviæ no external part was found wanting. How the large muscles of the claws were to be freed from their covering seemed the most insoluble part of the problem; but this was also effected without difficulty, the sutures dividing, the articulations having opened, allowing the soft muscles to be withdrawn. Every part of the shell is at last thrown off, the muscles being withdrawn even from the antennæ, and the case appears perfect and complete. This process, so observed in the cray-fish, is probably similar in all the other crustacea. The change when completed is followed like all violent muscular action by reaction. The animal is wearied as well as defenceless, and remains secluded in its hole till its strength returns and its shell is hardened. During this period it is quite incapable of capturing its prey. The whole shell is soft, and even the pincers are as pliant as parchment, so as to be unable to hold any object requiring the exertion of strength. The larger crabs when in this helpless condition may be easily taken by the naked hand in their holes among rocks at low water mark; and it is somewhat amusing to insert one's finger within the formidable looking forceps and observe the futile effort the poor animal makes to seize upon the aggressor.

One of the most singular faculties possessed by the crustaceans is the power of voluntary dismemberment. This faculty, however, is exercised by other animals. There are some species of lizards which on being alarmed, or even on being touched, strike off a considerable portion of their tails, and shuffle off apparently no worse for the loss of the important appendage. Some species of star-fishes have this faculty also: the brittle star, as described in a former chapter, being capable of separating itself into a great many pieces.

The lobster is said to shake off its claws at the sound of thunder or on the report of a cannon; and it is extremely probable that the act of so doing gives little or no pain. Their limbs are often lost or injured. A large crab on seizing a small one is capable of destroying its claws, and such mutilations must be fatal to the creature unless some provision be made to meet the exigency. The crab or lobster, therefore, is able to throw off the injured limb, and, according to the ablest comparative anatomists, it does so for two purposes, to stop the excessive flow of blood from the injured part and to lay bare the organ which reproduces the limb. The bleeding ceases whenever the damaged part is cast off, and a new limb shortly makes its appearance, and although at first it is much smaller than the other limbs, it attains its full dimensions on the first occasion of moulting.

If the hypothesis be correct that the crab suffers little or no pain on being injured, it is a circumstance which, combined with the marvellous reproduction of the limbs, cannot but be considered, in the case of a creature so much exposed to injury, as an instance of the benevolence which is so conspicuous in the designs of Infinite Wisdom and Goodness.

MOLLUSCA, OR SOFT-BODIED ANIMALS—
BIVALVES

CHAP. XX.

MOLLUSCA, OR SOFT-BODIED ANIMALS—BIVALVES.

Molluscs. — Bivalves. — Structure and Habits of various Species.—The common Cockle, &c.

In those districts of our sea-shores where the beach is covered with sand, or fine gravel, a very considerable variety of empty shells may often be found strewed along the limit of high-water. Many of these are bivalves, such as the common mussel, and many are univalves, like the periwinckle. All these shells, with the exception of those of crabs, which sometimes are cast ashore with the others, belong to a very extensive primary group of animals, called molluscs, from the Latin word signifying soft, a quality which distinguishes them from the jointed or articulated animals we have been considering.

The group of animals to which we are now to give our attention, exhibit great diversity, not only as respects size and shape, but as regards the places they inhabit.

Some of the shells of microscopic molluscs are so inconceivably minute as to pass readily through a hole pierced in paper with the point of a fine needle. Others, again, are of enormous dimensions; the Giant Clamp-shell, a huge bivalve, being said to attain the weight of about a quarter of a ton.

Every part of the ocean, both in the tropics, and in the arctic regions, is inhabited by members of the mollusc family; they abound likewise in fresh-water lakes and rivers, both having their own species. Some burrow in the sand and mud of our sea-shores, others crawl among the rocks and sea-weed, and several species are entirely terrestrial, like the garden-snail. The form and colours of many of the molluscs are so remarkable and beautiful, as to defy all attempts to describe them. But, without making the vain effort, we shall suppose our reader to examine for himself such specimens as he discovers during his visits to our sea-shores.

The mollusca have been divided into two distinct groups, to which naturalists have given appropriate names. The one group comprehends all molluscs destitute of heads, of which the oyster is a familiar example, and this group is therefore called the *Acephala;* the second group is denominated *Encephala,* because, comprehending animals furnished with heads, and of which the garden-snail affords a well-known type. Each of these two groups has been again subdivided into three classes; the first three belonging to the *Acephala,* being classified according to certain peculiarities in their gills, or in their integuments; the three last, pertaining to the *Encephala,* being classified according to certain modifications of their organs of motion. This brief statement will probably assist our reader in placing in its corresponding class those specimens which he discovers.

Of the three subdivisions of the headless molluscs, we shall omit the two first, the specimens of which are comparatively rare. The third class, however, contains a large number of familiar "shell-fish," and merits careful attention. It is known by the sesquipedalian title of *Lamellibranchiata*, which signifies that the gills are in the form of flat plates—*lamella* being the Latin word for a plate.

This subdivision comprehends a great many well-known bivalves, or animals with shells, having two separate sides attached together by hinges. Of these, the cockle, the mussel, the scallop, and the oyster, are the most familiar types.

Let us suppose it to be low-water on one of those sandy shores where the common cockle may be found. It is a spring-tide, and the waves have retreated far below their usual limit, leaving a wide extent of sand quite bare. Furnished with a trowel, we dig a little way below the surface, and our labour is at once rewarded with a handful of cockles. One of these will serve to illustrate the internal structure of several other species of bivalve molluscs.

The shelly covering of the animal consists, we perceive, of two pieces. In the cockle, the clam, and some others, each of these two pieces is almost hemispherical; in the oyster, the scallop, and others, they are, on the contrary, almost flat.

The hinge which unites them is a beautiful piece of mechanism, and affords an admirable illustration of that Infinite Goodness and Skill by which, even in the humblest creatures, the means are adapted to the end designed. The processes of the opposite parts of the hinge lock into each other, and are firmly kept together by a ligament of great strength, and yet so elastic as to act as a spring in opening the shell (whenever the animal relaxes the muscle which keeps it close), precisely as the spring of a watch-case throws it open, whenever the power keeping it shut is removed.

The hinge and ligament differ in form in different kinds of bivalves, and their modifications mark out differences of genera, according to the system of Linnæus. In some, as in the mussel and oyster, the hinge is very simple, and consists almost entirely of the ligament itself; in the mya, or gaper, the hinge is furnished with a thick, strong, and broad tooth; in the ligula there is a broad tooth on each valve, with a cavity for the reception of the cartilage or ligament which binds the parts together; the Venus-shell has a hinge of three teeth, and in the arca the hinge becomes a complicated piece of apparatus, consisting of numerous teeth or processes, inserted between each other. None of these differences are either unnecessary or undesigned. They are all intended and adapted to give such a degree of compactness to the hinge, as is suited to the circumstances of the creature inhabiting the shell, and there can be no doubt that, were we fully aware of the habits, the modes of life, the degree of exposure to danger, or other peculiarities of each of the bivalves, we should perceive that the special differences even in this apparently unimportant part of their structure, so far from being accidental, have been expressly intended for a certain purpose.

On opening the cockle, we perceive that the whole of the inner surface of the two valves, or shells, is lined with a smooth and delicate membrane, or skin. This membrane, because it encloses the body of the animal, is termed the mantle. It is found in all the molluscs, although subject to various modifications. It is, in fact, an essential part of their structure, and among the marvels of creative design there are few things more wonderful than the office which this apparently simple membrane performs. The mantle is an apparatus adapted to form the shell by which the mollusc is covered, and to deposit the colouring matter by which it is adorned. Simple as its structure appears to be, the manner in which it is fitted to effect this object, far exceeds the highest efforts of human ingenuity. It is composed of minute cells, differing in size, shape, and arrangement, in different species of molluscs, and containing calcareous matter secreted from the fluids of the animal. The edges of the membrane are occupied in adding continually to the edge of the shell, as its occupant increases in size, and the inner portions of it are, at the same time, employed in adding to the thickness of the shell, depositing the beautifully-smooth and pearly substance so remarkable in their inner surfaces. Thus, the fine mother-of-pearl on the inside of the oyster-shell, and the various patterns in yellow, blue, pink, brown, crimson, and other colours which ornament the exterior of other shells, is all the work of this simple, and efficient piece of mechanism. What the peculiarity of structure in the glands of this marvellous organ may be by which it elaborates the shelly matter, and deposits frequently in a regular pattern, the colours adorning it, and from what materials the lime and the colours are extracted, are all questions, which, while they demand for their solution the highest exercise of the naturalist's skill, display, at the same time, an instance of creative design which it is impossible too greatly to admire. The body of the cockle, besides containing the viscera, is furnished with a yellow-tipped instrument, which is by naturalists called its foot, being the means by which it moves, burying itself with ease in the sand.

The Scallop, the empty shells of which are frequently found scattered along the margin of the sea, is not found, like the cockle, buried in the sand, but is taken, like the oyster, in deep water, by means of a dredge. There are more than a dozen varieties peculiar to the British shores. This mollusc is well known to every visitor of the sea-shore, and its beautifully-marked, and regularly-fluted shell, is generally a

STRUCTURE OF BIVALVES. 289

great attraction to those who amuse themselves gathering specimens of our native shells. What has already been said of the mantle is equally applicable to that of the scallop. Around its margin, however, there are numerous pellucid, thread-like tentacula, which the animal can protrude or retract at will. But what is most remarkable is, that along its margin is a row of singularly beautiful eyes, so placed that each eye can look out upon the watery world through one of the grooves in the fluted shell. Unlike many bivalves, the scallop possesses the power of locomotion, a circumstance stated by Aristotle, and, although subsequently doubted, now confirmed by modern naturalists. The animal, by opening its shells, and suddenly shutting them, is enabled to propel itself through the water, and from the rapid movements of its variegated valves, it has been appropriately called the sea-butterfly. The beautiful figure of the Crouching Venus in the celebrated Maffei Collection is placed sitting in a shell of this kind, in correspondence with the classic myth that the sea-born goddess arose from the ocean in a scallop. The scallop-shell was, in the olden time, worn by pilgrims to the Holy Land, as an indication of their having performed their pilgrimage.

MOLLUSCA—WHELKS

CHAP. XXI.

MOLLUSCA — WHELKS.

*The Whelk and its Varieties.—Structure and Instincts, &c.—
The Limpet.—Structure, &c.*

THE bivalve molluscs are far from being the only members of the group they belong to which attract the attention of the visitor of the sea-shore. Numerous specimens of the second of the two groups into which the molluscs are divided present themselves to his notice. This second group is, as already mentioned, called the *Encephala,* and embraces all the molluscs furnished with heads. The group is itself farther subdivided into three classes in accordance with certain modifications of their locomotive organs.

The first of these three classes is that of the *Pterapoda,* a term which signifies " wing-footed," and which comprehends several species of molluscs of small size, specimens of which are so little likely to come under the reader's notice, that it is unnecessary to refer to them in a particular manner. We shall presume therefore that our reader's attention is given to the second class of molluscs, which are called *Gasteropoda,* or bellyfooted animals. Of these every rocky sea-shore affords numerous examples, such as the various kinds of whelks, limpets, wreath-shells and others.

All these, and a vast multitude of other animals of the same order, although differing from each other in many minute particulars, possess one peculiarity in common in their organs of locomotion, which consists of a broad muscular disk on the lower surface of the body. Of this peculiarity the common garden snail is a familiar example, its mode of progression being precisely similar to that of the aquatic members of the class to which it belongs.

The class of which we are now to notice some specimens is, as already stated, extremely numerous, and comprehends eight orders or subdivisions, differing from each other in some modification of their organs of breathing. It is not desirable in a work of this kind to enter into a minute description of the characteristics of each of these eight orders. Our purpose will be sufficiently accomplished by a description of some of the more familiar specimens of the class by which these orders are embraced.

The common whelk (*Buccinum undatum*) is a well-known example. It is to the empty shell of this mollusc that the poet Wordsworth refers, in his description of the effect produced on the imagination of a child by the murmuring sound heard from the shell when held close to the ear.

> "I have seen
> A curious child applying to his ear
> The convolutions of a smooth-lipped shell,

> To which in silence hushed, his very soul
> Listened intensely, and his countenance soon
> Brightened with joy; for murmuring from within
> Were heard sonorous cadences whereby,
> To his belief, the monitor expressed
> Mysterious union with its native sea."

The whelk is carnivorous, and one of the most interesting peculiarities in its structure is a powerful piece of mechanism by which it is enabled to bore into the shells of those molluscs on which it preys. This apparatus is a kind of proboscis acted upon by a beautiful and complex system of muscles, by means of which the animal can extend it, move it in any direction, or retract it within its shell. This proboscis consists of several parts. There is the external tube, to which the muscles for moving it are attached; in this tube there is a cylindrical implement which works in the tube as in a sheath. This implement opens at its extremity, and forms the mouth of the animal. This mouth is surrounded by two strong muscular lips, within which is the tongue armed with spines, the action of which, conjoined with that of the lips, can perforate the hardest shells. By means of this apparatus the whelk forms in the shells of other molluscs an orifice into which the tongue with its hooks being protruded, the body of the helpless victim is drawn out and devoured. This apparatus, it will be perceived, is extremely complicated. It is not only the tongue, the lips, the mouth, and the throat of the animal which uses it, but it combines in itself the multiple action of a centre-bit or auger, and a rasp and pincers. It would be difficult to point out a more striking instance of elaborate contrivance directed to a certain definite purpose: to that purpose it is adapted with unerring accuracy, and displays a beautiful instance of creative foresight.

The egg-clusters of the species of whelk now referred to are very remarkable, and may often be picked up on the shore after a storm, mingled with the froth of the sea, and the seaweed recently torn from the rocks. These clusters consist of a light sponge-like body, consisting of several globular subdivisions attached together, and about six or eight inches in length. They are composed of numerous little semi-transparent and flattish bladders united by their edges. The whole substance, to those unacquainted with its nature, seems to be some species of sponge. It is nevertheless a congeries of the eggs of the whelk, which inhabits deep water, and attaches these masses to the rocks, from which they are separated by the force of the waves.

Another, but a much smaller species of whelk, is a well-known inhabitant of the shallow pools left by the receding tide, and may be found attached to the rocks beneath the seaweed. It is the *Purpura lapillus,* or dog-whelk; it is about an inch in length; the shell is very hard and thick, and either white or ornamented with bands of yellow and brown.

This mollusc, like the murex, — a species of whelk, which yielded the Tyrian purple so celebrated in ancient times,—is also remarkable for furnishing a permanent dye, which, although not of the rich hue so highly prized in the classic murex, makes nevertheless an indelible marking ink of a purple colour. The colouring matter is contained in a vein or gland in the animal's body, easily found on breaking the shell. The fluid in this receptacle is of a pale yellow tint, but such is its chemical composition, that it is remarkably affected by light. If it be applied when fresh to white linen, and exposed to the sun, the pale tint becomes a brilliant yellow: soon afterwards it deepens into a delicate green, which grows darker in its shade; from green it gradually changes into blue, then successively into indigo, red, and finally purple. The relation which the rays of the sun bear to colour, is a highly interesting subject of study in chemical science, and probably a careful analysis of the fluid now referred to might disclose some new relation which the sunlight bears to certain substances, and might be of use in suggesting some process in the arts. Independently of any practical use, however, an investigation into the causes leading to the vicissitudes of colour we have just noticed, would be highly interesting in a scientific point of view.

The eggs of the *Purpura*, or dog-whelk, are still more remarkable than those of the buccinum, already described. They may be frequently discovered on the recess of the tide adhering to the surfaces of flat stones. These eggs are not attached together in clusters, but placed separate from each other. They are about a third of an inch in length, and are of a most singular form, being small urn-shaped bodies, supported by a foot, and bearing a striking resemblance to the wooden egg-cups sold in turners' shops. We remember with much interest our first discovery of these remarkable eggs, which for some time we looked upon as an unknown species of seaweed.

Unlike the buccinum, which preys on other animals of its own kind, many of the gasteropodous molluscs are herbivorous, feeding exclusively on marine vegetables. Such is the case as regards the periwinckle and its varieties, which pasture upon the bladder fucus and other algæ. The shells of those which thus feed on plants differ from those of the carnivorous species; they seem only to have circular orifices destitute of the *sulcus* or furrow seen in those of the whelk tribe; their mouths too differ, as may be supposed, from those of the predaceous kinds, as an examination with a lens will at once indicate. As they have to browse on plants, they do not require a formidable apparatus for cutting into the hard materials of shells; their mouths therefore are furnished with such cutting instruments only as the nature of their food renders necessary.

The limpet (*Patella vulgata*), of which every rocky shore furnishes several kinds, exhibits much that is remarkable in its structure. The circular disk by which it adheres to the rock is its organ of locomotion; for although it has been supposed to be permanently fixed to one spot, such is by no means the case, for, like other molluscs, it migrates from place to place. The tenacity with which it adheres to the rock is worthy of notice. This feat is performed on the same principle by which various fishes, such as the lump, the remora or the lamprey, are enabled to attach themselves to flat surfaces, and by exactly the same process as that by which the schoolboy's toy, called a leather-sucker, is fixed to stones or other smooth surfaces. The circular disk of the limpet's body or foot is applied to the smooth surface of the rock, and by means of the muscles, while the rim of the disk is pressed down very closely, the centre is raised up, thus creating a vacuum between the stone and the animal's body; the shell is therefore pressed down upon the rock by the weight of the superincumbent water and atmosphere, or if the tide be out, by the weight of the atmosphere alone. Thus a shell of which the mouth is but a square inch in diameter, may be pressed down upon the rock it adheres to with a weight of fifteen pounds, and as the conical form of the shell is the most favourable for resisting the external force of the waves, the limpet has the power of remaining unmoved and in perfect safety in the most violent storms. No candid and unprejudiced mind can avoid perceiving how remarkable an illustration is thus afforded of the doctrine of design and intention in the structure of animals. The circular disk of the limpet is constructed with express reference to the laws of fluid pressure, as exhibited in the ocean and in the atmosphere: the instinct of the creature itself is so adapted to its physical structure, that it can avail itself of those laws without being aware of their existence; and as it is the object of the limpet to remain fixed in one place, the pressure it can exert by creating a vacuum is obviously combined with the shape of its shell to give it greater stability. The purposes in view, and the means by which they are to be effected, are all distinct from each other, and clearly point out an intention on the part of one Intelligent Contriver, by which, with means various and distinct, the one end is brought about. No instance ever suggested by writers on Natural Theology can be more striking or more instructive than this.

We have already spoken of the proboscis of the larger species of whelk, the *Buccinum undatum:* the limpet is endowed with an instrument for obtaining its food, which, if less complex, is quite as well adapted to the creature's necessities. This instrument is its tongue, by means of which it is able to devour those marine plants which are adapted to its support. This tongue consists of a parchment-like strap, a couple of inches long and about half a line in diameter, having the end fashioned something like the bowl of a spoon. On subjecting it to the microscope this singular tongue is found to be along its whole length set with teeth, recurved like the top of a bill-hook, and disposed in rows, four teeth in each alternate row, and two differently shaped in the intermediate space.

By means of its tongue thus mounted, the

limpet is able to rasp through the outward tough skin of the algæ it feeds upon, with as much ease as a joiner cuts a piece of soft wood with a sharp saw. In order to have an idea of the efficiency of such an implement as the limpet's tongue, let the reader imagine a leather strap, of an inch in breadth, set with rows of fishing hooks and points of lancets alternately, and let him suppose this strap so prepared to be forcibly drawn over the object to be lacerated. Can any candid mind fail to admit that the implement thus furnished to the limpet has been adapted to the creature's wants by the exercise of design, as unquestionably as any tool used by the joiner is suited to the purpose for which it is applied?

MOLLUSCA — CUTTLE FISH

CHAP. XXII.

MOLLUSCA — CUTTLE-FISH.

Cuttle Fish: its Habits and Structure.—Varieties of Species.

THE second class of the encephalous molluscs, of which we have just been examining a few specimens, is, as already stated, extremely numerous; a vast multitude and variety of species being found on our sea-shores. The third and remaining class however, presents but few varieties. It is entitled the *Cephalopoda* or class of molluscs whose heads are the organs of locomotion, as the scientific term signifies.

Of this class the cuttle-fish is the only example to which we shall refer. This creature is in its organisation the most elevated of all the class to which it belongs. Its muscular and nervous system, its organs of respiration, and its internal skeleton contribute to give it a close analogy as regards its structure to those animals known to naturalists as the vertebrata, because possessed of internal skeletons, or strictly speaking because furnished with a backbone.

The cuttle-fish may often be found cast ashore after a storm. Let us suppose our reader to have discovered one and submitted it to an examination. The body, it will be perceived, is soft, although it feels not unlike a kind of cartilage. The arms or feet, eight in number, are arranged around the top of the head, and are covered with a multitude of small circular disks raised above the surface of the adjoining skin. From the midst of these arms extend two long tentacula, which are thickened at the ends and furnished, like the shorter arms, with similar disks or suckers. The mouth of the animal consists of a powerful beak like that of a parrot. The eyes are large and prominent, and when the creature is alive and in vigour are not only bright and staring, but have a look of intelligence and even of ferocity. The singular appearance of this creature is accompanied by habits no less remarkable. The members or limbs, already referred to, are used by it both as arms and legs. It walks at the bottom of the water with them, having its mouth and head downwards, and its body upwards; it also swims partly by these means, and employs them moreover in the capture of its prey, to which it attaches itself by means of the suckers before mentioned, which are furnished with muscles for creating a vacuum, as is the case of the disk of the limpet already referred to. As to its jaws or mandibles they are a very formidable weapon, and can easily break open many species of crustaceans and shell-fish. One would think that the soft body of the cuttle-fish would avail it little against the attack of a lobster with its formidable claws. There can be no doubt, however, that even a lobster is no match for a large cuttle-fish, naked and exposed although the latter appears to be. By means of its suckers it can easily tie together the pincers of the lobster so that they cannot open, and while its prey is thus rendered helpless, it can tear off with its powerful beak, as with a forceps, the crust in which its victim's body is encased.

On examining that part of the animal from which the head protrudes, a tube or funnel is discovered, which is connected with its branchiæ or breathing organs. To these organs the water is admitted, as it is admitted to the gills of fishes, but by a different apparatus. It gains access by valves which allow it to enter on the muscular dilatation of its body; and when the water so admitted has communicated its oxygen to the blood, it is expelled by the tube referred to; as in the case of fishes, it is driven out at the gills. But the cuttle-fish is said to employ this funnel or tube for another purpose; for, by ejecting the water from it with force, it is, by the reaction of the surrounding medium, enabled to dart backward with amazing velocity out of the reach of danger. While therefore it swims forward with rapidity by means of the fin-like expansion of its tail, it possesses in the hydraulic apparatus now mentioned an additional organ of locomotion in a contrary direction. It thus appears that the apparatus adapted primarily for breathing is applicable to an additional purpose under the impulse of instinct.

Another most remarkable peculiarity distinguishes the cuttle-fish. It is provided with an organ which secretes a black fluid by means of which it can darken the water so as to escape its pursuers. This ink is said to yield the Chinese or Indian ink, so well known to artists. In Italy a similar ink, although not so black, is prepared from it, and Cuvier is known to have used it to colour the plates for his memoir of these animals. It is interesting to add that the ink bag having been found in a fossil state in the Belemnite, a kind of Cephalopod which has been entombed in the solid rock for countless ages, Dr. Buckland presented some of it to Chantry, requesting him to ascertain its worth as a pigment, and a drawing having been made with it and shown to a celebrated artist he pronounced the sepia to be excellent, and inquired by what colourman it was prepared.

There are several species of cuttles, each differing in some respect from the specimen now referred to; these it is unnecessary to describe, but we cannot quit the subject without noticing a member of the family peculiar in form and habits even among the very peculiar race it belongs to. Let us fancy ourselves to have met with one of these on the beach. It is low water, and the creature has been left by the receding tide, but perhaps not unwillingly, for he is not only alive but moving along in an inverted position, and although at a leisurely pace, indeed, still making some progress. This is the celebrated polypus of the ancients, and is called the

Octopus, from its eight feet, or the common Poulpe. The body of this creature is almost globular; it is furnished with eight feet or arms, each having 240 suckers arranged in a double series. It is without the two long arms possessed by its relative the cuttle-fish; but it can walk with comparative facility, and in the water it can swim rapidly backwards. This animal, with its staring eyes and uncouth shape, is undoubtedly of a very repulsive aspect, and must not a little terrify the unhappy creatures it pursues and seizes upon with its suckers. The ferocity of its look is doubtless an accurate index of the fierceness of its disposition. This is illustrated by the following anecdote, which, although referring to a foreign member of the poulpe family, may perhaps indicate the character of our native species.

In his account of the "Natural History of the Sperm Whale," Mr. Beale mentions that on one occasion, while engaged in collecting specimens of shells on the shores of the Bonin islands, he encountered a most extraordinary animal, which was crawling on the rocks toward the water. It was creeping on its eight legs, which being soft and flexible bent under the weight of its body, and served indeed to raise it only a little from the surface along which it was moving. It seemed alarmed, and made great efforts to escape, but the naturalist had no idea of consenting to the termination of so unexpected an interview with the odd-looking stranger. In his first attempt to prevent its escape he placed his foot upon one of its legs, but so great was its strength that although he pressed upon it with considerable force it easily liberated itself. Determined however to secure his prize as a remarkable specimen of its class he then seized one of the legs in his hand, when the animal struggled with such vigour that it seemed as if the limb would be torn off in the contest. The animal in the mean time held itself fast to the rock by its suckers, and Mr. Beale gave it a sudden jerk to disengage it. This seemed to excite it into fury, and after successfully resisting the attempt it suddenly let go its hold of the rock and sprung on its assailant's arm, which was bare, and fixing itself by its suckers endeavoured to attack him with its powerful beak. The sensation of horror caused by this unexpected assault may be readily imagined. Mr. Beale states, that the cold and slimy grasp of the ferocious animal induced a sensation extremely sickening, and he found it requisite to call to the captain who was occupied in gathering shells at a little distance. Mr. Beale, aided by his friend, then made his way to the boat and the poulpe was at last destroyed with the boat knife, but it did not surrender till the limbs by which it so tenaciously adhered were successively cut off. The body of this cephalopod was not larger than a man's fist, but it measured four feet across its extended arms.

In the tropical seas the poulpe is said to arrive at an enormous size. Mr. Pennant, on the authority of a friend long resident among the Indian islands, and who was a diligent observer of nature, states that the natives affirm that some have been seen two fathoms broad over their centre, and each arm nine fathoms in length. It is also well known that the Indians, when navigating their little boats, are in great dread of those frightful monsters, and always provide themselves with an axe to cut off their arms, which if thrown across their boats would place them in imminent danger. The pearl divers too are said to be sometimes seized by these monsters of the deep, from whose grasp under such circumstances there is no release. Possibly the account given by Mr. Pennant's friend may have been exaggerated by the terrors of the Indians who are his informants; but besides the general fact that the tropical seas nourish creatures of far greater magnitude than those of temperate latitudes, authentic instances are recorded in which the octopus has actually been found of great size. During Cook's first voyage the carcass of one was discovered floating in the sea surrounded by aquatic birds which were feeding upon it, and having examined the remains of this animal, which were deposited in the Museum of the Royal College of Surgeons, Professor Owen stated that its body must have been four feet in length, and its arms at least three feet more. There is therefore the highest probability that the tropical seas are inhabited by monsters of far greater magnitude of the same species. Dr. Shaw thus speaks on the subject: " The existence of some enormously large species of the cuttle-fish tribe in the Indian northern seas can hardly be doubted; and though some accounts may have been much exaggerated, yet there is sufficient cause for believing that such species may very far surpass all that are generally observed about the coasts of European seas. A northern navigator of the name of Dens, is said some years ago to have lost three of his men in the African seas by a monster of this kind which unexpectedly made its appearance while they were employed, during a calm, in raking the sides of the vessel. The colossal fish seized three men in its arms and drew them under water in spite of every effort to preserve them: the thickness of one of the arms which was cut off in the contest was that of a mizen-mast, and the suckers of the size of pot-lids." A variety of statements have been made in different places and at various periods all tending to strengthen the belief that such enormous octopods exist, and it is not easy to avoid concurring in the opinion of a celebrated naturalist who has discussed the subject with great ability, that the different authorities who have referred to it "are sufficient to establish the existence of an enormous inhabitant of the deep,—a cuttle-fish possessed of characters which in a remarkable degree distinguish it from every other creature with which we are familiar;" and further, that it would be "contrary to an enlightened philosophy to reject as spurious the history of an animal, the existence of which is rendered so probable by evidence deduced from the prevailing belief of different tribes of mankind whose opinions it is evident could not have been influenced or affected by the traditions of each other, but must have resulted from the occasional appearances of the monster itself in different quarters of the globe."

The eggs of the cuttle-fish are almost as remarkable as the animal itself. They are oval, or rather spindle-shaped bodies, about the size of grapes, and somewhat like them in colour, one end of each egg is furnished with a fleshy stalk and the other is prolonged to a nipple-shaped point, and the skin is tough like india-rubber. By means of the stalk, the egg is attached to branches of seaweed, and numbers of them united to the same substance form a cluster by no means unlike a bunch of grapes, and appearing to an observer unacquainted with their real character to be some species of sea plant. These eggs or bladders contain at first a yoke of a white colour enclosed in transparent albumen, but as it advances toward maturity the contents assume the form of the young cuttle-fish, which is at length excluded, like the chick from the shell, by the opening of the envelope in which it is enclosed.

VERTEBRATA—FISHES

1

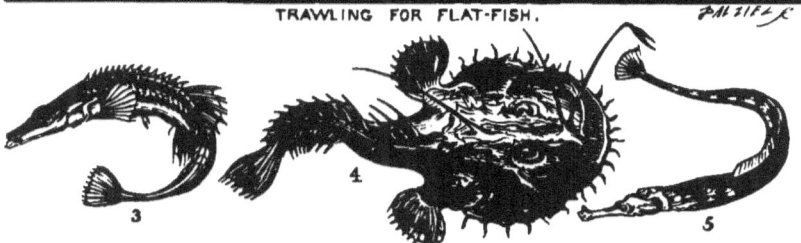

REMARKABLE FISHES.

1. Lamprey. 2. Lump Fish, or Lump Sucker. 3. Fifteen-spined Stickleback. 4. Fishing-Frog or Frog-Angler.
5. Pipe Fish.

(See Chapters 23, 24, and 25.)

CHAP. XXIII.

VERTEBRATA — FISHES.

Form of Fishes: its Adaptation.—External Covering.—Colours. Locomotive Powers.—Respiration, &c.

OUR readers have now been supposed, on their occasional visits to the sea-shore, to have seen a variety of examples from three out of the four great subdivisions or groups into which Cuvier has divided the whole animal kingdom, proceeding from the lowest rank of organised beings upwards to those of the highest grade. By this process they have now arrived at the great sub-kingdom of the *Vertebrata,* which comprehends within it all animals possessed of a vertebral column, or back-bone.

The group or sub-kingdom of the vertebrata is distributed into four classes: fishes, reptiles, birds, and mammalia. Of several of these classes a great variety of examples are either occasionally or permanently inhabitants of our sea-shores, and their structure, their instincts, and their habits afford most striking illustrations of that creative power, skill, and foresight which every reflective mind delights to recognise.

Our attention is naturally directed, in the first instance, to the lowest of the four classes now mentioned, which comprehends all the varieties of fishes, properly so called, and regarding which some considerations occur as suitable before giving attention to any particular specimens of the finny tribes.

Fishes exhibit great variety of form, but notwithstanding such special differences of shape as exist in different examples of the class, the general form which they all possess in common is in all instances such as to fit them for rapid and easy motion in their native element. Those whose motion is swiftest, such as the salmon, having precisely such a figure as may be shown, on the strictest principles of physics, to be that which presents the least resistance to the fluid through which they swim. Their centre of gravity too is so placed, and their specific gravity, or the weight of the fishes' body compared with an equal bulk of water, is such as to adapt them with the nicest accuracy to the fluid in which they exist. The unity of purpose and design which these considerations clearly exhibit can be referred to nothing else than that Infinite Intelligence to whom every physical law is known, and that Infinite Skill by which those laws can be directed and employed.

The external covering and the colours of fishes present to us many striking lessons to the same purpose. One of the distinctive characters of fishes is their scales, which constitute a covering peculiarly adapted to the element in which they live. These organs differ in form in various fishes; some are round, some oval, others are angular, and others are denticulated. They envelop the body so completely as to protect every part of it, and at the same time admit of that perfect flexibility which is requisite to those rapid and graceful motions for which the finny tribes are so remarkable. Among evidences of design the structure of the scales of fishes merits our careful attention. On examining them with a microscope, it is found that each of these organs is pierced by a minute hole, which is the extremity of a tube. Through this orifice is emitted a kind of mucus or slime, which is secreted by glands, and forms an external coating, which not only lubricates the body of the animal, but diminishes the friction of its transit through the water. The orifices are found to be more numerous and larger about the head of the fish than the other parts of its body, and in this we perceive an additional evidence of creative foresight acting in correspondence with the laws of physics; for, as Mr. Yarrell has observed, " whether the fish inhabits the stream or the lake, the current of the water in the one instance, or progression through it in the other, carries this defensive secretion backwards, and spreads it over the whole surface of the body." This provision is, as our readers will observe, analogous to that which is found in the structure of birds, in which a gland is made to supply the oily matter by which the feathers are smoothed and rendered impervious to moisture. We thus perceive, in both cases, an apparatus adapted to a similar use in elements and under conditions widely different, and thus exhibiting the unity of purpose in the one creative Mind.

The colours of fishes are likewise most remarkable. Nothing can exceed the beauty of the metallic lustre which some of them possess. The herring, for instance, when just taken from the water, presents a variety of iridescent hues; and there are many fishes the external decoration of whose scales exhibits the most brilliant tints of gold, silver, copper, blue, green, and scarlet, distinct or intermingled. The colours of fishes are all most brilliant when they are in full season, and at the period of reproduction; and it can hardly be doubted that those bright hues serve to promote the benevolent purposes of the Author of Nature by contributing in some manner to the happiness of those tribes which inhabit the world of waters.

The locomotive organs of fishes present to us several very striking lessons; they exhibit an admirable mechanical contrivance, adapted with the utmost nicety to the purpose in view. The tail, including the lower extremity of the body, is the principal organ of motion. By means of this apparatus the fish can turn to either side, or propel itself forwards. A stroke of the tail to the right or left turns the head of the fish in the opposite direction; a combination of strokes in both directions causes it to dart forwards. The action of the tail in causing progression is, our readers will observe, an illustration of what natural philosophers call the composition of motion, the two forces which separately would move the animal to the right or left, producing as their combined result motion in an intermediate direction, that is to say straight forwards. Human ingenuity has in various ways applied the same combination of force for a similar end. A boatman at the stern of a boat, by means of a single oar, turns the boat to the right or left, and by combining the two motions of the oar which separately produce that result, he imparts to the boat an onward motion. The screw placed at the stern of the steamship is an application of the same principle. But thousands of years before man existed the same natural laws, which he learnt to employ only after centuries of slow and painful progress, had already been taken advantage of by the All-wise Artificer in the structure and application of the fish's tail. The fins of fishes, which are analogous to the legs of quadrupeds, appear to be chiefly employed in balancing the animal's body, and their structure is no less admirably adapted to this purpose than the tail is to its own proper effect.

Related to the locomotive powers of fishes there is a peculiar organ possessed by many species, which cannot be too much admired as the evidence of an arrangement expressly adapted to a certain purpose. It has been already remarked that the weight of a fish's body is nearly the same as that of an equal bulk of water. This equality, where it is perfect, has the effect of causing any body immersed in a fluid to remain in one and the same place without sinking or ascending. An increase of the weight of the body in relation to the water causes it to descend, while a diminution of its relative gravity obliges it to rise toward the surface. Now, many fishes are furnished with an internal piece of mechanism, by which they are able in an instant to alter their specific gravity, and to ascend or descend without employing either fins or tail. This apparatus is called the air-bladder. It consists of a membraneous bag, filled with air secreted by the fish. This bag is surrounded with muscles, on which the fish can act at will. By relaxing those muscles the bladder becomes larger, the body is therefore specifically lighter, and ascends upwards; by pressing on the bladder with the muscles its size is diminished, and the animal sinks. This apparatus, although possessed by a great variety of fishes, is not universal. Many of those which live at the bottom of the water are not furnished with it, and for the obvious reason that they do not particularly require it. It is impossible not to perceive that this part of the animal's organisation proceeds from the express design of an Intelligence to whom are fully known those laws to which it is so wisely and accurately adjusted.

The gills, or apparatus for respiration in fishes, present a singularly beautiful adaptation of means to the end in view. These organs consist of arches on each side of the head, to which are attached a series of fringes, formed of minute blood-vessels, and so constructed that the water taken in at the mouth passes freely over them, imparting to the venous blood they contain the supply of oxygen necessary to its purification. These organs are precisely analogous to the lungs of terrestrial animals, and point out the same design adapted with equal precision to the element in which the animal breathes, and for a similar purpose.

The eyes of fishes exhibit several striking peculiarities pointing out special design and adaptation. As the medium in which the sense of sight is to be exercised is much more dense than air, the form of the lenses of the eyes is accommodated to the condition. The pupil also is large, so as to admit as much light as possible to enter. In terrestrial animals the organ of sight is furnished with glands, by which a fluid is secreted in order that the surface of the cornea may be kept perfectly clean. This fluid forms a wash which is passed over the eye by what is called the nictitating membrane. But in the fish this apparatus does not exist, because it is unnecessary. The element in which the animal lives performs the office of keeping the organs perfectly free from any substances which might impede the entrance of the rays of light. While, therefore, in terrestrial animals the arrangement of gland and membrane points out in a most striking manner, the design of Infinite Wisdom, the absence of the apparatus in the eyes of fishes is an equal evidence to the same effect.

If we now turn our attention to the instincts of fishes we shall perceive much that is calculated to point out the same divine wisdom and foresight which is manifested in their organisation. Without entering upon any discussion as to the nature of that marvellous power which we call instinct, we shall merely at present refer generally to one of the most striking instances of its exercise on the creatures we are now considering, that by which fishes are directed in the process of reproduction. In order to the vivifying of their eggs or spawn certain conditions are indispensable, which could not be attained in deep water, such as a certain degree of exposure to light, warmth, and the influence of the atmosphere. To accomplish this end, there is an instinct implanted precisely adapted to the object in view. Directed by this unerring impulse, fishes at the breeding season betake themselves to such stations as are best suited to the continuance of their species. The herring, for example, frequents the comparatively shallow waters of the coast, and the salmon enters the rivers from the sea and proceeds to the shallow parts of the streams, where the conditions necessary to the fruitfulness of its spawn can be obtained. This instinct, displayed as it is in a great variety of forms, must be regarded as arising from no perception on the part of the animals exercising it, as to the importance of the act they perform; it is accompanied by no knowledge whatever of those physical and chemical laws to which it is adapted. The tendency to act in a manner suited to those laws is a part of their constitution. It exhibits one of the most striking evidences that it is possible to conceive of overruling foresight on the part of that Infinitely Wise Being to whom all the laws of the material universe are known, and from whose special instruction alone, creatures, without any design arising from their own intelligence, act in the strictest conformity to those laws, and so answer the purposes for which they are called into existence.

The skeletons of fishes are formed either of cartilage, as in the skate, or of bone, as in the trout or perch. This circumstance has been adopted by the illustrious naturalist Cuvier as the basis of his classification. He has accordingly divided fishes into two primary groups, the one comprehending all the osseous fishes, the other all the cartilaginous tribes. These two groups admit of further subdivision with reference to certain peculiarities in the fins and other parts. It is, however, unnecessary minutely to describe the details by which those subdivisions are distinguished.

VERTEBRATA — FISHES

CHAP. XXIV.

VERTEBRATA — FISHES.

Fishes: Instances of remarkable Form, Structure, and Instincts.—The Lump-Sucker.—The Lamprey.—The Stickleback.—Pipe-fishes.—The Fishing-Frog.—Shark.—Rays, &c.

MANY of the finny denizens of our sea-shores are very remarkable, and in their structure, habits, and instincts, exhibit in a striking manner those great truths of natural theology to which we have so frequently referred. Without entering into such minute details as belong to the province of the naturalist, it will be sufficient for our purpose to describe such peculiarities as tend to illustrate our subject.

It has been already stated that various marine animals, such for instance as the limpet or the cuttle-fish, are furnished with disks, by which, in consequence of the law of atmospheric and fluid pressure, they are enabled to adhere with great tenacity to those objects to which their disks are applied. There are several kinds of fishes not uncommon on our coasts furnished with this very remarkable apparatus.

One of these is the lump-sucker (*Cyclopterus lumpus*), a fish frequently taken on various parts of our coast, and often found cast ashore. This is by no means a handsome fish. Its form is thick and clumsy, its skin rough and covered with tubercles, and although the various tints of blue, purple, and orange are mingled together over its surface, its general aspect is not pleasing. The flesh is rich, but it does not agree with all stomachs, owing to the quantity of oil it contains. Seals devour them with great avidity. This fish is extremely remarkable on account of the apparatus by which it can attach itself at will to the surface of other bodies. This apparatus which is popularly termed a sucker, is situated on the lower part of the creature's body between the pectoral and ventral fins, and consists of an oval-shaped disk or flat surface, furnished with muscles by which a vacuum can be created between the disk and the object to which the fish adheres. Such is the tenacity with which it is able to fix itself by this means that one of these fish having been placed in a bucket of water, it attached itself so firmly to the bottom that the whole vessel, containing several gallons and of considerable weight, could be lifted from the ground on using the fish's tail as a handle. It is difficult to ascertain all the purposes which are served by this part of the creature's structure, but one purpose appears evident. The lump is not an active or powerful fish, and its shape exposes it in no ordinary degree to the power of the waves. By means of its sucker, however, it can bid defiance to their utmost force, and remain amidst the agitation of the water free from all danger of destruction. We are entitled to regard the sucker in this particular instance as a compensation which makes up for want of greater activity and power. The spawn of the lump-sucker is deposited among rocks and seaweed within low-water mark, and the male fish is said to watch the spawn after its exclusion until the young fry are hatched, when the latter instantly employ their suckers by fixing themselves on the sides and back of their parent, by whom they are carried into deeper water. We may truly consider the mechanical apparatus with which this fish is furnished as one of those innumerable instances with which the wise and beneficent Creator has provided for the safety of some of the humblest of his creatures.

There are other fishes which are provided with "suckers," constructed on precisely the same principles as that of the fish now mentioned, but apparently employed for different purposes. One of the most remarkable of these is the lamprey (*Petromyzon marinus*), specimens of which fall under our notice on various parts of the English coast much more frequently than on the shores of Scotland and Ireland. This fish has an eel-shaped body, and is from two to three feet in length; its colour is a yellowish-brown marbled with a dusky hue. It is, like the salmon, a migratory fish, passing a portion of the year in the sea, and entering the rivers in spring for the purpose of spawning. The remarkable peculiarity in its structure is the mouth, which is circular, surrounded by a flexible lip, and armed with a very singular tooth. The lamprey feeds, like the eel, on any animal matter it finds; but it occasionally attacks other fishes fastening upon them with its sucker-shaped mouth, and cutting into their flesh with its tooth-like processes evidently adapted to the purpose. This is not, however, the only use to which its sucker is applied. The fish is imperfectly adapted for swimming, having neither air-bladder nor pectoral or ventral fins; by means of the sucker, therefore, it can in no small degree remedy the defects of its natatory powers, by attaching itself to stones, and thus not only obtaining rest, but perfect security against the strength of the current. Another and very distinct use of the sucker remains to be mentioned. The lamprey, prior to depositing its spawn in the rivers, finds its necessary to prepare a place for its reception, and this it does by removing the small stones from the spot in which the roe is to be laid. In the rivers they frequent the male and female lamprey may often be observed from a bridge, busily occupied in this, to them, important process. To those who are not aware that substances immersed in water are much lighter than in air, it is quite marvellous what large stones the lampreys contrive to carry from the place which in their parental instinct they are preparing for their progeny. The structure of the lamprey's mouth is precisely analogous to that of the little apparatus called a leather sucker used by boys at school, or to the mouth of an exhausting syringe. It is, however, like all instances of natural mechanism, much more perfect than any artificial apparatus can ever be. In this particular instance we find the mouth serving not only for the reception of food, but for a variety of purposes, to any of which, if its form were similar to that of other fishes, it could not be applied, and for which, even if its shape were circular, it would be unfit if unaccompanied by an apparatus for creating a vacuum, and by an implanted instinct adapted both to the structure and to the wants of the animal. Can any consideration more clearly evince the design of Divine skill and benevolence?

Our readers are all, doubtless, acquainted with those active little fishes called sticklebacks, from their being armed on the back with spines. There are several varieties of these, but they inhabit fresh water, although some of the species are found on the brackish water at the mouths of our larger rivers. There is, however, one species which is entirely a salt water fish, and is found in a great variety of places on the coasts of Britain and Ireland. It is the fifteen-spined stickleback, and is sometimes called the sea-adder. It inhabits places where there are rocks and stones covered with seaweed, among which it takes refuge when alarmed. The most interesting circumstance regarding this little fish is its nest-building instinct. The nest may often be discovered during spring and summer in the rock-pools between tide marks. The structure is about eight inches in length, pear-shaped, and formed of branches of seaweed, intermixed with confervæ and corallines. To unite these materials together, the little architect forms a thread as fine as silk, and strong as well as elastic, for which purpose it is furnished with a secretion capable when drawn into a thread of resisting the water. With this thread, which is frequently of great length, the fish binds together the sea weeds forming its nest, carrying it through and around them in all directions. In the middle of this nest the spawn is deposited in irregular masses, containing many hundreds of eggs of a whitish or amber colour, and about the size of small shot; the masses of eggs in the same nest are met with in different stages of advancement towards maturity, from which it appears that the fish deposits its spawn at various times in the same place. The care of the little creature does not cease with the deposition of its spawn; it watches the scene of its parental toils, with anxious solitude guarding it from all danger, so far as its limited powers will allow, till the young fry are excluded. In this instance we perceive that the parental instinct, the tendency to build, and the possession of a substance secreted to form a thread, without which the nest could not be constructed, all exhibit unity of design in that Creative Power which implanted the instincts and gave the corresponding structure.

The family of Pipe-fishes (*Sygnathidæ*) is represented in our seas by some species, specimens of which are to be found in various parts of our sea-shores. The appearance of all this tribe is most remarkable; their bodies are long and slender, their snouts much elongated, and the whole body is covered with plates, like a coat of mail, and the plates are so disposed that the body is rendered angular. They possess no ventral fins, and in the majority of cases neither pectoral nor caudal fins. But what is more remarkable still is the the fact that, like the kangaroo, these fishes are furnished with a marsupial cavity, into which their young may retreat. Of this tribe there are seven species known on our shores, and differing from each other in various minute respects. Perhaps the most remarkable of these is the species known as the short nosed sea-horse, which is a kind of pipe-fish, somewhat rare on the British shores, although frequent on the continental coasts. The name is suggested by the resemblance which the head of the fish bears to that of a horse. The animal, it appears, is accustomed to use its tail as a prehensile instrument, for which the shape and position of the plates by which it is covered, adapt it; and it is enabled to twist it round marine plants, and wait with its head free, ready to dart upon any object it desires to make its prey. It is said to swim in a vertical attitude, with the tail ready to catch any object within its reach. Two of these singular fish sometimes engage in combat, when they twist tails round each other, and struggle with great violence. The eyes have the faculty of moving independently of each other, and this, along with the brilliant iridescence about the head and its blue bands, gives it a considerable resemblance to the chameleon. Among the most remarkable fishes which can attract our attention is the Fishing-frog, or Angler (*Lophius Piscatorius*), a creature whose structure and instincts are very marvellous. This fish is frequently taken three or four feet in length, and is said occasionally to be found of the dimensions of seven, and even ten feet in length. Its head is flat, and of enormous breadth and size, its surface exceeding that of all the rest of the fish, and the mouth is prodigious, and armed with numerous teeth. But the most singular part of the animal's structure are three tentacula, which arise from the head. Two of these filaments arise from above the upper lip, and the third from the back of the head. The first of these, on the upper lip, is nearly half the length of the fish's body; at its base it is accommodated with a joint, which admits of its motion in every direction, and at the extremity it is surmounted by a little membrane of a brilliant metallic lustre. This filament constitutes the rod, line, and bait, by which the fishing-frog entices its prey. It swims with difficulty, and instead of pursuing its prey it has recourse to a degree of craft rivalling that of a disciple of Walton himself. Crouching close to the ground, it stirs up the sand and mud with its fins, and thus concealed from the sight of its victims, it elevates its fishing-rod and bait, moving the coloured membrane about in all directions. This attracts the fishes in its vicinity, who hasten to seize upon tempting spoil, but they no sooner attempt to nibble at the apparent worm than the angler withdraws the lure, and elevating his enormous mouth, seizes his unsuspecting prey, and, swallowing it in a moment, immediately holds out the bait to capture another prize.

Many authentic anecdotes are related of the voracity of this fish, a quality which the extraordinary magnitude of its mouth unequivocally indicates. A fisherman had hooked a large codfish, and while drawing it up he felt a much heavier weight attach itself to his line. This proved to be a large angler, which had seized the cod, and which the fisherman compelled to quit its prey only by giving it some heavy blows on the head. On another occasion, an angler seized a large conger-eel, which had taken the hook, and was in the act of swallowing the huge morsel, when the prey escaped from the angler's jaws by finding its way out by the gill-covers behind the mouth; and in this condition both were drawn up together. Another of those fishes, pressed by hunger, is known to have seized at the top of the water a large cork buoy employed as a float for a deep sea-line; and it is said that some fishermen near Queensferry, in Scotland, observing the water much discoloured at one particular spot where it was not very deep, rowed to the place, and, on poking the bottom with a long handled mop, found it taken hold of by an angler, who was, doubtless, busily engaged plying his vocation, and who, mistaking the mop for a fish, seized it, with the intention of swallowing the savoury morsel; the woolly substance of the mop, however, caught in his teeth, and being unable to extricate himself in time he was hauled into the boat, the victim of his own inordinate appetite.

It is to the structure and instincts of this singular creature, however, that we would especially direct the reader's attention. From what has already been stated, the mechanism of the fishing-rod, as we may call the filament with which it entices its prey, is adapted with extreme nicety to its purpose. The peculiar form of the joint by which it is fixed admits of its being moved in every direction, and it is supplied with a set of muscles under the control of the animal's will, while the size and position of the mouth, and the the situation of the eyes with reference to the membrane or bait at the end of the rod, are precisely such as to be most efficient. To these peculiarities, we must add the instinct and craft, without which the structure could not be available; but what is more, the structure and the instinct are both adapted to the instinct of other fishes, who, in pursuit of food, mistake the angler's lure for some living object, such as they are wont to pursue. This latter adaptation is entirely independent of the angler itself, and the whole arrangement points in the clearest manner to the design of that Supreme Intelligence by whom alone the structure and the instincts could be adapted to each other.

Specimens of almost every species of the shark family—*Squalidæ*—have been found on the British coasts, but the largest and most formidable of the tribe are rare. Most visitors of our sea-shores, however, must be familiar with one or other of the minor species of shark, called dog-fish, of which there are several kinds, and which frequent some parts of our coasts in immense multitudes, occasioning great havoc among the nets and fishing lines, and often tearing to pieces the best fish on the hooks. A very remarkable example of beneficent care has been observed in relation to the teeth of the shark. In the larger specimens the teeth, from their extraordinary and indiscriminate voracity, must be exposed to frequent injury, and without some provision by which those terrible weapons of destruction may be renewed the shark tribe would have become extinct, or their peculiar functions, that of thinning the number of the inhabitants of the deep, would be rendered impossible. Accordingly the teeth of shark are not fixed in sockets, but attached to a cartilaginous membrane. This membrane grows outward; the outer row of teeth in due time drop out, and another row which has been gradually advancing occupies the place of the first; this in due time disappears and other sets follow in succession. By this means, even in the oldest of these monsters of the deep, the teeth are always in the most perfect condition for the work of destruction for which they are destined.

The family of fishes, known as Rays or Skates—*Raiidæ*—are also numerous in our seas. They belong, like the sharks and lampreys, to the cartilaginous division of fishes. Of the rays there are many varieties, some scarce, and others occurring in great plenty.

Several of the shark tribe bring forth their young alive; but others produce eggs, as also do the rays, and these are not deposited in large multitudes, like those in the spawn of other fishes, but in comparatively very small numbers, and each egg is contained in a case formed of a substance like thin horn, and of a very remarkable shape. Those produced by the skate are about four or five inches in length, of a dark brown colour, similar indeed to the darkest sea weed when dried; their shape is as near as possible that of a four-handed barrow, but with these our readers are probably familiar, as they are frequently found empty on the sea-shore: they are called mermaids' purses or skate-barrows.

Those belonging to the dog-fishes are very much like the purses of the skate, but are of a clear yellowish horn-colour. From each of the four corners of the purse issues a long tendril which coils round the sea weeds or other substances near which the parent fish deposits it, and it is thus so fixed as to be free from danger of being driven ashore by the waves. Both kinds of purses are furnished with openings at the ends through which the sea water flows while the young fish is being matured, and by which it eventually issues forth from its very singular envelope.

Remarkable, however, as these "sea-purses" are in form and structure, there is one particular regarding them which presents us with a most striking instance of a provision made for the wants of the young fish before it is able to quit its prison. During its embryo state it cannot use its gills for the purpose of breathing, any more than an infant before birth can employ its lungs in breathing. Yet in order to the development of the fish, it is indispensable that through its circulating system the blood shall pass purified by the action of the water, and supplied with oxygen as it is required. Without this process the young fish must perish. And how is this accomplished? By a very marvellous expedient. From the gills of the young fish project certain threads or filaments; each of these contains a minute blood-vessel, and as the water has free ingress to the interior of the receptacle, these blood-vessels serve the purpose of gills. They are, however, entirely temporary; they cease to exist after the gills are capable of acting. The purpose they had to serve is accomplished otherwise, and by an apparatus possessed of a degree of efficiency suited to the enlarged powers of the fish. Can any mode be devised by which to account for the admirable appropriateness of this structure, but that of referring it to the wisdom and skill of the Creator? The supply of a temporary breathing apparatus to be used while the gills were imperfect and only gradually assuming a condition fit for their future purpose; the orifices in the egg-purse allowing the water access to that temporary breathing apparatus, and the fact that the apparatus itself ceases to exist when it is no longer required; these and other considerations cannot fail to point out the design of that Divine Intelligence to which all the conditions that require to be provided for are known, and that Divine Skill by which the details requisite to the result intended are carried out in an unerring correspondence with natural laws.

VERTEBRATA — FISHES

CHAP. XXV.

VERTEBRATA — FISHES.

Edible Fishes.—The Cod Family.—Flat Fish.—The Herring and Pilchard Family.—Pilchard Fishing.

HAVING given our attention to some of those fish most remarkable for their structure, or some other peculiarity, we shall now notice a few specimens of those whose immense numbers and whose edible qualities render them of the greatest value to mankind.

Among the most valuable of this class of fishes are those comprehended in the cod and haddock family—*Gadidæ*—which include several varieties, such as the haddock, coal-fish, rockling, ling, and various kinds of whitings, hake, and others of the same order. It will suffice to mention the cod properly so called, as being a familiar type of the order to which it belongs.

These fishes are to be found on every part of the shores of Britain and Ireland, and appear to be most plentiful off the northern coasts of Scotland. They chiefly inhabit places where the water is from forty to fifty fathoms in depth. They are extremely voracious, devouring fish of all kinds, molluscs and crustacea, crabs of considerable size being often found in their capacious stomachs, no fewer than thirty-five crabs, none of them smaller than a half-crown piece, having been taken from one fish. No fish is of greater utility. The flesh is white, firm, and of excellent quality, and every part of the fish is capable of being turned to some useful purposes. The tongue, either salted or fresh, is a great delicacy. The gills are employed as baits in fishing; the liver furnishes an enormous quantity of excellent oil, applicable to a variety of useful purposes, and possessing highly nutritive qualities, and peculiarly suited as an article of nourishment to persons of feeble health; the swimming-bladder furnishes isinglass equal in quality to that yielded by the sturgeon; and even the head furnishes the fisherman and his family with food. The Norwegians, on whose coast the cod is very abundant, give it together with marine plants to their cows, for the purpose of producing a greater quantity of milk. In Iceland the bones afford nourishing food for cattle, and the people of Kamschatka feed their valuable dogs with it. On the desolate shores of the Icy Sea the same parts when thoroughly dried are employed as fuel.

The fecundity of the cod is amazing. Nine millions of eggs have been counted in the roe of a single fish of middling size, and if the enormous multitudes which must be thus produced and which must survive the devastation of their enemies, be taken into consideration, along with the useful and valuable properties which this fish possesses, it is impossible not to admit that among the purposes for which it has been designed, we are entitled to reckon that of supplying many of the wants of the human race.

Another family of fishes, of which many of the various species are familiar to our readers, is that of the *Pleuronectidæ*, so called from the remarkable circumstance of their swimming on one side. These are what are popularly known as flat fish, and comprehend eighteen or twenty kinds, including among them the plaice, the flounder, and its varieties, the halibut, the turbot, and several kinds of sole. The characters peculiar to this race of fishes are so distinct as to render it one of the most marked and insulated of all the families into which the finny tribes have been subdivided. There is a singular want of symmetry in some parts of the figure of the flat fish. The head appears as if forcibly twisted to one side, in consequence of which the mouth appears distorted. The body is compressed, and almost surrounded by the dorsal and anal fins as with a fringe. The habitation of these fishes is the bottom of the sea, and they are not furnished with the air-bladder so frequently forming part of the structure of those fishes which frequent the higher parts of the water. Reference has already been made to the very remarkable resemblance which fishes present in their hues to that of the ground they frequent. In no instance is this more striking than in the tribe of fishes to which we now refer. While the side next the ground is white, the upper side, which is exposed to the light is of some dark shade, either brown, or greyish sand colour, and in some instances this general hue is broken by blotches, light or dark, blackish or reddish, which not only present a resemblance to under-shades caused by inequalities of the ground, but to the different tints that occur upon it. Flat fish too seem to be endowed with the power of altering their colour, so as to correspond with the prevailing tints of the ground, and even when the sand is of a very light colour, they so nearly resemble it, that even in very clear and shallow water, a flat fish may be immediately under the observer's eye without being perceived. But that this is one among many similar instances of design in the Author of Nature, by which an express provision is made for the safety of the creatures endowed with the faculty and with the general and permanent resemblance in question cannot be disputed.

The *Clupeidæ*, which comprehend the herring, the pilchard, and several other species, is a family of fishes of the highest importance, and in several respects of great interest. Familiar as we are with the herring, we are by no means fully acquainted with its natural history. On this subject some of the statements that have been made appear from recent observation to have been purely imaginary. The herring has been described as having its permanent abode within the arctic circle, from which it migrates southwards towards the British Islands in a shoal of countless myriads, at certain periods of the year, and when the shoal reaches the Shetland Isles, it separates into two vast bodies, one of which proceeds eastwards, filling with their numbers the creeks and bays on the east coasts of Britain, while the other passes along the west, visiting the various lochs and bays on that part of Scotland, the Irish Sea and the Irish Coast. This, however, appears to be a fabulous account. The herring does not possess its habitual place of abode in the arctic seas, where it is said to be extremely rare, and not only are there no herring fisheries of any importance in Greenland, or even in Iceland, but no notice has been taken of this fish by voyagers to the frozen seas.

That the herring does perform a migration is of course unquestionable, for it entirely disappears at certain times and revisits our coasts afterwards; but the extent of its migration is understood to be very limited, and the best naturalists are of opinion that it inhabits the deep water of our coasts all the year, and only approaches to the shallow water of the shores for the purpose of reproduction, in this respect being similar to other tribes of fishes. The opinion thus expressed is corroborated by several circumstances. The herring is known frequently to occur in great abundance in some southern localities before its appearance in those more to the north, and this fact is not consistent with the theory that they arrive on the British coast from the arctic regions. And the accuracy of opinion in question is rendered still more probable by the circumstance that the pilchard, a fish nearly allied to the herring, is now known to reside permanently in the British seas, and although at one time supposed, like the herring, to migrate to the north, is extremely limited in its range.

The pilchard is a smaller fish than its relative the herring, and is by no means of such general occurrence along our coasts. Its chief locality is the south coast of England, and especially that of Cornwall and Devonshire, and although a few stragglers may sometimes be obtained along the eastern shores of the island, yet the range of this fish seldom extends on the east beyond the Straits of Dover, and on the coast beyond the parallel of the southern shores of Ireland. The prodigious multitude of both these kinds of fishes which are annually caught in the British seas has rendered the herring and pilchard fisheries of the greatest value and importance, employing as they do many thousands of fishermen, affording support for their families, and supplying a large quantity of food.

But what is especially worthy of our remark is the instinctive impulse by which these fishes quit the deep water and approach the shore. This instinct, which is possessed by them in common with many others of the finny tribes, is, like all other instances of it, how differently soever directed, a blind and unintelligent impulse. The shallower parts of the shores, probably because of the higher temperature of the sea in such places, the greater amount of light which reaches the spawn, and the increased supply of oxygen which it obtains, are the only suitable localities in which the ova could be rendered productive. But of this the herring and the pilchard know as little as of the chemical and vital agencies thus brought into operation. Without the continual reproduction of their kinds the whole race must perish, and with them doubtless many other animals which subsist upon them, while even man himself would not a little feel the loss; but directed by an unreasoning impulse these fishes draw near the shore free from all intention or purpose either of preventing their species from becoming extinct or administering to the important purposes referred to. The migratory instinct, independent as it is of all knowledge or intelligence, can be referred only to that Being to whom all the chemical, physical, and vital laws relating to the humblest of His creatures are fully known, and from whom alone could proceed an impulse, which, although blind itself, is adapted to produce its result, with a degree of precision and accuracy far exceeding that which the most exalted human reason can attain. When we take this marvellous instinct into view, whether we regard it as intended to produce a result or a combination of different results, it is impossible not to reflect upon it with that reverential admiration with which we recognise the design of Infinite wisdom, knowledge, and beneficence.

The mode of fishing for the herring and the pilchard is much the same. The herring is taken by means of a net of great length and of considerable depth. These nets are suspended perpendicularly from a rope extending along the surface of the water, on which it is floated by means of buoys. These nets are run across the usual course which the shoal of herrings takes, and the fish run their heads into the meshes from which the threads entering behind the gills, render it impossible for them to withdraw, while the size of the mesh makes it equally impossible for them to pass through the net. These nets are made to extend a great distance from the boat, and having been left floating are often found, on being taken up, to contain as many herrings as will completely fill the boat to which the net belongs.

The pilchard is taken by the same method as that employed in the capture of the herring, but the largest quantities are obtained by means of the net called the seine or sean, a form of net of great antiquity, the name of which has come down to us from the Greek language. The seine is a net of great length, which may either be shot from the shore or from a boat. In the latter case, other nets are used called stop nets, which are shot in such a manner as to prevent the escape of the fish already enclosed in the seine itself, by completing the circle in which the fish are enclosed. In some instances several seines are united together, and when fully extended, enclose a great space and frequently capture a corresponding quantity. On such occasions, several boats are employed, and when a large shoal of fish is discovered and the direction in which they are moving ascertained, the greatest activity prevails, and no small degree of skill is manifested by the fisherman. The extent and course of a shoal of pilchards is frequently much more correctly ascertained from an elevated part of the shore, and the experienced eye of the fisherman who takes his station on an eminence enables him, from certain indications in the water which would escape the notice of others, to discover those particulars regarding the shoal necessary to a successful cast of the nets. This he easily communicates by preconcerted signals to the fishermen in the boats, who act on the suggestions thus conveyed to them. A graphic and spirited account of the process is given in an eminent periodical*, with a quotation from which we will close this part of our subject. " On an eminence above the sea, and probably on a narrow path, paces a strong rough Cornishman in apparently a meditative mood. He carries a branch of a tree or of furze in his hand. He carefully scrutinises the sea, and now and then shades his eyes with his large hand, as if he would descry a far sail. A well laden boat now shoots out to sea, and at this the solitary watcher gazes. Does it hold his son or his daughter? Is he full of fatherly anxiety for his son as he is about to emigrate? Mark him! He now frantically waves his branch and his arm in one wide sweep. The folks in the boat see this; and strange to say, are swayed by this mad motion. He again sweeps round the

---

* Athenæum, Dec. 1859.

branch, and as they look up to him he directs their course by it, as if it were their compass. What can this mean? Why the supposed madman is sane and sagacious enough. He sees a faint bluish line on the surface of the waters and *there* are the pilchards in one fluctuating, changeful, life-abounding shoal. See how they leap, they play, they shift, they sink, they rise again! Swiftly row the oarsmen, down bend the seiners in less time than common men would think possible, down goes fathom after fathom, and heap after heap of the seine, up float the bordering corks, clash, dash, splash go the long oars again. The cliff watcher is now doubly frantic. He waves and raves, and runs and stamps, and jumps; the shoal is shifting, warping, eluding, the boat is turned, the telegraphic branch is again eyed and obeyed; and now the cliff-watcher is satisfied. He lowers his branch, he nods, he assents by every primitive symbol and significant action that can be imagined. The entire seine is gradually lowered into the sea, the men bend over and you dread a capsize, and even more and more when you see their motions reversed. Now they no longer let down but haul up. A hearty shore-resounding and echo-awakening shout is their mutual encouragement—up comes bit by bit of the seine. How heavy! How joyfully full! Fishermen's heads almost touch the brine, their backs alone are broadly apparent. Now one strong combined haul and nearer together is the seine drawn. What hundreds of glancing, leaping, struggling fish spring up from within that spot! The shore is soon lined with assistants. Some row off with 'tuck nets' to the great boat and let the said small tucks down inside the large seine. The waters are beaten with oars and loaded ropes, and thus the fish are frightened into a narrower space. Listen to the discordant noises on the shore! Boys shout shrilly; dogs bark loudly; and women chatter, and all these sounds mingle with the deep-toned nautical 'Yo! heave ho! yo! hoy! hoy! hoy!' at sea. Though yourself a calm reticent student when in London you catch the Cornish enthusiasm, and as if your whole venture was in pilchards you yourself shout and shriek, and jump and rave. Never mind; all is right. To shore comes the little crowd of boats, and out on the bare beach is poured one teeming, struggling, leaping, panting mass of silvery scales!"

VERTEBRATA — MARITIME BIRDS

MARITIME BIRDS.

1. Terns, or Sea Swallows.   2. Puffins.   3. Sheldrake.   4. Smew.   5. Gannet (adult and young).   6. Diver.

(See Chapter 26.)

CHAP. XXVI.

VERTEBRATA — MARITIME BIRDS.

Swimming and Wading Birds. — The Curlew. — The Sandpiper. — Divers. — Grebes. — The Gannet: its remarkable Structure.

AMONG the most interesting objects which present themselves to our notice during a ramble along the sea-side are those birds of which our shores are either the occasional or permanent abode. Many of the feathered tribes belonging to the inland country may be found inhabiting the woods, the groves, or the fields near the coast, but to any of these it is not our intention to refer; our object is to point out a few of those which are characteristic of the sea-shore. A few general remarks will, however, be necessary in the first instance.

Birds form one of the four great classes into which all the vertebrated animals have been subdivided. They possess a higher rank as regards organisation than either fishes or reptiles, and like the mammalia, they breathe by means of lungs and are warm-blooded. Naturalists have divided the class into several orders, each order comprehending birds possessed of some general characteristic sufficient to distinguish them from others. Thus the first order includes all birds of prey; the second, birds which perch; the third, those that scrape; the fourth embraces all wading birds, and the fifth, all the swimmers. It is to the two last of these five orders that we are now to turn, selecting a few examples from some of the many groups which they contain.

Various species of gulls are common to our sea-shores, building in the precipitous cliffs near the sea, or resorting to a solitary island in some distant lake for the same purpose. All of these are remarkable for the ease and elegance of their motions when on the wing, and for the power with which they are able to make their way amidst the storm. To the gull family belongs the Tern, a bird which merits its popular name of sea-swallow on account of its shape and its rapidity of flight; the Kitty-wake, so called from its peculiar note; the Fulmar, a large grey and white species; and the Storm-petrel, so dreaded by the mariner as the forerunner of a tempest. In addition to these, there are many birds which frequent those parts of the sea-shore when the tide recedes to a great distance leaving bare a long tract of sand or mud in which they find an ample supply of marine worms and other kinds of food. Among these there are Curlews, Sandpipers, Plovers, and other birds; they are, however, as a general rule, so shy, and keep at so great a distance, that it is impossible to observe their actions.

The swimming birds that frequent our shores

are also highly interesting. Of these a few may here be referred to. The Sheldrake is a very handsome bird, belonging to this family, and very common on some of our shores, where it builds its nest in old rabbit holes. The body of this bird is diversified with patches of chestnut, white, and black; its bill is bright red, its head is glossy green, and its legs are flesh coloured. The Scoter is another familiar bird on some of our coasts, but it differs much from the sheldrake, being uniformly black in its plumage, but like the former it frequents the sea-shore, often in considerable numbers, when it seeks its food, which consists of small molluscous animals.

Besides these there are the tribe of Mergansers, of which there are four species known on our shores. Of these the Smew is the smallest, as well as the most common. Its colour is white, diversified with black and grey, the bill is slate-coloured, the face is black, and the head, neck, and breast, white; on the head is a crest of feathers, partly greenish-black and partly white. Another and larger species is the Red-breasted Merganser. The head and throat of this bird are green, the lower part of the neck and the breast are chestnut colour, and the body and wings are diversified with white, black, and brown. The largest species is the Goosander, which in its colours bears a considerable resemblance to the last-mentioned species.

The divers and the grebes have also their representatives at various parts of our shores.

These are all easily distinguished from the tribes of aquatic birds above referred to by the long conical bill, and by the position of the legs, which are placed so far back, that when on the land these birds appear to stand upright. The divers are very common on almost every part of our coast, and may be readily distinguished by the expertness with which they carry on their piscatory labours, diving incessantly after their finny prey. The Great Northern Diver is a very handsome bird. The upper part of the body is dark mottled with white, the head and neck are black tinted with green, and having two rings of mottled feathers, the under surface is white. This bird is the largest of the tribe to which it belongs, and visits our shores during the winter months, retiring during the breeding season, like the gulls, to some remote and little frequented inland lake, on whose borders it rears its young.

Another family of maritime birds comprehends the guillemots, auks, razor-bills, and puffins, all of which are gregarious, inhabiting the rocky headlands and islets, especially on our northern coasts, in immense multitudes. In those inaccessible places these birds congregate at the breeding season, each of them producing a single egg, which some of them place upon the bare rock, and hatch by sitting upon it in their singular erect posture during the requisite period. Such is the fidelity with which these birds, especially the guillemots, devote themselves to the all-important duty of incubation, that they will suffer themselves to be seized rather than quit their post. The puffin, however, a round little bird, with black and white plumage, and a parrot-shaped bill, ribbed with orange, lays its single egg in a burrow which it digs with its bill, if it is unable to discover one already made by a rabbit, and there for a month it sits with the utmost patience, till the young puffin at length breaks the shell. The structure of all these birds, their instincts and their habits, are such as illustrate in a most striking manner the observations already made, exhibiting in the evident correspondence subsisting among them the obvious designs of Infinite Wisdom.

On this subject we must, however, content ourselves with one illustration, furnished by the structure of the gannet or solan goose. This bird is very abundant on our northern shores, and has various favourite breeding places in the inaccessible precipices both on the eastern and western coasts of Scotland. In seeking its appropriate food the gannet flies at no great distance from the surface of the water, but on perceiving a fish it immediately rises into the air, and descends with extraordinary force upon its prey, sometimes by the mere impulse of its descent penetrating the waters to a depth of twenty or even thirty fathoms. Incredible as this may appear, it is certain that these birds have occasionally been found in great numbers entangled in the fishing nets sunk in the sea to the depths now stated, having darted into the water in pursuit of fish. This power of penetrating to so great a depth beneath the surface is rendered all the more marvellous when the extreme buoyancy and lightness of the bird are considered. The gannet floats very high in the water, differing in this respect from some aquatic birds, whose bodies when they are swimming are almost wholly immersed, so that only the neck and head seem to be raised above the surface. Now the cause of the extreme lightness of the gannet's body has been ascertained by anatomists. It appears that a system of air cells exists both along the sides and the inferior part of the body, and that these all communicate with each other, and can be completely inflated at the will of the bird. It also appears that there exists an air cell in the front of the breast four inches in diameter, in direct communication with the lungs, which the bird can inflate in an instant. Over all these air-vessels, however, a system of muscles are stretched, by means of which the gannet can in a moment press upon the vessels, and completely expel the air they contain. When afloat, therefore, or when flying aloft, the gannet inflates all these air vessels. The specific gravity of its body is thus reduced, and it swims high on the wave, or soars with comparative facility in the air. On perceiving its prey, however, and darting down upon it, the air-vessels are immediately compressed, the size of the bird becomes greatly reduced, its weight and specific gravity are increased, and these circumstances, united with the velocity of its fall, enable it to sink deep beneath the wave and secure its prey, an act which would have been physically impossible if the bird still retained its former buoyancy. Having captured the fish, the gannet again comes to the surface, instantaneously inflates its air-vessels, and soars away with the captured prey with a degree of facility which, had it still maintained its increased density, would have been unattainable. Can any arrangement be conceived more clearly evincing an express design, a design carried out with the most precise and accurate reference to the laws of physics? Can any design better display the thorough knowledge of those laws which the wise and Beneficent Designer possessed?

VERTEBRATA — SEASIDE MAMMALIA

THE SEAL FAMILY.

1. Common Seal.   2. Gray Seal.   3. Walrus.   4. Harp Seal.

(See Chapter 27.)

CHAP. XXVII.

VERTEBRATA — SEASIDE MAMMALIA.

The Cetacea, or Whale Tribe.—The Dolphin.—The Sea Unicorn. The Common Whale.—Remarkable Adaptations of Structure, &c.—The Seal Family: Form and Habits.—Adaptations of Structure.—Conclusion.

THE class which occupies the highest rank in the animal kingdom is that of the *Mammalia*, and of this class there are several marine animals which make our sea-shores either their occasional resort or their permanent abode.

The mammalia is the class to which man himself belongs, and the scientific term being derived from the Latin word *mamma*, a teat, indicates the characteristic which distinguishes the mammalia from all the other animals, viz. that they suckle their young. In this class the whale, the seal, and their varieties are comprehended.

Of the order *Cetacea*, to which the whale belongs, there are several examples more or less known in our seas. The Dolphin is one of these; but it is only occasionally met with. The Narwhal or Sea-unicorn, which Cuvier comprehends in the family of the *Delphinidæ*, and which is remarkable for having a spirally twisted tusk projecting from

B B

its snout five, seven, and even ten feet in length, sometimes finds its way to our shores from the dreary regions of the North Sea, where it habitually resides. The Beluga or White Whale has, although very rarely, paid us a visit, and some of the more common species not unfrequently enter our bays and estuaries. Of all the cetacea, however, the porpoise is the most common.

There are many considerations of the greatest interest connected with the natural history of all these animals. But we shall refer only to one or two points regarding their structure, many of the peculiarities of which evince in a most striking manner the design of the great Author of Nature.

There is a remarkable peculiarity in the structure of the tail in the cetacea, which distinguishes all the order from fishes properly so called. The tail of the fish is vertical in its direction, while that of the whale family is horizontal. Now the reason of this peculiarity becomes obvious at once if we consider that all the whale tribe breathe by means of lungs in the same manner as quadrupeds. They require, therefore, to have direct access to the atmosphere, and although living in the sea and capable of remaining submerged for a considerable length of time, must at certain intervals visit the surface in order to breathe. Now the horizontal position of the tail is, of all others, the best suited to this purpose. The structure, therefore, has a direct reference to the necessity under which the animal is laid to obtain easy and swift access to the atmosphere, and it refers us at once to that Being to whom the physical necessities of all His creatures are known, and by whose wisdom alone those necessities can be appropriately supplied.

A similar remark may be made with respect to the structure of the mouth in the common whale. This animal, as is well known, feeds upon the minute crustaceous and molluscous animals, and the gelatinous medusa that abound in the northern seas. Its jaws are accordingly furnished, not with teeth, but with a series of horny laminæ, called whalebone, or baleen. These plates are attached to the upper jaw in rows parallel to each other, and are furnished at their edges with fringes to the number of several hundreds. These fringes form a strainer through which the water, taken into the animal's mouth, is made to pass, leaving behind multitudes of the creatures which form its food. To an animal thus nourished, teeth would not constitute a suitable apparatus; but the huge strainer in question is precisely adapted to the whale's requirements, its food requiring no mastication. Here we possess a very striking instance of a structure strictly adapted to a peculiar and indispensable purpose, for which nothing but the intention and design of Infinite Skill can account.

We arrive at a similar conclusion when we consider another peculiarity in the structure of the whale. What is called the blubber has been ascertained by anatomists to be the true skin of the whale. This skin consists of a mass of fibres interlacing each other, as in ordinary skin; but the texture is much more loose and open, and thus affords room for the fatty matter, or oil, deposited in it, and varying in thickness from that of several inches to between one and two feet. The integument, or skin, thus thickened is adapted in such a manner to the requirements of the animal as to excite the utmost admiration.

The skin is, as already stated, not only open in its texture, and of great thickness, but it is filled with a substance the specific gravity of which is considerably less than that of sea water. This substance envelops the whole body of the animal, and serves the important purpose of rendering buoyant a fabric so huge, of which even the bones are of very great weight compared with those of fishes.

But this skin, so peculiar in its structure, performs another office. It is an extremely bad conductor of heat, inasmuch as there is no circulation among the particles of which the deposited oil is composed. Hence the animal heat of these warm-blooded animals is not transferred to the surrounding waters, or, which is the same thing, the external cold cannot penetrate. By this means the whale can with perfect safety inhabit the coldest water. This arrangement of its skin is necessary to its existence, because of its being a warm-blooded animal; if, on the other hand, the whale possessed cold blood, like a fish, such a protection would have been unnecessary. Is it possible to avoid the conclusion which a contemplation of this admirably adapted structure forces upon us, that the Supreme Intelligence in originating the structure intimately knew and carefully provided for the laws of the transmission of caloric?

But it remains to be added that the integument in question answers a third purpose. It is extremely elastic, and it is well known that elastic substances, and even air itself, which possesses great elasticity, present an increasing resistance with every increase of pressure. Thus the more elastic the substance is the more does its reaction equal the compressing power to which it is exposed. Now the whale is wont to descend to an immense depth in the ocean, and this would expose it to destruction, were it not for the resistance which the structure of the skin presents to the enormous compression of the surrounding water. At a great depth below the surface every square inch of the animal's body may be pressed upon with a ton weight, making an aggregate compressing force of many thousands of tons. This immense power must necessarily diminish, to a certain degree, the whale's body; but the compression extends, it is certain, only a limited distance from the surface of the skin, and cannot, therefore, extend to any of the vital organs. Does not this use of the peculiar structure of the skin clearly indicate the design of Supreme Wisdom?

The *Phocidæ*, or Seal family, are represented on our sea-shores by some four different species, of which the most familiar is the common seal.

The common seal is a gregarious animal, and, although the water is its chief abode, it haunts caverns and recesses among the rocks, in which it brings forth its young, which are generally two in number, and are nursed by their mother with great assiduity and tenderness. The favourite food of this animal when inhabiting coasts at a distance from rivers consists of almost any of the larger kinds of fish, and it is said especially flat fish; but when it frequents the estuaries of our larger rivers it makes terrible havoc among the salmon, which it often pursues even into the nets of the fisherman. The common seal is remarkably intelligent and docile. It is capable of being tamed, and it evinces great affection for its master. But one of the most remarkable of its peculiarities is its marvellous fondness for music. Laing mentions, in his "Account of a Voyage to Spitzbergen," that the tones of his violin would generally draw around him an audience of seals who would follow his boat for miles. In the "Naturalists' Library" the following statement is made by an excellent writer:—"The fondness of these animals for musical sounds is a curious peculiarity of their nature, and has been to me often a subject of interest and amusement. During a residence of some years in one of the Hebrides I had many opportunities of witnessing this peculiarity, and, in fact, could call forth its manifestation at pleasure. In walking along the shore in the calm of a summer afternoon, a few notes of my flute would bring half a score of them within twenty or thirty yards of me; and there they would swim about with their heads above water, like so many black dogs evidently delighted with the sounds. For half an hour, or indeed for any length of time I chose, I could fix them to the spot; and when I moved along the water's edge they would follow me with eagerness, like the dolphins, who, it is said, attended Arion. I have frequently witnessed the same effect when out on a boat excursion. The sound of a flute, or of a common fife, blown by one of the boatmen, was no sooner heard than half a dozen would start up within a few yards, wheeling round us as long as the music played." Another author mentions the remarkable fact that when the bells of the church of Hoy, which stands on the sea-shore, were rung for divine service, all the seals within hearing made directly for the shore, where they kept looking about them as if surprised at the sounds. This peculiarity in the seal has often been regarded as fabulous, but there is no reason whatever to doubt its accuracy.

The element in which the seal chiefly dwells is the sea, and although on land its movements are awkward in the extreme, no aquatic animal is more admirably adapted to move in the water. If we examine its structure we perceive that its trunk bears no inconsiderable resemblance in its general figure to the body of a fish. It is elongated and conical, tapering from the chest to the tail; the hinder limbs are directed backwards so as to terminate the body, and consist of broad webbed and powerful paddles; the whole structure of the body combined with the animal's great muscular power adapting it, like a fish, to make its way with extraordinary ease and rapidity through the element in which it chiefly lives, and to seize upon its finny prey, notwithstanding the swiftness of their movements.

The structure of this creature's body exhibits several other most striking instances of adaptation, one or two of which we cannot refrain from pointing out. Water is the principal element in which the seal has its abode, and in order to capture its prey it is frequently necessary for the animal to remain immersed for a considerable length of time. Its respiration accordingly corresponds with this necessity, differing materially from what is observed in most other animals. It is able to remain at least twenty minutes under water, during which time the nostrils are closed, so that during its immersion no water can enter the air passages. Even when on land the period intervening between the inspirations has been found to be of great length, two minutes often occurring between each breath; but the great quantity of air taken in upon each breath makes up for the small number of the animal's respirations.

But not only its respiration, and even its nostrils, are accurately adapted to its subaqueous habits, but the eye itself is so accommodated. It is specially adapted for seeing in the water, and as the seal is often at great depths exposed to unusual pressure, a provision for the protection of the eye is made by an appropriate mechanism, consisting of an additional eyelid, placed at the inner angle of the cornea, which at the will of the animal may be drawn over the whole eye. It appears moreover, that even the apertures of the ears may be closed, a structure existing for this purpose, by which they are rendered impervious, however great the pressure of the surrounding fluid may be. Can any causes be assigned for arrangements so specially adapted to the required conditions other than the design and purpose of that Being who gave to the material world its peculiar laws, without a suitable adaptation to which animal life could not subsist? Can any arrangements in the body of an animal be pointed out more clearly indicative at once of Divine intelligence, power, and goodness?

Having thus confined our attention, with few if any exceptions, to illustrations of our subject, derived from the natural history of the sea-shore, and having presented to our readers a variety of examples derived from the chief branches into which that delightful science is divided, we now bring our volume to a close, and we do so in the belief that such studies as those which it is the purpose of this work to suggest, are capable of adding immeasurably to the charms of a visit to the coast, by furnishing the mind with cheerful and ennobling contemplations, and aiding the thoughtful observer to convert the simplest object which engages his attention into a lesson on Seaside Divinity.

THE END.

LONDON
PRINTED BY SPOTTISWOODE AND CO.
NEW-STREET SQUARE

BOOKS

PUBLISHED BY

JAMES HOGG AND SONS

LONDON

The Female Characters of Holy Writ.

By the Rev. HUGH HUGHES, D.D., Rector of St. John's, Clerkenwell, and Lecturer of St. Leonard's, Shoreditch. A New and revised Edition. One vol. 8vo. cloth, 10s. 6d.

"THE plan of this work differs from all others of the kind in the following requirements:—1. To present all the Female Characters of Holy Writ with scarcely an exception or omission of any. 2. To present the Female Characters of the Canonical books without intermixing with them any of the Apocryphal biographies. 3. To deduce from each of them distinct practical instruction. 4. To exhibit them chronologically, and to connect them by a chain of reference, so as to keep in view the stream of Sacred History and the varying aspect of the Church in different ages of the world.

"As combining these several requisites to unity, comprehensiveness and completeness, this attempt will be seen to bear features which distinguish it from all other attempts in the same field of Sacred Literature."—*Extract from the Preface.*

The English Gentlewoman;

or, A Practical Manual for Young Ladies on their Entrance into Society. Third Edition. Revised and enlarged by the Author. Fcp. 8vo. cloth, floral gilt edges, 4s.

"THIS work is intended chiefly for young ladies of the upper classes of English Society. The object of the writer is, by the experience of a life passed in those circles which constitute what is called 'the world,' to supply those who are entering into a new and busy sphere with some of the practical benefits of observation and reflection, to propound the elements of that species of knowledge, which, contrary to other sciences, is usually acquired by blunders and errors; the lessons of which are often received with mortification, and remembered often with regret. This little book, which pretends to no deeper learning than that which the heart and the memory can impart, is therefore offered to the young who are destined, not for the happy duties of an humble and narrow sphere, but for the arduous introduction into a career usually deemed more perilous. It is for those who must live, more or less, in communion with the gay and the opulent, but who wish 'to live unspotted in the world.' It is meant to resemble the warning voice of the nurse who sees the children of her care sporting on the brink of a sedgy pool, all green with aquatic plants, and calls to them to beware."—*Extract from the Preface.*

The English Matron;

or, A Practical Manual for Young Wives. By the Author of "The English Gentlewoman." Third Edition. Revised and enlarged by the Author. Fcp. 8vo. cloth, floral gilt edges, 4s.

"TO recall the serious purpose of an English matron's life; to warn, advise, inform her; to stimulate her best aims; to place even in solemn terms the miseries of failure, was the object of this work. Its merits, such as they are, were never more needed than now. It is offered with earnest prayers for the well-being of the young matron; in all faithfulness, in all sincerity to her is proffered such counsels as a mother would give to a beloved daughter entering on the all-important career of married life."

Extract from the Preface to the Third Edition.

Sketching Rambles;

or, Nature in the Alps and Apennines. By AGNES and MARIA E. CATLOW, Authors of "Popular Field Botany," "Garden Botany," "Popular Conchology," "Scripture Zoology," &c. Illustrated with Twenty Views, from Sketches by the Author. Two vols. 8vo. cloth, 21s.

The Young Poet's Guide:

Hints on the Structure of English Verse. Accompanied by Examples from the Works of different Authors, together with a Rhyming Dictionary, and Explanatory Observations on the Selection and Use of the Rhymes. Crown 8vo. green and gold, 4s. 6d.

The Leighs; or, The Discipline of Daily Life.

By Miss PALMER. With Illustrations by Walter Ray Woods, printed on toned paper. Small crown 8vo. cloth extra, 3s. 6d.

The Long Holidays; or, Learning without

Lessons. By H. A. FORD. With Illustrations by C. A. Doyle, printed on toned paper. Small crown 8vo. cloth extra, 3s. 6d.

Aunt Agnes; or, The Why and Wherefore

of Life: An Autobiography. With Illustrations, printed on toned paper. Small crown 8vo. cloth extra, 3s. 6d.

The Wave and the Battle Field.

By Mrs. STEWART, Author of "Atheline; or, The Castle by the Sea," "Bradmere Pool," &c. With Illustrations by Henry Saunderson, printed on toned paper. Small crown 8vo. cloth extra, 3s. 6d.

The Busy Hives around Us:

A Variety of Trips and Visits to the Mine, the Workshop, and the Factory; with Popular Notes on Materials, Processes, and Machines. With Illustrations by Harvey, &c., printed on toned paper. Small crown 8vo. cloth extra, 3s. 6d.

The Printer Boy;
or, How Benjamin Franklin made his Mark: An Example for Youth. By WILLIAM M. THAYER. With Illustrations by Julian Portch, the Frontispiece and Vignette coloured. Small crown 8vo. cloth extra, 3s. 6d.

Men who have Risen:
A Book for Boys. With Illustrations, printed on toned paper. Small crown 8vo. cloth extra, 3s. 6d.

Women of Worth:
A Book for Girls. With Illustrations, printed on toned paper. Small crown 8vo. cloth extra, 3s. 6d.

Friendly Hands and Kindly Words:
Stories Illustrative of the Law of Kindness, the Power of Perseverance, and the Advantage of Little Helps. With Illustrations, printed on toned paper. Small crown 8vo. cloth extra, 3s. 6d.

Roses and Thorns;
or, Five Tales of the Start in Life. With Illustrations, printed on toned paper. Small crown 8vo. cloth extra, 3s. 6d.

Pictures of Heroes,
And Lessons from their Lives. With Illustrations, printed on toned paper. Small crown 8vo. cloth extra, 3s. 6d.

Favourite Passages in Modern Christian
Biography. With a Group of Portraits. Small crown 8vo. cloth extra, 3s. 6d.

The Popular Preachers of the Ancient Church,
their Lives, their Manner, and their Work. By the Rev. WILLIAM WILSON, M.A. With Illustrations by Henry Anelay, printed on toned paper. Small crown 8vo. cloth extra, 3s. 6d.

The Book of Children's Hymns and Rhymes.
Collected by the DAUGHTER of a CLERGYMAN. Illustrated with numerous Engravings on Wood. Small crown 8vo. cloth extra, 3s. 6d.

THIS is a Comprehensive Collection of what may be called the "Children's Favourites."

Todd's Lectures to Children;
A Complete Edition of the First and Second Series, with a Memoir of the Author, from Authentic Sources, and Twelve full-page Illustrations, printed on toned paper. Small crown 8vo. cloth extra, 3s. 6d.

The Angel of the Iceberg and other Stories and
Parables, Illustrating Great Moral Truths. Designed chiefly for the Young. To which is added TRUTH MADE SIMPLE: A System of Theology for Children. With Twelve Illustrations by R. W. Sherwin, printed on toned paper. Small crown 8vo. cloth extra, 3s. 6d.

The Pilgrim in the Holy Land;
or, Palestine, Past and Present. By the Rev. HENRY S. OSBORNE, A.M. With Twelve Illustrations of various Objects of Interest in the Holy Land, printed on toned paper. Small crown 8vo. cloth extra, 3s. 6d.

The Pilgrim's Progress.
By JOHN BUNYAN. A Complete Edition, presenting a clear handsome Text, with Twelve choice Illustrations by C. A. Doyle, printed on toned paper. Small crown 8vo. cloth extra, 3s. 6d.

Hints on the Culture of Character.
Small crown 8vo. cloth extra, 3s. 6d.

CONTENTS.

PART I.

The Cultivation of the Intellect, a Divine Duty of Man. By the late Rev. GEORGE CROLY, LL.D., Rector of St. Stephen's, Walbrook, and St. Benet's.

Christian Bearing at Home and in Society. By the Hon. and Right Rev. the BISHOP OF DURHAM.

The Principle of Christian Stewardship. By the Rev. THOMAS DALE, M.A., Canon Residentiary of St. Paul's.

Christian Membership. By the Rev. HENRY MELVILLE, B.D., Chaplain in Ordinary to the Queen, and Canon Residentiary of St. Paul's.

PART II.

Selections from the Works of Divines of the Church of England: embracing readings from Sumner, Whately, Tait, Blomfield, Thirlwall, Wilberforce, Hampden, Wordsworth, Trench, C. J. Vaughan, Moberly, Hare, Gleig, Hussey, Jelf, Millman, Sydney Smith, Warter, Berens, Whewell, Arnold, Heber, Robinson.

Small Beginnings;
or, The Way to Get on. With Illustrations, printed on toned paper. Small crown 8vo. cloth extra, 3s. 6d.

A Handy Book of Medical Information and
Advice: containing a Brief Account of the Nature and Treatment of Common Diseases; also Hints to be followed in Emergencies; with Suggestions as to the Management of the Sick Room, and the Preservation of Health; and an Appendix, in which will be found a List of the Medicines referred to in the Work, with their Proper Doses and Modes of Administration. By a PHYSICIAN. Small crown 8vo. cloth extra, 3s. 6d.

IN addition to the simple, every-day knowledge which is useful to all, and particularly to the Head of a Household, this little Volume is specially intended as a Safe and Ready Guide to those Resident in Country Places, and generally under circumstances where Medical Advice is not instantly available.

The Habits of Good Society:

A Handbook of Etiquette for Ladies and Gentlemen; with Thoughts, Hints, and Anecdotes concerning Social Observances, Nice Points of Taste and Good Manners, and the Art of making One's-self agreeable. The whole interspersed with Humorous Illustrations of Social Predicaments, Remarks on the History and Changes of Fashion, and the Changes of English and Continental Etiquette. With a Frontispiece. Small crown 8vo. cloth extra, 3s. 6d.

The Vicar of Wakefield.

By OLIVER GOLDSMITH. A Complete Edition, presenting a clear handsome Text, with Twelve choice full-page Illustrations, printed on toned paper. Small crown 8vo. cloth extra, 3s. 6d.

The Star of Hope and the Staff of Duty:

Tales of Womanly Trials and Victories. With Illustrations by Julian Portch, printed on toned paper. Small crown 8vo. cloth extra, 3s. 6d.

Noble Traits of Kingly Men;

or, Pictures and Anecdotes of European History; with a Bird's-eye View of the Grander Movements and their Leaders. With Illustrations by S. A. Groves, printed on toned paper. Small crown 8vo. cloth extra, 3s. 6d.

The Sea and her Famous Sailors:

A History of Maritime Adventure and Exploration; with Incidents in the Lives of Distinguished Naval Heroes and Adventurers. With Illustrations, printed on toned paper. Small crown 8vo. cloth extra, 3s. 6d.

THIS volume, whether viewed as a careful, concise Ocean History, or as a compact series of Tales and Adventures, possesses many attractive as well as useful features. It embraces the rise and full of Maritime Greatness in connection with the annals of various nations—the enterprise and endurance which won and obtained Naval Power, and the innumerable episodes of brilliant daring which mark the career of our Early Adventurers.

Hughes's Graduated Reading-Lessons, in Four

Books: A Series of Advanced Reading Lessons. Edited by EDWARD HUGHES, F.R.A.S., F.R.G.S., Associate of the Institute of Civil Engineers, and late Head Master of the Royal Naval Lower School, Greenwich. Embracing Original Contributions to the various branches of Knowledge by Eminent Writers, profusely Illustrated with 430 Engravings on Wood. Each volume is sold separately, strongly bound in cloth, boards, 3s. 6d., and contains about 450 pages of fcp. 8vo.

AMONGST Educational Works, this carefully edited Series of Lessons (the *first*, and still the most elaborate, of all "Graduated" Series) occupies a conspicuous position, and deserves the attention of all who are interested in Tuition. The range of subjects is comprehensive; the various Articles and Treatises are by Authors distinguished in Science, Literature, and Art; the Illustrations are numerous and exact; while the whole has been methodised and arranged for practical use by a Teacher of acknowledged eminence in his profession.

The objects have been at once "clearness of explanation, general adaptation to the purposes of sound education, and the closest attention to practical utility." To attain these ends, no expense has been spared in securing the assistance of the most competent Writers in each department, and in the free use of good Illustrations to enhance the value of the text.

The progressive nature of the plan, the compact arrangement, and the thoroughness of the information (for which the names of the Authors, as given in the Work, are a sufficient guarantee) combine to afford a systematic body of knowledge—graphic, recent, accurate, and well digested. *Taken as a whole, the four volumes may be termed an Elementary Cyclopædia reduced to a form convenient for daily instruction.*

The Rose-bud Stories:

A New and attractive Series of Juvenile Books, each volume Illustrated with coloured Engravings. Sixteen varieties, uniform in size and style, 1s. 6d. each. Every volume contains one or more Tales complete, is strongly bound in cloth boards, with Four coloured Engravings on Wood, designed and engraved by Dalziel Brothers, and 124 pages of clear, bold letter-press, printed upon stout paper.

The Tales are written by various Authors, most of them expressly for the Series, and for cheapness, attractiveness, and sterling interest, they present, perhaps, one of the most pleasing and useful collections of Stories in modern Juvenile Literature.

> As the fresh rose-bud needs the silvery shower,
> The golden sunshine, and the pearly dew,
> The joyous day, with all its changes new,
> Ere it can bloom into the perfect flower;
> So with the human rose-bud; from sweet airs
> Of heaven will fragrant purity be caught,
> And influences benign of tender thought
> Inform the soul, like angels, unawares.
> MARY HOWITT.

Ally and her School-fellow:
A Tale for the Young. By Miss M. BETHAM-EDWARDS, Author of "Holidays among the Mountains," "Charlie and Ernest," &c. With Four coloured Pictures. Royal 18mo. cloth lettered, ornamental side, 1s. 6d.

Loyal Charlie Bentham.
By Mrs. WEBB, Author of "The Beloved Disciple," "Naomi," "Idaline," &c. And THE CHILDREN'S ISLAND: A True Story. Edited by L. NUGENT. With Four coloured Pictures. Royal 18mo. cloth lettered, ornamental side, 1s. 6d.

Simple Stories for Children.
By MARY E. MILLS. With Four coloured Pictures. Royal 18mo. cloth lettered, ornamental side, 1s. 6d.

A Child's First Book about Birds.
By a COUNTRY CLERGYMAN. With Four coloured Pictures. Royal 18mo. cloth lettered, ornamental side, 1s. 6d.

Prince Arthur;
or, The Four Trials. By CATHERINE MARY STIRLING. And TALES BY THE FLOWERS. By CAROLINE B. TEMPLER. With Four coloured Pictures. Royal 18mo. cloth lettered, ornamental side, 1s. 6d.

The Story of Henrietta and the Ayah;
or, Do Not Trust to Appearances. And MY LITTLE SCHOOL-FELLOW; or, One Good Turn deserves Another. By Madame DE CHATELAIN. With Four coloured Pictures. Royal 18mo. cloth lettered, ornamental side, 1s. 6d.

THE ROSE-BUD STORIES—*continued.*

Stories from English History.
For Young Children. Edited by the Rev. ROBERT HENNIKER, M.A., Incumbent of South Charlton, Northumberland. With Four coloured Pictures. Royal 18mo. cloth lettered, ornamental side, 1s. 6d.

Twelve Links of the Golden Chain.
By ANNA J. BUCKLAND. With Four coloured Pictures. Royal 18mo. cloth lettered, ornamental side, 1s. 6d.

Easy Talks for Little Folks.
By the Author of "A Visit to the Seaside," "Cousin Elizabeth," "Little Crumbs," &c. And MAY-DAY; or, Anecdotes of Miss Lydia Lively. Edited by L. NUGENT. With Four coloured Pictures. Royal 18mo. cloth lettered, ornamental side, 1s. 6d.

Susan and the Doll;
or, Do Not be Covetous. And THE LITTLE ORPHAN'S HISTORY; or, Everything for the Best. By CAROLINE LEICESTER. With Four coloured Pictures. Royal 18mo. cloth lettered, ornamental side, 1s. 6d.

Juvenile Tales for Juvenile Readers.
By CHARLOTTE ELIZABETH. With Four coloured Pictures. Royal 18mo. cloth lettered, ornamental side, 1s. 6d.

The Life of Robinson Crusoe.
In Short Words. By SARAH CROMPTON, Author of "A Plan to Combine Education with Instruction," "Life of Columbus," "Life of Luther," in Short Words, &c. With Four coloured Pictures. Royal 18mo. cloth lettered, ornamental side, 1s. 6d.

A Winter's Wreath of Illustrative Tales.
Edited by Lady CHARLOTTE LAW. And SYMPATHY: A Tale. By E. A. M. With Four coloured Pictures. Royal 18mo. cloth lettered, ornamental side, 1s. 6d.

Little Paul and his Moss-wreaths;
or, The King and the Boy who kept his Word. By ANGELIKA VON LAGERSTRÖM. Together with the STORY OF LITTLE GEORGE BELL. With Four coloured Pictures. Royal 18mo. cloth lettered, ornamental side. 1s. 6d.

Six Short Stories for Short People.
By the Rev. F. W. B. BOUVERIE, Author of "Life and its Lessons," &c. With Four coloured Pictures. Royal 18mo. cloth lettered, ornamental side, 1s. 6d.

The Captive Sky-Lark;
or, Do as You Would be Done by? A Tale. By Madame DE CHATELAIN. With Four coloured Pictures. Royal 18mo. cloth lettered, ornamental side, 1s. 6d.

C C

Studies of Christian Character.

By BITHA FOX, Author of "Pictures of Heroes," "The Yews," &c. With Illustrations by James Godwin, printed on toned paper. Crown 8vo. elegantly bound in cloth, labelled boards, gilt edges, 6s.

CONTENTS.

Signal Fires.
The Fair Pietist.
"The Tenth Muse."
The Lamp in the Cell.
The Red Silk Banner.

Watchers for the Dawn.
The Artists of the Reformation.
The Cobbler-Poet of Nuremberg.
The Friendships of the Reformation.

The Golden Casket:

A Treasury of Tales for Young People. Edited by MARY HOWITT. With Illustrations by John Palmer, printed on toned paper. Small crown 8vo. elegantly bound in cloth, gilt edges, 5s.

CONTENTS.

The Elchester College Boys. By Mrs. Wood, Author of "Red Court Farm," "Danesbury House," &c.
The Delft Jug. By Eliza Meteyard (Silverpen).
The Boy and the Man. From the German of Christopher von Schmidt.
William and his Teacher. By Mrs. S. C. Hall.
The Story of Luke Barnicott. By William Howitt.
The Castle East of the Sun and West of the World: A Story from the Old Danish.
My First Cruise. By W. H. G. Kingston.
The Holidays at Barenburg Castle. By Ottilie Wildermuth.
Some Passages from the Child-Life of Lucy Meredyth. By the Author of "An Art Student in Munich."
The Touching and Marvellous Adventures of Prince Hempseed and his Young Sister. From the French of Léon Gozlan.

Fit to be a Duchess;

With other Stories of Courage and Principle. By Mrs. GILLESPIE SMYTH, Author of "Selwyn," "Life and Times of Olympia Morata," "Probation," "Tales of the Moors," &c. With Illustrations by Corbould and Absolon, printed on toned paper. Crown 8vo. elegantly bound in cloth, gilt edges, 5s.

Men who were Earnest:

The Springs of their Action and Influence: A Series of Biographical Studies. With Illustrations by Frederick Borders, printed on toned paper. Crown 8vo. elegantly bound in cloth, gilt edges, 5s.

The Art of Doing our Best,

as seen in the Lives and Stories of some Thorough Workers. By HALWIN CALDWELL. With Illustrations by John Absolon, H. K. Browne, and the Brothers Dalziel, printed on toned paper. Fcp. 8vo. elegantly bound, cloth, gilt edges, 5s.

The Old Favourites:

A Treasury of Tales for Young People. Edited and Written by MARY HOWITT. With Illustrations by Zwecker, printed on toned paper. Small crown 8vo. elegantly bound in cloth, gilt edges, 5s.

THE Volume contains an Original Tale, entitled "Rockbourne Hall," introducing the Young Folks' Readings, and their Conversations about Old Favourite Tales. The course of the Narrative embraces many Stories by various Standard Authors, given in a carefully Revised and sometimes Popularised form.

A Treasury of New Favourite Tales for Young

People. Edited and Written by MARY HOWITT. With Illustrations by Coleman and Palmer, printed on toned paper. Small crown 8vo. elegantly bound in cloth, gilt edges, 5s.

CONTENTS.

The Lords of Wyvon. By Mary Howitt.	The Secret Society. By Mrs. De Morgan.
Jonas on a Farm. By Jacob Abbott.	The Rainy Day. By Fanny Fern.
The Gray African Parrot. By Harry Gringo.	The Chimæra. By Nathaniel Hawthorne.
The Travelling Tinman. By Miss Leslie.	Making Something. By Mrs. Child.
Red-headed Andy. By Fanny Fern.	The Boat Club. By Oliver Optic.
My Little Lizzie. By Miss Gillies.	The Little Peacemaker. By Mary Howitt.

Every Boy's Stories:

A choice Collection of Standard Tales, Rhymes, and Allegories. In One thick Volume, with Twelve full-page Illustrations, printed on toned paper. Small crown 8vo. cloth, 5s.

The Brave Old English Confessors.

With Illustrations by L. Huard, printed on toned paper. Crown 8vo. elegantly bound in cloth, bevelled boards, gilt edges, 5s.

Mornings with Mama;

or, Scripture Dialogues for Young Persons from Ten to Eighteen Years of Age. By Mrs. GILLESPIE SMYTH, Author of "Selwyn," "The Life and Times of Olympia Morata," "Probation," &c. Third Edition, revised and Illustrated. In Six Volumes, fcp. 8vo. green and gold, 2s. 6d. each.

TITLES OF THE SIX VOLUMES.

I.	IV.
THE LIFE OF MOSES AND THE EARLY HISTORY OF THE ISRAELITES, &c.	LIVES OF THE KINGS AND THE PROPHETS, &c.
II.	V.
LIVES OF JOSHUA, SAMSON, AND RUTH; THE EARLY DAYS OF SAMUEL AND SAUL, &c.	THE GOSPELS:—The Angel's Message —St. John—The Transfiguration— Parables, &c.
III.	VI.
THE LIVES OF DAVID AND SOLOMON, &c.	THE GOSPELS:—Lessons of the Parables—The Crucifixion, &c.

VARIOUS eminent Clergymen encouraged the preparation of these favourite Dialogues; and the late Dr. CHALMERS (to whom, by permission, the volumes were originally dedicated) made daily use of them in his own Family. Each volume is Illustrated by highly-finished Engravings on Wood by Dalziel (printed on Toned Paper), chiefly from choice Compositions of the Old Masters.

Mornings with Mama

may also be had in three vols. thus:—

THE OLD TESTAMENT SERIES.

I.	II.
EARLIER LIVES AND NARRATIVES.	LATER HISTORY AND BIOGRAPHY.

THE GOSPEL SERIES. 1 VOL.

Fcp. 8vo. bevelled boards and gilt edges, 5s. each.

The Book of Drawing-Room Plays and Evening

Amusements: A Comprehensive Manual of In-door Recreation, including all kinds of Acting Charades—Mute, Comic, Poetic, Fairy, Dramatic, Historic, and Classic; Proverbs, Burlesques, and Extravaganzas; comprising Novel and Original Ideas, numerous Skeleton Plots and Dialogues; Descriptions of Continental Court Tableaux hitherto unnoticed in this Country; Intellectual, Active, Catch, and Trick Games; Forfeits, Board Games, Puzzles, and Parlour Magic. The whole interspersed with Practical Directions concerning Costume, and Hints on Management and Accessories. By HENRY DALTON. With Scenic Illustrations by Corbould and Du Maurier, printed on toned paper, and upwards of 120 Diagrams on Wood; accompanied by a copious Index. Small crown 8vo. elegantly bound in cloth, gilt edges, 6s.

Sketches of Foreign Novelists.

By GEORGINA GORDON. A Series of Tales and Sketches from recent Works of the Popular Novelists of Germany and France, including Mühlbach, Auerbach, Mügge, and Hygare-Carlin; Feuillet, Sandeau, and Dumas. Post 8vo. 10s. 6d. CONTENTS.

A Royal Marriage.
Cinderella of the Black Forest.
A Peasant Prince.
The Story of Chateau Laroque.

Louisanne's Stratagem.
The Jailer's Daughter.
The Smugglers.

De Quincey on Self-Education.

With Hints on Style and Dialogues on Political Economy. Fcp. 8vo cloth, 6s. CONTENTS.

Letters to a Young Man whose Education has been neglected.
Language.
Style.
Rhetoric.

Conversation.
Superficial Knowledge.
Dialogues of Three Templars on Political Economy.

"THESE Dialogues are unequalled, perhaps, for brevity, pungency and force. They not only bring the Ricardian Theory of Value in strong relief, but triumphantly repel, or rather annihilate, the objections urged against it by Malthus in the pamphlet now referred to and his Political Economy, and by Say and others. They may, indeed, be said to have exhausted the subject."—*J. R. M'Culloch—Literature of Political Economy.*

WORKS BY GEORGE GILFILLAN.

1. The Bards of the Bible.

Fifth Edition. Crown 8vo. cloth, 5s.

2. Christianity and our Era:

A Book for the Times. Demy 8vo. cloth, 10s. 6d.

3. Galleries of Literary Portraits.

(First, Second, and Third.) Fourth Edition, complete in Two Volumes. Crown 8vo. cloth, 10s.

The Romance of Diplomacy:

Historical Memoir of Queen Carolina Matilda of Denmark, Sister to King George the Third; with Memoir, and a Selection from the Correspondence (Official and Familiar) of Sir Robert Murray Keith, K.B., Envoy Extraordinary and Minister Plenipotentiary at the Courts of Dresden, Copenhagen, and Vienna. By Mrs. GILLESPIE SMYTH. Second Edition, revised, with Portraits engraved on Steel. Two vols. post 8vo. 14s.

www.ingramcontent.com/pod-product-compliance
Lightning Source LLC
Chambersburg PA
CBHW050846300426
44111CB00010B/1141